THE TEN GREATEST REVIVALS EVER

THE TEN GREATEST REVIVALS EVER

From Pentecost to the Present

ELMER TOWNS
DOUGLAS PORTER

SERVANT PUBLICATIONS
ANN ARBOR, MICHIGAN

Vine Books is an imprint of Servant Publications especially designed to serve evangelical
Christians.

All Scripture quotations in this publication are from The New King James Version, copyright ©
1979, 1980, 1982, Thomas Nelson, Inc., Publishers.

Published by Servant Publications
P.O. Box 8617
Ann Arbor, Michigan 48107

Cover design: Paul Higdon

00 01 02 03 10 9 8 7 6 5 4 3 2

Printed in the United States of America
ISBN 1-56955-217-7

LIBRARY OF CONGRESS CATALOGING-IN-PUBLICATION DATA

Towns, Elmer L.
    The ten greatest revivals ever / Elmer Towns and Douglas Porter.
        p.   cm.
    Includes bibliographical references.
    ISBN 1-56955-217-7 (alk. paper)
    1. Revivals—History.   I. Porter, Douglas, Dr.   II. Title.

BV3770.T69   2000
269'.24'09—dc21   00-040859

THE TEN GREATEST REVIVALS EVER

1. The 1904 Revival, Beginning in Wales
Evan Roberts, Korea, Manchurian Revival, Azusa Street

2. The First Great Awakening, 1727–50
Zinzendorf, Wesley, Whitefield, Jonathan Edwards

3. The Second Great Awakening, 1780–1810
Cane Ridge

4. The General Awakening, 1830–40
Charles Finney, Hawaii, Jamaica

5. The Layman's Prayer Revival, 1857–61
Phoebe Palmer, Lanphier, D.L. Moody

6. The World War II Revival, 1935–50
Billy Graham, Duncan Campbell, New Zealand

7. The Baby Boomer Revival, 1965–71
The Jesus People, The Prairie Revival, Asbury

8. The Pre-Reformation Revival, 1300–1500
Lollards, Wycliffe, Hus, Savonarola

9. The Protestant Reformation, 1517
Martin Luther, John Calvin, Zwingli, Knox

10. Pentecost: The Beginning of Revival, A.D. 30
Peter, Ephesus, Paul

CONTENTS

The order of *The Ten Greatest Revivals Ever* was determined
by the following, who read the manuscript:

Bill Bright, Gerald Brooks, David Yonggi Cho, Robert Coleman, James O. Davis, Lewis Drummond, Dale Galloway, Eddie Gibbs, Jack Hayford, Charles Kelly, D. James Kennedy, Ron Phillips, Alvin Reid, Chuck Smith, Tommy Tenney, C. Peter Wagner, and Steve Wingfield.

PREFACE

There have been instances in the history of the Church when the telling and retelling of the wonderful works of God have been used to rekindle the expectations of the faithful intercessors and prepare the way for another Awakening.

J. Edwin Orr

Pray for revival in America." So read a sign in a Dallas restaurant not long ago, spotted as we were writing this book. In our spirit we say, "Amen!" But we wonder if the folks in that restaurant know what they're praying for.

When most people pray for revival, they're probably asking for a wonderful experience at church next Sunday at 11:00 A.M. But revival is more than a Sunday morning experience. When you pray for revival, you're asking God for life-shaking experiences that will cost you plenty.

Revival is agonizing: It so terrorizes you over your sin that you repent deeply. Revival is consuming: It leaves you no time for hobbies, for chores around the house, for work, for sleep. Revival wrecks your appointment calendar, interrupts TV times, demands your full attention ... and wears you out.

Usually when we pray for revival, we're thinking about the bad guys, and we're telling God to "sic 'em." Little do we realize that revival begins with us, the people of God. As a matter of fact, we've got a suggestion for those who want revival: Don't pray for revival. Just repent of all known sin, do everything you're supposed to do, give God all—not part, but all—your time, and you'll experience revival.

If you need some inspiration for such repentance, we know of no better place to find it than in the records of earlier revivals. For that reason, this book describes *The Ten Greatest Revivals Ever* and their influence.

The stories of the revivals revisited in this book are written by men sympathetic to revival. Each is, in fact, the product of revival. Elmer Towns was converted to Christ during a revival experienced in a Presbyterian church in Bonna Bella, Georgia. Douglas Porter yielded to God's call on his life to preach the gospel during a similar revival experienced at a youth conference.

Each prays for God to send "the greatest revival since Pentecost!"

Our choice of which ten revivals rank as the "greatest" is based on years of study. Douglas Porter's doctoral dissertation was a close analysis of evangelical revivals and their implications for evangelism. Elmer Towns was his mentor for that study, and Towns himself has written the book *Rivers of Revival* with Neil Anderson, as well as several books on related subjects.

The reader will note that the most recent revivals described in this book are more than thirty years old. Does this mean the age of revivals has come to an end? That's not the view of the authors. Even as this book was written, we received reports of significant revivals around the world.

Some current revivals, like those in Toronto and Pensacola, Florida, have received much attention internationally. Others have been promoted widely in their region but are mostly unknown beyond their state or national borders. Some revivals appear to be having a profound impact on their country, especially in such Latin American countries as Argentina. Others, such as those recently reported at Wheaton College and Cornerstone College, appear to have had a profound impact on college campuses. We rejoice in all the reports of God at work among his people, even though we may not be able to endorse everything that happens in these revivals.

Some contemporary revivals haven't been described because sufficient time has not yet passed to measure their impact on a generation. The dramatic events surrounding the initial outpouring of the Holy Spirit are only part of the story that makes a revival great. The real impact of a revival is realized in the ministry of a revived church in an awakened community.

This takes time. In fact, in the opinion of the authors, it takes a generation for the story of a revival to unfold fully. We're better able, a generation later, to evaluate, for example, the impact of the Asbury College Revival in 1970 than were those caught up in the enthusiasm of the revival itself. It thus remains the task of the next generation to revisit the revivals of this generation.

This is not a history book for scholars, but was written rather to touch the hearts of readers and to challenge them to revival. We've therefore left out the footnoting system used in scholarly pursuits. For the same reason, though we've relied on primary sources and quoted from them, we've attributed them to their sources as a modern newspaper might present a story. The scholar seeking further research should consult the bibliography. If you wish to correspond with us about revival or comment on this book, contact us by e-mail: Elmer Towns at www.elmertowns.com or Douglas Porter at porter.palace@sympatico.ca.

The psalmist wrote, "I will open my mouth in a parable; I will utter dark sayings of old, which we have heard and known, and our fathers have told us. We will not hide them from their children, telling to the generation to come the praises of the Lord, and His strength and His wonderful works that He has done" (Ps. 78:2-4). This is our account of some of "His wonderful works that He has done." The stories gathered in this volume are included as models of what God has done and is doing in our world. We've retold them with the hope that they might motivate Christians to prepare their hearts and lives for revival.

May God use this book to stir hearts to pray one more time, "Will You not revive us again, that Your people may rejoice in You?" (Ps. 85:6).

Elmer Towns   Douglas Porter

Virginia, United States   Ontario, Canada

The Reality of Revival

But there have been certain seasons called revivals—when God has "poured His Spirit out on His people." These times—also called awakenings—occurred when the presence of God is experienced in powerful manifestations of the Holy Spirit.

J. Edwin Orr

The evening prayer meeting had been over for about an hour. Students of Liberty University and members of the Thomas Road Baptist Church in Lynchburg, Virginia, were milling around the front of the sanctuary. It was late—10:30 on a Wednesday night—so most of the ushers and pastors had gone home.

Suddenly a lone student rose and walked to the pulpit, weeping, to confess sins. The microphone and pulpit lights were off, but God was there. That student's passionate repentance captured the attention of those who were still in the auditorium.

Someone began singing. Someone else ran to play the piano—softly, so as not to interrupt the sacred sound of tears. People dropped to their knees beside the altar and front pews.

Shortly, another broken person approached the pulpit to confess sins. Soon there were others. After two hours, frantic phone calls went out to the pastor and deacons: *"Revival's hit the church!"*

Church members, awakened in the middle of the night, dressed hurriedly and drove through the dark streets of Lynchburg. All came back to the church building expecting to experience God. No neckties ... no Sunday morning dresses ... just believers eager for a divine touch. Soon the glory of the Lord flooded the church auditorium.

People stayed at the church from Wednesday night until Saturday morning. All normal activities in their lives shut down. Classes were canceled. Most of those involved didn't leave for work; some didn't eat. When drowsiness couldn't be fought off, students slept in the pews in the back of the auditorium, or even under the pews.

No one wanted to leave the sanctuary, because when they left the building, they were leaving an almost tangible presence of God. They didn't want to miss anything that God was doing.

Like the tide that ebbs and flows, the intensity of the experience came in waves. There were louder times when people were publicly confessing their sins, then quieter times of soft weeping and private prayer around the altar.

How did the revival end? Early Saturday morning one student rose to confess his sins, but he seemed to be bragging about what he had done when he had sinned; there was no shame, no brokenness. The Holy Spirit—who knows the heart—departed the meeting. Within one hour, everyone knew the revival was over. They left, went home, and went back to their daily activities.

Revivals: A Long History

What happened in our church and university back in the fall of 1973 was just a small taste of what God has done many times in the history of the church. "When the Day of Pentecost had fully come" (Acts 2:1), the Scripture tells us, God moved in a remarkable manner among his people. He continued his miraculous movement as the church was established. In the days since, God has repeatedly moved among his people in these "special seasons," resulting in great blessing to both the church and the secular community.

In the early centuries of Christian history, God accomplished similar works: through Gregory "the Illuminator," resulting in the conversion of Armenia; through Frumentius, in Ethiopia; through Patrick, in Ireland; through Columba, as he preached the gospel to the Scottish Picts; and through Methodius, in his ministry among the Slavs. In later centuries, the ministries of reformers such as Savonarola, Wycliffe, and Knox revealed a similar supernatural working of God among his people. Place names such as

Hernhutt, Northhampton, Fetter Lane, and Cane Ridge are still remembered by Christians as sites where a significant movement of God once took place.

During the eighteenth and nineteenth centuries especially, many communities experienced an outpouring of the Holy Spirit. This was the era of celebrated preachers and evangelists such as David Brainerd, Jonathan Edwards, John Wesley, Charles Finney, Jeremiah Lanphier, and Dwight Lyman Moody. While these names remain well known among contemporary Christians, God used a host of others as well to bring significant revivals to churches and communities.

Some say that revival is an American phenomenon, a unique cultural event experienced only south of the Mason-Dixon line. Yet the brief history we've just noted argues otherwise. In fact, even those revivals best known to Americans for their fruits in this country, such as the First Great Awakening and the Second Great Awakening, actually began in Europe before they spread across our continent in the North as well as in the South.

The present time in particular confirms that revival is indeed a global phenomenon. This is the age of the Asuza Street explosion, the Welsh Revival, the Korean Pentecost, and the Manchurian Revival. Great revivals have occurred in India and East Africa; in Los Angeles and the Hebrides Islands of Scotland; in East Timor, Indonesia, and Saskatoon, Saskatchewan; at Asbury College in Kentucky, and in the towns of New Zealand. Although this age has declared God dead, he's shown himself very much alive when his people humble themselves, pray, seek his face, and turn from their wicked ways.

What Is a Revival?

The eternal human quest is to know and experience God.

Some want God to split open the heavens and descend to earth so they can see him. Others want God to write his message in the sky or on a mountain so they can see it and know for sure what to do. Still others want to hear the voice of God shouting like thunder. And still others want God to "zap 'em" so they'll quiver on the floor or jump like a kangaroo. Though most won't admit it, in one way or another they want God to quit playing hide and seek, to come show himself, to visit his people.

True believers want God to intervene in their humdrum experiences. But for most, God can't be felt or touched. Many feel that God isn't with them.

A Working Definition

One way God responds to this basic human longing is to manifest himself in a revival. But what exactly do we mean by that term? A variety of definitions have been offered by pastors, theologians, and historians, but we would describe it this way:

> An evangelical revival is an extraordinary work of God in which Christians repent of their sins as they become intensely aware of his presence in their midst, and they manifest a positive response to God in renewed obedience to the known will of God, resulting in both a deepening of their individual and corporate experience with God, and an increased concern to win others to Christ.

This view of revival recognizes several distinctives, common to historic revivals, that we should keep in mind as we study them:

- An extraordinary work of God should be distinguished from the more ordinary work of God in the life of the believer.
- The realization of the unique presence of God during times of revival is consistently reported in the testimonies of the revived.
- Revivals naturally lead to a significant evangelistic outreach and harvest of souls in the community touched by the revived church.

While there may be isolated exceptions, these are the manifestations connected with the normal experience of a Holy Spirit outpouring as we read about examples of it in Scripture.

Nine "Faces" of Revival

All people have the same basic facial features, yet these features are arranged differently. In a similar way, revivals display the same essential features as they reflect God's presence, yet they have different "faces"; that is, revival is expressed in different ways. The nine "faces" of revival have been described in an earlier book, *Rivers of Revival* (written by Elmer Towns with Neil Anderson, Regal Books, 1998; see pp. 116-17). That list of revival types, each with its characteristic focus, is worth repeating here:

- The *repentance revival* emphasizes a moral cleansing of individual lives and of society as a whole.
- The *evangelism revival* focuses on winning souls to Christ.
- The *worship revival* centers on magnifying God.
- The *deeper life revival* emphasizes the experience of God's indwelling.
- The *spiritual warfare revival* devotes its energies to battling Satan and the other demons.
- The *Holy Spirit revival* is characterized by extensive manifestations of the Spirit.
- The *reconciliation revival* leads to the removal of barriers to racial and ethnic harmony.
- The *liberation revival* focuses on gaining freedom from corporate and personal bondage to sin.
- The *prayer revival* displays considerable efforts at intercession and other forms of prayer.

Though any given revival may manifest several of these characteristics, most revivals tend to display one trait more prominently than the others. Just as the face of a child often reflects a blending of the faces of both parents (and grandparents), so the "face" of a particular revival often reflects a blending of two or more of the revival types listed above.

Choosing the Ten Greatest Revivals

Choosing the ten greatest revivals in history was no easy task. We began by setting criteria for our choices. Five questions were asked of each revival, and the answers helped guide us in our selection.

Guidelines to Ranking Revivals

- Does the experience fit the biblical portrait of revival?
- Was there a demonstration of God's presence?
- Was the larger body of Christ awakened to its New Testament task?
- Was the surrounding culture impacted positively by the revival?
- Are there reliable sources that demonstrate the greatness of the revival?

First, *does the experience fit the biblical portrait of revival?* In other words, does it fit the definition we've already given based on scriptural accounts?

Second, *was there a demonstration of God's presence?* Since revival happens when God pours himself on his people, those involved typically experience an extraordinary yet unmistakable sense of the divine presence. Sometimes this is called "atmospheric revival," in which people give testimony to feeling, experiencing and sensing that God is present. However, a revival that fits the New Testament pattern is never measured by feelings alone; there must be a demonstration of New Testament fruit as well.

We should note that strange and controversial phenomena are often associated with revivals: the "jerks," shouting, being "slain in the Spirit," speaking in tongues, barking, dancing in the Spirit, and more. Since none of these extraordinary manifestations have appeared in all revivals, we conclude that none of them are mandatory for a spiritual awakening. True revival can happen without them.

Nevertheless, most of these unusual phenomena occur more than once in these accounts. What, then, do we think is the cause of such occurrences? We agree with those observers who have concluded simply that when the divine is poured into the human, we can expect the human to react in extraordinary ways.

Some of these phenomena, we believe, are prompted by God. At other times they are just the exuberant expressions of those who are experiencing God's presence. For that reason, we offer a few words of caution to those who read about the various displays of emotions while they pray for revival in our own day.

First, don't seek the extraordinary signs of revival, for these unusual expressions are not what revival is about. Second, don't measure the success of a revival by the number or intensity of extraordinary signs; if you do, you'll miss the whole purpose of a revival. Third, seek the Lord, because it is he who revives our hearts.

Measure a revival by God himself. Is God present? Focus on what he's doing, not on what people are doing. What has God accomplished?

If we aren't careful, the significance of the revival experience itself can work to hinder the progress of revival. Some see revival as an end in itself, rather than an opportunity to know God. When extraordinary experiences become the goal, revivals become inclusive and sectarian, sometimes even taking on cultic or occult traits.

Since the days of Pentecost there is no record of the sudden and direct work of the Spirit of God upon the souls of men that has not been accompanied by events more or less abnormal. It is, indeed, on consideration, only natural that it should be so. We cannot expect an abnormal inrush of Divine light and power, so profoundly affecting the emotions and changing the lives of men, without remarkable results. As well expect a hurricane, an earthquake, or a flood, to leave nothing abnormal in its course, as to expect a true Revival that is not accompanied by events quite out of our ordinary experience.

A.T. Schofield

The Scope and Fruits of Revival

Another important criterion of a great revival is the fruit it bears beyond the experience itself. Thus a third question to ask in evaluating a revival refers to the scope of its influence: *Was the larger body of Christ awakened to its New Testament task?*

While revivals often begin in a small group, congregation, or single denomination, every great revival spills over its natural boundaries. The Moravian Revival began in the little village of Herrnhutt, Germany, but it touched the world. There were only about five dozen people at Fetter Lane, but it gave birth to the Methodist Church. Asuza Street was a small church by contemporary standards, but the Pentecostal movement for which it was the catalyst has exploded worldwide. Each of the revivals described in this book spilled out of its context into a broad arena.

A fourth question, also with regard to the fruit of a revival, involves its effects on the wider society: *Was the surrounding culture impacted positively by the revival?* When a revived church is mobilized to preach the gospel, individual lives of both believers and the unsaved are transformed by the power of God. When many individuals are brought into conformity with Jesus Christ, the culture is transformed.

The First Great Awakening in England, for example, resulted in Sunday school and educational reform, changes to labor and child welfare laws, significant prison reforms, and the abolition of slavery. During the Welsh Revival, the culture was so transformed that new mules had to be secured to work in the coal mines: The old mules wouldn't respond to miners who no longer cursed and abused the animals! In these and many other ways, revivals in England, America, and other nations have historically shaped those societies into more Christian communities.

A final question, critical to the credibility of our rankings, regards the records of a revival: *Are there reliable sources that demonstrate the greatness of the revival?* We've tried wherever possible to rely on the primary historical sources of eyewitnesses, newspaper accounts, journals, and other written observations of the revivals. When secondary sources have been consulted, we have tried to eliminate biased accounts in which writers had a reason to exaggerate, or records that were in some other way less than objective.

You may well disagree with our choice of the ten greatest revivals or with the order in which we've presented them—after all, we ourselves disagreed over these issues at times. Since we don't have complete records of revival, and no one knows everything that God did in all the revivals that have taken place throughout history, only God knows which were truly the ten greatest. In fact, there may well have been greater revivals than those described in this book—events we know nothing about because no one wrote down what happened.

Nevertheless, here are the ones on which we've chosen to focus:

- The Revival of 1904
- The First Great Awakening, 1727
- The Second Great Awakening, 1780
- The General Awakening, 1830
- The Laymen's Prayer Revival, 1857
- The World War II Revival, 1935
- The Baby Boomer Revival, 1965
- The Pre-Reformation Revival, 1300
- The Protestant Reformation, 1517
- Pentecost, the Beginning of Revival, A.D. 30

Please note that these are not listed in chronological order, but rather in the order of our assessment of their intensity and results. Keep in mind as well that these are ten revival *eras*, not just isolated revival places or revival events. The dates of their beginning are noted, but not dates of their conclusion, because the influence of each revival continued long after its inception.

These are called revival eras because each time God poured out his Spirit, he did so on "all flesh" (see Acts 2:17)—meaning that the revival sprang up in several places at the same time, like a stream that disappears underground only to burst to the surface at another location. In the First Great Awakening, for example, revival sprang up generally at the same time in New England under the influence of Jonathan Edwards, in England with Wesley and Whitefield, and in Germany at Herrnhutt.

When we identify the "ten greatest revivals ever," then, we're speaking of the ten time periods when God gave the greatest manifestation of himself through worldwide "times of refreshing ... [that] come from the presence of the Lord" (see Acts 3:19). We'll begin our close-up studies of revival history with a look at what some scholars consider the greatest spiritual awakening of all time: The 1904 Revival.

CHAPTER ONE

The 1904 Revival

There is a Divine mystery about Revivals. God's sovereignty is in them. I may not live to see it, but the day will come when there will be a great Revival over the whole earth.

Alexander Whyte

A blaze of evening glory at the end of the Great Century"—that's how the 1904 Revival has been described by church historian J. Edwin Orr. For good reason: By some estimates, more than five million people were won to Christ within two years. Aspects of this revival have become legends in the spiritual heritage of evangelicals the world over.

A Response to Prayer

As the nineteenth century came to a close, two evangelical ministries, the Moody Bible Institute in America and the Keswick Convention in England, called their two nations to prayer for revival. The large prayer movement organized by these ministries was matched by an even larger, apparently unconnected movement of prayer worldwide. On mission fields as far away as India, the Far East, Africa, and Latin America, missionaries and national churches began praying for revival in their respective lands. Most of those praying had never seen revival on the mission field; many had never experienced revival themselves. Yet they prayed that God might do for them what they had read about in the stories of history's great revivals.

The Prisoner of War Revival
In response to this prayer movement, the first manifestations of revival began

in a most unlikely place: among prisoners of war held in camps halfway across the world from each other. The Boer War (1899-1902) in South Africa had pitted the Boers (Afrikaners), of Dutch ancestry, against the British. Some of the Boers taken prisoner were held on Bermuda (a British island colony off the southeastern coast of the United States) and some on Ceylon (an island in the Indian Ocean).

According to one observer, the Prisoner of War Revival, as it came to be called, was characterized "by extraordinary prayer, by faithful preaching, conviction of sin, confession and repentance with lasting conversions and hundreds of enlistments for missionary service." With the return of the prisoners to their homeland, revival swept through South Africa as well, which was in the grips of an economic depression.

Japan and Australia

A Japanese awakening began in 1900 as part of a decade-long intensive evangelistic campaign. Campaign organizers had called the evangelical church to prayer as preparation for the evangelistic effort. This prayer resulted in a revival in Japanese cities. The total membership of the churches almost doubled within the decade, despite the interruption of a war with Russia four years into the campaign.

American evangelists R.A. Torrey and Charles M. Alexander were surprised to find a widespread prayer movement during their highly successful campaign in Australia and New Zealand in 1901. The campaign produced more converts than ever before experienced by the churches of that region. When the American evangelist Wilbur Chapman replaced Torrey, revival continued.

British evangelist Rodney ("Gipsy") Smith saw the same results during his mission of peace in South Africa in 1901. The South African Awakening under Smith's ministry was so significant that Smith extended his ministry in that nation an additional six months, yet the greatest manifestation of the 1904 Revival was yet to come.

Wales

During this time a man named Evan Roberts felt impressed by God that revival was coming to his native Wales. He told a friend, "I have a vision of all Wales being lifted up to heaven. We are going to see the mightiest revival that Wales has ever known—and the Holy Spirit is coming soon, so we must get ready."

Though only a young student, Roberts claimed God would give him "a hundred thousand souls" if he were obedient, and before long his preaching was stirring great crowds. But that was only the beginning. Although Roberts became the acknowledged leader of the Welsh Revival, the revival itself extended far beyond his ministry. Churches were filled for two years across the entire nation. Just as he had predicted, a hundred thousand converts were added to the church.

The Rest of the British Isles and the Continent
News of the revival encouraged those praying for revival throughout Great Britain to intensify their efforts. The Archbishop of Canterbury of the Church of England called for a national day of prayer. When one bishop told of confirming 950 converts in a single country parish church, thirty others declared their support for the revival. Outside the Anglican Church, Protestants in England increased their number by 10 percent between 1903 and 1906. Revival swept through Ireland and Scotland as well.

The European continent also experienced an unusual movement of God in response to news of the Welsh Revival. The awakening begun under the ministry of evangelist Albert Lunde in Norway was later described by Norwegian Bishop Berggrav as "the greatest revival of his experience." That revival spread through Sweden, Finland, and Denmark. Lutherans described the revival as "the greatest movement of the Spirit since the Vikings were evangelized." Germany, France, and other European nations were also touched.

North America
News of the Welsh Revival provoked a similar response in America in 1905. Ministers gathered in various conventions to prepare for the coming awakening. In Philadelphia, Methodists soon reported 6,101 new converts in trial membership. The pastors of Atlantic City churches claimed there were only fifty unconverted adults left in that city. On a single Sunday in New York City, 364 were received into membership and 286 were converted to Christ.

The revival also swept through the South. First Baptist Church in Paducah, Kentucky, added a thousand people within a couple of months. Across the Southern Baptist Convention, baptisms increased by 25 percent in a single year.

In the Midwest, Methodists reported "the greatest revivals in their history." Every store and factory in Burlington, Iowa, closed to allow employees to attend prayer meetings. When the mayor of Denver declared a day of prayer in that city, churches were filled by ten o'clock. At 11:30, virtually every place of business in the city closed as 12,000 gathered for prayer meetings in downtown theaters and halls. Every school in town, and even the Colorado State Legislature, closed for the day.

In the West, interdenominational meetings attracted up to 180,000 attendants. One evening in Los Angeles, the Grand Opera House was filled by midnight with drunks and prostitutes seeking salvation. In Portland, Oregon, the entire city virtually shut down between 11:00 A.M. and 2:30 P.M. for noon hour prayer meetings.

A similar movement occurred throughout Canada. Urban and rural churches alike organized prayer meetings and evangelistic campaigns. Thousands gathered nightly during Torrey/Alexander campaigns in major Canadian cities, including Winnipeg and Toronto. Among the converts of Torrey's Toronto meetings was a young man named Oswald J. Smith, who would one day become known as "the greatest missionary statesman of the twentieth century."

Out of these revivals grew Bible institutes and Bible colleges, and an intense movement to offer training in the English Bible to laypeople and those called into Christian service. The purpose was to equip people for lay service in the church and to educate candidates for church and missionary service.

India and the Far East

News of the Welsh Revival also encouraged those praying for revival in India to increase their efforts. The resulting awakening touched every province in that nation. The Christian population increased by 70 percent during the Indian Revival, sixteen times as fast as did the Hindu population. In many places, meetings lasted five to ten hours.

Missionaries in Burma reported an "ingathering quite surpassing anything known in the history of the mission." Among the Burmese ethnic group known as the Karens, two thousand were baptized in 1905, ten times the usual number. In a single church, 1,340 of the Shans, another ethnic group, were baptized in December of that year.

Korea experienced three waves of revival in the first decade of the new century, the best known being the 1907 "Korean Pentecost." Church membership quadrupled during the decade. One of those touched by the Korean revival was a Canadian missionary serving in China, Jonathan Goforth. He returned to Manchuria as a carrier of revival. The national awakening that followed doubled the Protestant population of that nation to a quarter of a million, despite the persecution surrounding both the Boxer Uprising and the 1911 Revolution.

The Pacific Islands, Africa, and Latin America

Revival swept through the island nations of the Pacific as well. In Indonesia, 100,000 evangelicals in 1903 became 300,000 strong within the decade. On the island of Nias, two-thirds of the population was converted to Christ. In Malagasia, Protestant church membership increased by 66 percent.

While the revival had limited effect in South America, both Brazil and Chile were exceptions to the rule. The growth of the evangelical church in those nations began during the revival and continued uninterrupted throughout the century. Approximately one hundred years later, both nations boasted more evangelicals than Roman Catholics attending church in what had once been predominantly Catholic nations.

According to the Edinburgh World Missionary Conference, "more progress had been made in all Africa in the first decade of the twentieth century than experienced hitherto." Between 1903 and 1910, the number of Protestants living in the African continent increased from 300,000 to 500,000. Still, the full impact of the Welsh Revival in Africa was yet to be manifest. As revived missionaries made their way to Africa, the growth rate of the African evangelical church continued to be twice that of the general population for the following half century.

The Pentecostal Movement

As noted earlier, news of the Welsh Revival encouraged many in Southern California to pray to intensify their efforts. In 1907, a small church in Los Angeles saw the crowds grow at their meetings until the converted house in which they met collapsed. They moved into a vacated Methodist church on Asuza Street. During the revival that followed, people began speaking in tongues, a phenomenon that attracted international attention.

The Asuza Street church quickly became a revival center visited by Christians from around the world. The Pentecostal movement was born, and it became the fastest-growing Protestant movement of the century. In fact, religion writers in an Associated Press survey in 1999 voted the Asuza Revival as one of the hundred most important religious movements of the millennium.

This overview of the awakening that shook the world after the turn of the twentieth century should demonstrate clearly why we've included it among the top ten revivals in history. In terms of sheer numbers of conversions alone, it warrants attention, but the scope and fruits of this revival were extraordinary as well. Now we'll look more closely at what happened in some of the places where God's presence became powerfully manifested.

The Welsh Revival (1904)

At the annual gathering of the British Keswick Convention in 1904, those assembled experienced a growing sense that a mighty outpouring of the Holy Spirit was on the horizon. Many Keswick speakers reported that Christians were surrendering themselves more deeply to Christ and committing themselves to pray for revival. Among those speakers was Seth Joshua, an evangelist who conducted many of his meetings in neighboring Wales.

Christians in Wales had witnessed the rapid spread in their land of worldliness and humanistic philosophy, which produced a deadening effect in the churches. One church leader observed, "While the church sleeps, the enemy busily sows tares among the wheat. Nothing short of an outpouring of the Spirit from on high will uproot them, and save our land from becoming prey to atheism and ungodliness."

In response to the conditions around them, Welsh pastors began a season of intense prayer. As they prayed, a small group claimed to experience God's power in their preaching as they challenged their congregations. Among the group was pastor Joseph Jenkins, who led a church in New Quay, Cardiganshire.

Jenkins' New Quay Church was among the first stirred by a touch of revival. The pastor had organized a special conference in January 1904, in which many in his church had begun experiencing personal revival. The spirit of revival continued under the preaching of Seth Joshua. Later that year, Joshua preached in the town of Blaenannerch. During his meetings there, students from the nearby Methodist Academy attended.

Evan Roberts

Evan Roberts was among the academy students who attended Joshua's meetings. At a prebreakfast meeting on Thursday, September 29, the evangelist concluded, crying out in Welsh, "Lord, bend us." When Evan Roberts later recalled that morning, he explained, "It was the Spirit that put the emphasis on 'bend us.'"

"That is what you need," said the Spirit to Evan Roberts. Evans began praying, "O Lord, bend me."

The next meeting that morning was scheduled for nine o'clock. Several students prayed aloud when given the opportunity. Roberts himself knelt with his arms stretched out, perspiration soaking his shirt as he agonized over committing himself to God. Finally he prayed aloud, "Bend me! Bend me! Bend me!" Later that day, Joshua made an entry in his journal recalling the young man's cry.

Roberts felt himself overwhelmed by the love of God. A verse he had learned immediately came to mind: "But God demonstrates His own love toward us, in that while we were still sinners, Christ died for us" (Rom. 5:8).

The motto of the revival in Wales was born out of Roberts' experience that day: "Bend the church and save the world." Though still young, this new evangelist was about to become God's agent to carry the spirit of revival throughout his homeland.

Although he was already twenty-six years old, Roberts had just begun his course of study to train as a minister. As a boy growing up in Loughor, Wales, he'd had a compelling desire to "honor God in every aspect of his life." He knew God was calling him into the ministry, but he resisted enrolling in a formal course of instruction, fearing the training might quench his zeal for souls.

That zeal intensified in the spring of 1904 following a unique encounter with God:

> One Friday night last spring, when praying by my bedside before retiring, I was taken up to a great expanse—without time and space. It was communion with God. Before this I had a far-off God. I was frightened that night, but never since. So great was my shivering that I rocked the bed, and my brother, being awakened, took hold of me thinking I was ill. After that experience I was awakened every night a little after one o'clock. This was most strange, for through the years I slept like a rock, and no disturbance in my room would awaken me. From that hour I was taken up into the divine fellowship for about four hours. What it was I cannot tell you, except that it was divine. About five o'clock I was again allowed to sleep on till about nine. At this time I was again taken up into the same experience as in the earlier hours of the morning until about twelve or one o'clock.

According to Roberts, this experience lasted for three months.

Roberts' fellowship with God grew following the Blaenannerch Conference. He spent hours engaged in personal Bible study, prayer, and worship. The nervousness he'd previously experienced in preaching now seemed to pass.

In addition, Roberts began experiencing visions of large numbers of people coming to Christ. He felt a revival was coming to his native Wales and that he must prepare for ministry. He formed a ministry team with several friends, telling them God was sending a revival that would reach a hundred thousand people for Christ.

Roberts and his team conducted meetings in the area, but he viewed them primarily as preparation for something much larger to come. He knew the revival would come soon, and when it came, he would be busy. Before it arrived, he also knew he needed to return home to gain the support of his family and friends.

The Loughor and Gorseinon Meetings

At the end of October, Roberts took the train home to be with his family and conduct a week of meetings among the youth in his home church. From the train, he wrote various friends to tell them what he was doing and to solicit their prayer support. When he arrived in Loughor, he went to his pastor to request permission to conduct the meetings. The first meeting was scheduled, and he was given permission to speak to any youth who agreed to stay after the usual Monday evening meeting.

At the meeting, Roberts urged that "any who were unwilling to submit to the Holy Spirit" should be free to leave the meeting. As a result, only seventeen remained to hear him. For almost three hours, the zealous evangelist led the group in worship and prayer, calling on God to break down any hardness of heart that might hinder revival. During the meeting, each of those present, including the evangelist's brother and three sisters, experienced the convicting power of the Holy Spirit, confessed their sins, called on God for mercy, and magnified God in praise.

The results that evening convinced Roberts revival would come in its fullness to Loughor if he would remain faithful. Attendance at the meetings began to increase each night. By Friday, those attending Roberts' meetings included people from several other congregations in town.

Although he knew he had commitments as a student, the young man decided to continue the meetings a second week. Furthermore, he would expand the ministry beyond Loughor to other chapels in nearby Gorseinon. Without any formal publicity, by Wednesday people were crowding the church, and those who arrived late stood in the vestibule to listen through the open doors.

On Thursday evening, a service was held in Brynteg Chapel in Gorseinon. Many people went directly to the church from work to insure they would get a seat. A newspaper reporter wandered into the service two hours after it began. In his story, published in the *Western Mail* on Saturday, November 12, he reported:

The meeting at Brynteg congregational church on Thursday night was attended by those remarkable scenes which have made previous meetings memorable in the life history of so many of the inhabitants of the district.

The proceedings commenced at seven o'clock and they lasted without a break until 4:30 ... on Friday morning. During the whole of this time the congregation were under the influence of deep religious fervor and exaltation. There were about 400 people present in the chapel when I took my seat at about nine o'clock.... There is nothing theatrical about [Roberts'] preaching. He does not seek to terrify his hearers, and eternal torment finds no place in his theology. Rather does he reason with the people and show them by persuasion a more excellent way. I had not been many minutes in the building before I felt that this was no ordinary gathering. Instead of the set order of proceedings to which we were accustomed at the orthodox religious service, everything here was left to the spontaneous impulse of the moment. The preacher too did not remain in his usual seat. For the most part he walked up and down the aisles, open Bible in hand, exhorting one, encouraging another, and kneeling with a third to implore blessing from the throne of grace.

Seven and a half hours after the meeting began, the newsman noted,

In the gallery a woman was praying and she fainted. Water was offered her, but she refused this, saying the only thing she wanted was God's forgiveness. A well-known resident then rose and said that salvation had come to him. Immediately a thanksgiving hymn was sung, while an English prayer from a new convert broke in upon the singing. The whole congregation then fell upon their knees, prayers ascending from every part of the edifice, while Mr. Roberts gave way to tears at the sight.

When the reporter left about 4:30 the next morning, dozens of people still stood outside, "discussing what had become the chief subject of their lives."

The meetings continued that week, with evidence of the Holy Spirit moving mightily among those gathered. Evans wrote to a fellow student, telling him of his decision not to return to school. "Perhaps we shall have to go through the whole of Wales," he suggested. "If so, thank Heaven! What a blessed time!"

Two days later, Roberts was invited to preach at Bryn Seion Chapel in Trecynon, Aberdare. He immediately accepted and asked several friends from Loughor to assist him in the campaign. Once again, the Holy Spirit was poured out and the church experienced a significant reviving. By the time the campaign ended, powerful revivals were being reported throughout the nation.

Other Welsh Preachers

Roberts was not the only preacher in the Wales Revival. His friends Sidney Evans and Joseph Jenkins carried the revival to other communities as well. Seth Joshua also experienced revival in his meetings. In one place, Joshua noted in his journal, "There is a wonderful fire burning here. The ground is very prepared, thank God.... Even in the morning a number were led to embrace the Savior. In the afternoon the blessing fell upon scores of young people.... Numbers confessed Jesus, but it is impossible to count."

As revival broke out across the nation, pastors saw their churches fill with people coming to Christ. In the village of Egryn, near Harlech, a farmer's wife named Mary Jones led more than seventy of her neighbors to personal faith in Christ. The revival continued for more than two years, even in places Roberts and others associated with him had not visited.

The Revival's Impact

With regard to the impact of the revival on the wider culture, historian J. Edwin Orr has noted:

> Drunkenness was immediately cut in half, and many taverns went bankrupt. Crime was so diminished that judges were presented with white gloves signifying that there were no cases of murder, assault, rape or robbery or the like to consider. The police became unemployed in many districts. Stoppages occurred in coal mines, not due to unpleasantness between management and workers, but because so many foul-mouthed miners became converted and stopped using foul language that the horses which hauled the coal trucks in the mines could no longer understand what was being said to them. (J. Edwin Orr, *The Flaming Tongue: Evangelical Awakenings, 1900* [Chicago: Moody, 1975], pp. 192-93)

Not surprisingly, news of the revival was widely published both within Wales and beyond.

Soon church leaders were coming from around the world to see for themselves. Common people were also drawn to the revival by the reports they read. Because of the spontaneous nature of the revival, many began their journey not quite sure about where they were going.

One man and his daughter went to the railway station and bought train tickets to attend revival meetings. When they asked the porter at the station how to find the meeting, he responded, "You'll feel it on the train. Go down that road and you'll feel it down there."

The Welsh by nature are a musical people, and they often expressed their new joy in the Lord in song. In many meetings, the people would gather just to sing. During the singing, the Holy Spirit would begin working, and revival would come even when there was no preaching.

The emphasis of Roberts' message could be summarized in four principles. First, he insisted Christians must put away any unconfessed sin. Second, he called on them to renounce any doubtful habit. Third, he told them, "You must obey the Spirit promptly." Finally, he urged people to confess Christ publicly.

Historian J. Edwin Orr describes the revival as "the farthest reaching of the movements of general awakening, for it affected the whole of the evangelical cause in India, Korea and China, renewed revival in Japan and South Africa, and sent a wave of awakenings over Africa, Latin America and the South Seas." Visiting pastors from Norway, Japan, America, India, South Africa, and Korea were all deeply moved in the Welsh Revival and became carriers of revival to their nations as they returned home.

The Azusa Street Revival (1906)

William Joseph Seymour had come to Los Angeles to preach, but now the church doors were locked. He'd travelled from Texas to Southern California at the invitation of the pastor, but the message he preached had caused the pastor to change her mind. The views espoused by this African-American preacher were questionable at best, at least in the pastor's mind. There was no way she would allow that message to be preached in her church. She couldn't stop Seymour from preaching, but she could and would stop it from being preached in her church.

Still in his mid-thirties, Seymour was well acquainted with rejection. He began life as the son of recently freed slaves in Centreville, Louisiana. The South was in transition following the Civil War, but despite the liberation of slaves, in 1870 it was a society still steeped in class distinctions.

In those days, receiving a good education was nearly out of the question for an African American. If Seymour was going to learn how to read and write, he would have to teach himself. The fact that he did so is a commentary on his strength of will and determination.

Still, as a young man in his twenties, Seymour had had enough. He left the South and headed north to Indianapolis. For several years, he waited on tables in a prominent hotel. By the time he was thirty, he was living in Cincinnati.

Early in life, Seymour had been drawn into the Holiness movement then sweeping through the South. In Indianapolis he attended the local Methodist Episcopal church, a church that emphasized the ministry of Christ indwelling the life of the believer. By the time he was thirty, he'd been "saved and sanctified" through the ministry of a revivalistic group called "the Evening Light Saints."

This latter group believed human history was coming to an end and anticipated Christ's imminent return to establish his kingdom. Just before that happened, the group believed, there would be a fresh outpouring of the Holy Spirit, a "latter rain" (see Hos. 6:3). To prepare for this, the group encouraged Christians to leave existing denominations to become part of a pure and interracial church God was beginning to raise up.

Speaking in Tongues

Despite the attractive interracial idealism of the Evening Light Saints, Seymour soon found himself back in the South, in Houston, in a black church. He had little choice: In Houston at the turn of the century, if you were black and attended church, you attended a black church. It was while in this church that Seymour witnessed something he'd never before seen: He heard a woman praying in what seemed like another language.

It was widely held by Holiness groups of that day that "speaking in tongues" was a sign that would accompany the arrival of the last days.

Seymour sensed this woman had something he longed for but hadn't yet found. He knew he had to talk with her.

When he met with Lucy Farrow, the woman who had spoken in tongues, he learned she had recently worked as a governess in Topeka, Kansas. Her employer had been a man named Charles Fox Parham, a white preacher who ran a Holiness Bible school, Bethel College, in the same city. Parham had introduced her to the experience he called "the baptism of the Holy Ghost," which led to speaking in tongues.

Before long, Seymour headed to Topeka to seek out Parham. When he found him, he begged to be admitted into the school. In making his request, however, Seymour was once again brought face-to-face with the realities of life in America at the turn of the century.

While Parham was always looking for students and welcomed the zeal of Seymour, Parham was also a Ku Klux Klan sympathizer. He wasn't sure he was ready to welcome a black student into his school. On the other hand, how could he turn him away? That just didn't seem to be the Christian thing to do, either.

Finally, Parham arrived at a compromise. He would allow Seymour to listen to his lectures from a chair outside by an open window. In the event of rain, Seymour would be allowed to move his chair into the hall, and the door would be left ajar so he could hear.

Seymour agreed to the terms established and began attending Parham's lectures. Earnestly he sought the "baptism of the Holy Ghost," but without success. He continued preaching at black missions while waiting on God for his own "second blessing," as the experience was also called.

On to California

A lady visiting from Los Angeles heard Seymour preach in one of those meetings and recommended him to her pastor back home in California. That recommendation led to an immediate invitation to preach in a little storefront church on Santa Fe Avenue. The church had been started as a split from a local black Baptist church over the doctrine of the second blessing. When the invitation arrived, Seymour saw it as his own version of the apostle Paul's "Macedonian vision" calling him to a new place of ministry (see Acts 9–10). He borrowed train fare from Parham and made his way west.

At his first meeting, Sister Julia W. Hutchins, pastor of the church, recognized significant differences between the preaching of Seymour and her own views of the second blessing. She considered Seymour extreme in his doctrine of the Holy Spirit, perhaps even heretical. It was clear the two could not continue to work together.

When Seymour later arrived at the church to preach at an afternoon meeting, he found the church doors locked. He was no longer welcome in the little storefront church on Santa Fe Avenue. Undaunted, he agreed to preach in a home on Bonnie Brae Avenue.

Several from Sister Hutchins' church attended the meeting along with others in the shabby neighborhood north of Temple Street. Most of the congregation was composed of domestic servants and women who took in laundry. As word of the home meetings spread, the crowds grew. People came to hear a preacher who had never spoken in tongues tell how the blessing of God would come soon when all would have this unique gift.

As Seymour was preparing to go to the meeting on April 9, 1906, an acquaintance named Edward Lee told him he'd received a vision. He claimed the apostles had come to him and told him how to receive the gift of tongues. Together the men prayed, then made their way to the meeting. That night, "the power fell" on those assembled and several, including William Joseph Seymour himself, began praising God in "unknown tongues."

The Apostolic Faith Mission

As news of the outpouring spread through the community, the little home on Bonnie Brae Avenue soon became too small. The weight of the crowd gathered on the porch outside was so great that the porch collapsed. While there were no serious injuries, everyone knew a more adequate meeting place had to be found.

An abandoned church building at 312 Azusa Street was available. It had most recently been used as a warehouse and livery stable. The building was swept out, and Seymour's Apostolic Faith Mission moved to its new home on Easter Saturday, April 14, 1906.

Seymour preached an apocalyptic message, assuring his listeners the end of the world was at hand. It was his view that Jesus was coming very soon to judge the world and establish his kingdom on earth. Prior to that coming, there would be a "latter rain" outpouring of the Holy Spirit. The evidence that the Spirit had indeed come would be "speaking in tongues." Everything seemed to be happening just as Seymour had said.

Then, on the morning of April 18, 1906, four days after the Apostolic Faith Mission had begun holding services on Azusa Street, nine days after the first manifestation of tongues in their midst, the earth itself shook. A major earthquake along the San Andreas fault almost completely destroyed the city of San Francisco. Its impact was felt throughout Southern California. As the ground shook beneath their feet, the lives of many who had ignored Seymour's message were shaken also.

Daily services at 312 Azusa Street quickly filled with both blacks and whites seeking salvation and "the baptism of the Holy Ghost." One white preacher from the South commented, "The color line was washed away by the blood" of Christ. As the young church witnessed what they perceived to be evidences of the end of the world, their worship of God was noisy and enthusiastic.

A skeptical reporter with the *Los Angeles Times* heard about the meeting and attended. The next day, his report described "wild scenes" and a "weird babble of tongues." He was the first of many to publish negative descriptions of the revival. But not all who investigated the story left as antagonistic. Before long, reports were being circulated in Pentecostal circles of those who "came to scorn and stayed to pray."

News of the Azusa Street Revival soon began drawing others from across America and around the world. Seymour himself began publishing an occasional paper describing the progress in the spread of his Pentecostal message. *The Apostolic Faith* attracted readers across America and beyond. In it, Seymour described the doctrines of the movement and published reports of tongue-speaking around the world.

As many as 300 soon crowded into the forty-by-sixty-foot frame building. On occasion that crowd doubled, forcing worshipers to gather in the doorway and around the building outside. Many who came to investigate the revival were themselves touched and received the Azusa Street blessing. They became the pioneers of the Pentecostal movement of the twentieth century.

In their earliest days, the meetings at Azusa Street were multiracial in character. Though Seymour initially taught that speaking in tongues was the evidence of the baptism of the Holy Spirit, he felt increasingly uncomfortable with Christians who spoke in tongues yet still harbored racial prejudice toward people of color. He soon began preaching that the dissolution of racial barriers "was the surest sign of the Spirit's pentecostal presence and the approaching New Jerusalem." Unfortunately, not everyone in the emerging Pentecostal movement agreed.

Concerns Over Race
Charles Parham, Seymour's mentor in his pilgrimage to Pentecost, arrived in Los Angeles in October 1906 to investigate the revival for himself. Seymour welcomed the arrival of his teacher and invited him to preach in his pulpit. For years, Parham had preached about the need for a new dispensation of the Spirit, so he came to Azusa Street with great expectation. But what he saw there was far different from his own vision of the coming revival.

Parham shuddered to see blacks and whites praying at the same altar. When a white woman "slain in the Spirit" (that is, overcome by the power of God) fell back into the arms of a black man, he was horrified at what he called a "darkey revival." When he began preaching, he accused those gathered of practicing animism and rebuked them for their disregard for racial distinctions.

The elders of the Azusa Street Mission, both black and white, rejected Parham's condemnation. What Parham considered a work of the devil was perceived by them to be the work of the Holy Spirit. Parham was asked to leave and barred from returning.

Unfortunately, he wasn't the only white Holiness preacher sympathetic to the Pentecostal message who was unable to break from the cultural values of the day. Soon after the revival began, Pentecostal denominations began to be formed along racial lines. Yet even though they broke with Seymour and his vision of the social outworking of Pentecostalism, they didn't abandon the Pentecostal experience of speaking in tongues they had seen at Azusa Street.

Emerging Pentecostal Denominations
Several major Pentecostal denominations, including the Assemblies of God in Springfield, Missouri, trace their historic roots to the impact of the Azusa

Street Revival on their founders. Leaders of a black denomination who called themselves simply "the Church of God" attended the Azusa Street church for several weeks in June 1907; they returned home to transform their entire denomination into what is still the largest black Pentecostal denomination in America, the Church of God in Christ.

Another Church of God denomination, this one white, became Pentecostal when G.B. Cashwell, an Azusa Street convert, described the Azusa Street Revival at the national convention of that denomination. During that meeting, the General Overseer of the group of churches, A.J. Tomlinson, listened attentively. Then, suddenly, Tomlinson fell out of his chair and began speaking in tongues at Cashwell's feet. While a few churches left the movement, most embraced the Pentecostal message. By the end of the century, the Church of God of Prophecy was a fast growing white denomination in America.

The influence of the Azusa Street Revival spread far beyond the national boundaries of America. The Pentecostal Assemblies of Canada recognize their spiritual indebtedness to Seymour and the Azusa Street mission, especially in the earliest manifestations of charismatic phenomena in Winnipeg and Toronto. Many of their founding fathers first experienced the Pentecostal blessing under Seymour's preaching, or were mentored by him in their early Pentecostal experience.

The spread of the Pentecostal message to South Africa also grew out of the Azusa Street Revival. John G. Lake visited the Azusa Street Mission prior to taking the Pentecostal message to South Africa in 1908. Within five years he'd established 500 black and 125 white Pentecostal churches in that nation. Others took the Pentecostal message to Europe and Asia. *The Apostolic Faith* soon reported:

> The Pentecost has crossed the water on both sides to the Hawaiian Islands on the west, and England, Norway, Sweden and India on the east.... We rejoice to hear that Pentecost has fallen in Calcutta, India.... We have letters from China, Germany, Switzerland, Norway, Sweden, England, Ireland, Australia and other countries from hungry souls that want their Pentecost.... In Stockholm, Sweden ... the first soul came through tonight, receiving the baptism with the Holy Ghost with Bible evidence.... In Christiana, Norway—God is wonderfully demonstrating His power.

In this way the Azusa Street Revival, rippling out across the globe, continued for about three years.

The awakening's views of race relations proved to be too much even for revived Christians at the beginning of the twentieth century. The emphasis on the imminent end of the world also hindered its ability to endure. When Seymour married Jenny Moore, a black leader in his church, some of his strongest supporters objected that marriage was unwise so close to the end of the world. They left to begin a rival group in Portland, Oregon.

Seymour himself died in 1922. The Azusa Street church was closed a few years later, demolished to make way for a new plaza, but the influence of the Azusa Street Revival has been felt around the world now for almost a century.

The Korean Pentecost (1907)

Although Korea was one of the last nations in the Far East to hear the gospel, a series of revivals early in the twentieth century quickly turned the Korean church into a powerful force for God. These awakenings transformed Korean culture and society and reached beyond its borders to other nations in Asia.

In 1890 Dr. R.A. Hardie, a Canadian Colleges medical missionary, arrived in Korea, a nation that was just beginning to hear the gospel from foreign missionaries. In 1898 he associated with the Methodists. About that time, missionaries first began reporting a turning to Christianity on the part of Korean nationals. While missionaries rejoiced in the interest shown, they lamented the fact that these new converts showed no evidence of conviction of sin followed by repentance and saving faith. It appears the first "converts" were entering the church "as interested disciples rather than regenerated members."

In August 1903, seven missionaries gathered in the city of Wonsan for a week of study and prayer. Dr. Hardie confessed he "had not seen any examples of plain, unmistakable, and lasting conversion" in his thirteen years of ministry in Korea. Believing the ministry was being hindered by his own failings, he confessed his faults before both the missionaries and the Korean congregation, with others making similar confessions.

Just a few months later, in October of 1903, missionary advocate Fredrik Franson arrived in Korea and was invited to preach. The meetings were marked by open confession of sins. Many admitted to theft and offered to make restitution. Church members insisted that restitution be made to the Lord rather than to themselves. As a result, funds were raised for evangelism in the area. During his stay in Korea, Franson impressed upon Hardie and his fellow workers the necessity of prevailing prayer.

In 1905, Japan's victory over Russia resulted in the Japanese occupation of Korea, provoking a new Korean nationalistic spirit. Christians looked to the church to organize resistance. Instead, missionary and church leaders preached forgiveness and forbearance. This preaching was followed by a second wave of revival in 1905 and 1906, described as "a spreading fire" and "a continuing religious awakening."

Hundreds were converted, more than in any previous year in the history of the Korean mission. In Pyongyang, 700 conversions were recorded in a two-week period. Still, the best was yet to come.

The blessing of God continued in 1906. In Pyongyang, a New Year's Day evangelistic crusade drew 4,000 people to the meetings, 20 percent of the city's entire population. A united evangelistic thrust in the nation's capital, Seoul, resulted in 1,000 conversions.

As had been their custom in recent years, the missionaries gathered at Pyongyang for a week of prayer and Bible study in August 1906. Speaker Dr. Howard Agnew Johnston told Korean missionaries of the Welsh Revival and other awakenings in India. Half of the missionaries then in the nation were Presbyterians and were deeply moved by accounts of revival among Welsh Presbyterians and Presbyterian missionaries in Asia.

News of the other revivals motivated missionaries to intensify their prayer for a similar outpouring in Korea. Throughout the fall of 1907 and the following winter, missionaries gathered in the church each morning at five o'clock to pour out their hearts to God. During one week together, the missionaries studied the First Epistle of John, which later became their textbook for revival.

The New Year's Day Bible Conference

It was the custom of the Korean church leaders to gather at Pyongyang each New Year's Day for a ten-day Bible conference. In January 1907, 1,500 men gathered together, representing the leadership of hundreds of churches. For almost six months, missionaries had been praying for a mighty movement of God among the Korean church, and anticipation grew as the meetings began.

On Monday afternoon, several missionaries gathered together for prayer. They pleaded with God to move among them. One of their number later testified, "We were bound in spirit and refused to let God go till He blessed us." That night as they entered the church, it seemed the entire building was filled with the presence of God.

After a brief message, Mr. Lee, a Korean leader, took charge of the meeting and called for prayer. So many men wanted to pray that Lee announced, "If you want to pray like that, all pray." Across the church, the whole congregation began praying at the same time.

The result was not the confusion one might expect, but rather, as one observer noted, "a vast harmony of sound and spirit, like the noise of the surf in an ocean of prayer." (Later this practice came to be called a "concert of prayer.") In the midst of the prayer, many of the men became deeply convicted of their sin. One after another rose to his feet in deep agony to confess his sins and cry out to God for his mercy.

On Tuesday, the missionaries gathered at noon to discuss what had happened the night before. Only a few had been present at the meeting. One who had been present expressed a personal concern, because it was common knowledge that two church leaders had a hostile relationship.

On Monday evening, a Mr. Kang had confessed his hatred for a Mr. Kim, but Kim had remained silent. Several missionaries were concerned about Kim's unwillingness to reconcile. That evening, God answered the prayers of the missionaries in a most unusual way.

As the meeting progressed, Kim sat with the elders behind the pulpit with his head bowed. Suddenly he came to the pulpit. Holding it firmly, he confessed, "I have been guilty of fighting against God. I have been guilty of hating not only Kang You-moon, but Pang Mok-sa." Kim's animosity toward Kang was well known, but Pang Mok-sa was the Korean name of the missionary who had urged others to pray for him.

The revelation of hatred toward the missionary came as a complete surprise to all gathered. Turning to the missionary, Kim continued. "Can you forgive me?" he asked. "Can you pray for me?"

The missionary stood to pray in Korean. He began, *"Apage, Apage"* ("Father, Father"). That was as far as he got. "It seemed as if the roof was lifted from the building and the Spirit of God came down from heaven in a mighty avalanche of power among us," the missionary later reported. "I fell at Kim's side and wept and prayed as I had never prayed before."

Across the auditorium, hundreds stood with arms stretched out toward heaven calling on God. Others lay prostrate on the floor. Hundreds cried out to God for mercy.

While they had been praying for revival for months, when it came the missionaries were terrified. Many in the church were in deep mental anguish. Others struggling to resist God were seen clenching their fists and banging their heads against the ground.

Some feared that allowing the meeting to continue would result in some people going crazy, yet they knew they dared not interfere with the work of the Holy Spirit. Finally, they agreed to end the meeting at two o'clock in the morning, six hours after it had begun. Throughout the rest of the conference, similar events were repeated daily.

The Impact of the Revival

The deep reviving of the Korean church leadership had an immediate impact on both the churches and the communities those churches sought to reach. The men returned to their homes as *carriers of revival*. When the story of the Bible conference revival was retold, a similar revival swept the churches.

As the churches were revived, they were gripped by a burning passion to reach the lost in their community. Everywhere, revived churches began to see "drunkards, gamblers, adulterers, murderers, thieves, self-righteous, Confucianists and others" transformed into new creatures in Christ.

The revival had an almost immediate impact in the nation's Christian colleges. Ninety percent of the students at Union Christian College in Pyongyang professed conversion in February 1907. Many also sensed God's call upon their lives as evangelists. They carried the revival beyond the city and into village churches throughout Korea.

From 1905 to 1910, the Korean churches recorded 79,221 additions in membership. That was more than the total number of Japanese church members after fifty years of missionary effort. It was also twice the number of Chinese Protestants after eighty years of missionary labors. By 1912, there were about 300,000 Korean Protestant church members in a nation of twelve million people.

The Korean Pentecost was quickly recognized as a movement of God by Christian leaders around the world. The Edinburgh World Missionary Conference of 1910 declared, "The Korean Revival ... has been a genuine Pentecost, for Korean church membership quadrupled in a decade."

The Student Volunteer Movement, an American voluntary association promoting world missions, cited six evidences of "the present day work of the Holy Spirit in Korea" the same year. These evidences included: "(1) the unity and cooperation which prevailed among Christians, (2) the remarkable numerical growth of the churches, (3) the wonderful religious awakening of 1907 which affected 50,000 converts, (4) the noteworthy interest in the Word of God, (5) the dedication of national Christians to service, including generous giving, and (6) the wonderful prayer life of the Korean Church."

Although the Korean church represented only about 1 percent of the entire population in Korea, its influence in daily life was far greater because of two unique conditions imposed upon new converts. First, missionaries required illiterate Korean adult converts to learn to read Korean in a simple phonetic alphabet before they could be admitted to membership. Second, Korean patriots viewed Christians as Japanese collaborators because they cut their hair as the missionaries and Japanese did rather than in the traditional Korean style. To distinguish between collaborators and Christians, the patriots required Christians to recite chapters from the Bible to prove they were Christians. The result was a 100 percent literacy rate among Christians in a largely illiterate nation. Their ability to read made Christians the natural leaders of the Korean society.

Prayer and Fasting

The Korean Revival was born out of intense prayer, and prayer remained an integral part of Korean church life throughout the twentieth century. In many churches, "concerts of prayer" are still practiced in Sunday morning services, with the whole church confessing their sins to God and then calling on God in unison for his blessing. In what have come to be called the "Dawn Meetings," many Koreans still gather every morning at their churches at five o'clock for prayer. Friday nights are devoted to all-night prayer meetings.

Fasting with prayer is widely practiced. More than 5,000 "prayer mountains" have been established—mountain retreats where Christians go for days or weeks of prayer. The prayer life of the Korean church remains a role model for Christians around the world. No wonder that by the year 2000, a third of the Korean population had become members of a Christian church.

The Manchurian Revival (1908)

If there was ever a man whose very life was defined by revival, it was Jonathan Goforth. As a student at Toronto's Knox College in 1887, his life was impacted by a college revival conducted by the American evangelist D.L. Moody. Later, when he was a missionary in China, news of the Welsh Revival created a deep hunger for a similar movement of God in his own ministry. Once he learned of the Korean Pentecost, he travelled to see it for himself. After Goforth returned to China, he became a carrier of revival who brought awakening to Manchuria.

As a young man preparing for ministry, Goforth read Hudson Taylor's book describing missionary work in China. He was already involved in work at an area rescue mission, but he was so impressed by what he read that he committed his life to serving God in China. Rather than join Taylor's China Inland Mission, Goforth and his wife Rosalind served under the sponsorship of their local Presbyterian church.

When they were assigned to serve in Honan Province, Goforth contacted Taylor to ask for advice. The China Inland Mission had tried unsuccessfully to establish a work in that province, so Taylor rejoiced to learn that another group was bringing the gospel to that part of the Asian nation. Knowing the work would be difficult, Taylor wrote back urging the younger missionary to "go forward on your knees."

The Boxer Rebellion

Much of Goforth's early ministry in China involved training hundreds of Chinese pastors and evangelists. He and other missionaries served at a time when many European businessmen were exploiting China. An indigenous movement known as the "Boxers" rebelled at the abuse China was suffering at the hands of these unethical businessmen. Unfortunately, the Boxers' hatred for foreigners didn't distinguish between missionaries and the unethical English businessmen.

On December 31, 1899, the Boxers murdered a British missionary. The empress of China issued an order that all foreigners should be executed. In the bloodbath that followed, over a hundred missionaries were killed. The Goforths were wounded in the uprising, barely escaping with their lives.

The world responded to the Boxer Revolt with military might, capturing Peking and crushing the old order. While the revolt had been directed primarily at foreigners, hundreds of national Christians also lost their lives at the hands of the Boxers. Their bravery in the hour of persecution and martyrdom later bore fruit. As peaceful conditions returned to China, the Chinese people began flocking to church to learn more about Christianity.

Three Phases of Awakening

According to J. Edwin Orr, the Chinese awakening occurred in three phases. From 1900 through 1905, a significant prayer movement emerged in many parts of the nation. These prayer meetings actually preceded the Boxer uprising, and many who were involved in the prayer movement became martyrs in the revolt. The years 1906-07 were marked by a widespread awakening as large numbers of Chinese nationals responded to the preaching of the gospel. The third phase of the awakening, an extraordinary revival, began in 1908 and continued up to 1911.

In 1907 Goforth made a tour of Korea, something he'd wanted to do ever since he'd heard the first reports of the Korean revival. While there, he was deeply moved by what he experienced. He realized the movement in Korea was "no wild gust of religious enthusiasm," but rather a deep, moving work of the Holy Spirit. He was also challenged by the prayer life of the Korean missionaries and national church leaders. Believing God was "no respecter of persons," Goforth began praying for a similar outpouring of the Holy Spirit in China.

On his way back to Honan from Korea, Goforth stopped one evening in Mukden to share what he had seen in Korea with a group of missionaries. They were deeply impressed, and they asked Goforth to return the next February to conduct a special week of meetings.

When Goforth returned to Mukden for the scheduled meetings, things didn't look promising. The evening Goforth arrived, his host took the opportunity to speak critically of a friend of Goforth, claiming, "his theology is as old as the hills." After the service, Goforth learned that his host's wife had been so opposed to having the special meetings that she had arranged to visit out of town during the campaign. In addition, Goforth learned that no prayer meetings had been organized as he'd requested. As he prepared to go to bed that evening, he wept and cried out to God.

"What is the use of my coming here?" he asked. "These people are not seeking after Thee. They have no desire for blessing. What can I do?"

No sooner had he begun to pray when it seemed as though a voice came back to him, saying, "Is it your work or Mine? Can I not do a sovereign work?" Then a verse Goforth had memorized years earlier came to his mind: "Call to Me, and I will answer you, and show you great and mighty things, which you do not know" (Jer. 33:3).

Confession and Reconciliation

The next morning, one of the elders of the church came to see Goforth before the scheduled morning meeting. As soon as the two were alone, the elder began to weep uncontrollably, telling his story:

> In the Boxer year, I was treasurer of the Church. The Boxers came and destroyed everything, the books included. I knew I could lie with safety. There were certain Church funds in my keeping which I swore I had never received. Since then I've used the money in my business. Yesterday, during your address I was searched as by fire. Last night I couldn't sleep a wink. It has been plain to me that the only way that I can find relief is to confess my sin before the Church and make full restitution.

Following Goforth's message that morning, the elder made his confession.

Suddenly, a member of the group issued a piercing cry, but he wouldn't say anything. Others, however, moved to tears, one after another began praying and confessing sin. The conviction continued to spread the next day. An older missionary who had been part of the Scottish Revival of 1859 claimed he was seeing that revival reenacted in China.

On the fourth day, Goforth concluded his message with his usual invitation for the people to pray as God would lead them. When he did so, a man came to the front of the meeting place with tears flowing down his face. It was the elder who two days earlier had cried out, yet had resisted confessing his sin. Now the Spirit of God had broken through earlier barriers. He turned to face the congregation and began his confession.

"I have committed adultery," he confessed. "I have tried three times to poison my wife." Then, looking at the bracelets and rings he was wearing, he took them off and placed them in the offering plate. "What have I," he said, "an elder of the Church, to do with these baubles?" Then he reached into his pocket and took out his elder's card. He tore it in pieces and scattered them on the floor.

"You people have my cards in your home. Kindly tear them up. I have disgraced the holy office. I herewith resign my eldership."

Several others confessed sin and recognized their unworthiness before God. That morning, all the elders and deacons of the church resigned from their offices as they confessed sin they felt disqualified them. Then the pastor stood before his congregation.

"It is I who am to blame," he insisted. "If I had been what I ought to have been, this congregation would not be where it is today. I'm not fit to be your pastor any longer. I, too, must resign."

With the resignation of their pastor, the church felt it was time to begin a ministry of reconciliation in their midst. From different parts of the congregation came the cry to reappoint the pastor. It seemed as if the whole church was expressing its confidence in the pastor. He was restored to his office. Then the elders were also restored to their offices, as were the deacons.

The revival then spread from the church to the missionaries. During a prayer time the next morning, Goforth's host ran forward in the meeting, crying, "Oh, pray for us missionaries; for we need it more than any of you." The man's wife returned early and was also touched by the revival in the final days of the campaign.

On the last day of the meetings, a national pastor addressed the people. "You know how many elders and members of this congregation have drifted away," he began. "Oh! if there were only some way of bringing them back." Then the congregation rose to their feet in unison and began crying out to God for those who had drifted from the church. By year's end, hundreds had returned to the fold. Most confessed they had never been converted.

The meeting at Mukden was the first of several similar meetings conducted by Goforth throughout China. In two years, Goforth completed thirty campaigns in six provinces of China. He never asked anyone to confess publicly, yet public confession of sin was common in the Manchurian Revival. He simply concluded his message with the statement, "You people have an opportunity to pray."

In many meetings that invitation was followed by open confession of sins. The list was long: idolatry, theft, murder, adultery, gambling, opium smoking, disobedience to parents, hatred, quarrelsomeness, lying, cheating, gambling, fraud, division, misappropriation of funds. Through such confessions, the revival led to deep and lasting change in the lives of those touched by it.

The revival also gave missionaries working with the usually stoic Chinese new insights into the people with whom they worked. One British missionary reported, "We know now that Chinese are emotionally susceptible in matters of religion. We know now that 'instantaneous conversions' may be seen in China as was seen in Chicago or London. We know that when people long for the filling of the Spirit, and they are willing to sacrifice all, God will revive them in Shensi, China, as in Keswick."

The Manchurian Revival also helped establish the indigenous Chinese church. Chang Ling-sheng, a Presbyterian elder active in the Shantung Revival, embraced the Pentecostal experience when missionaries from the Azusa Street revival came to China. He teamed up with two others to establish the True Jesus Church, an indigenous sabbatical Pentecostal denomination.

Years later, Nee To-sheng, better known outside of China as Watchman Nee, was influenced by a single British missionary, Margaret E. Barber. In 1909, Barber had submitted to believer's baptism and left her Anglican mission to become an independent faith worker. She conducted "breaking of bread" meetings similar to those of the Christian Brethren. Nee To-sheng organized the Little Flock, a Brethren-style indigenous Chinese denomination. The True Jesus Church and Little Flock soon had more adherents than all other mission-sponsored churches combined.

The Mizo Outpouring (1906)

When news of the Welsh Revival of the early nineteenth century reached India, many Christian missionaries began praying for a similar outpouring on their own field of service. As a result, a significant revival broke out in the Khasi Hills, which eventually brought an end to paganism in that region. It was news of that indigenous Indian revival that first stimulated interest in revival among the Mizo Christians in Lushai, India.

Early in 1906, ten dedicated young Christians hiked through a mountain jungle for two weeks to get to an outlying district church. When they arrived, they quickly became disappointed, because the entire ministry was in Khasi, a language which none of the Mizo Christians understood. They observed and sensed a strange power at work in the meetings, but with no one to explain what was happening, it had little apparent impact on their own life.

They left the meetings to return to their homes, pausing at the village of Chatlang to pray. During that prayer, they "felt their hearts filled with a strange joy." Some regard this as the beginning of the Mizo Outpouring.

When they got home, they gathered Christians every night to pray for revival. After a week of intense prayer, nothing had happened. "Perhaps God would not send revival after all," they reasoned. It was easy to assume God would withhold revival blessings because of the widespread paganism in their region.

Nevertheless, as the Mizo Christians were saying farewell to three friends, revival came. According to one observer, while the group sang the hymn "God Be With You Till We Meet Again," "the Spirit was poured upon them in a remarkable manner." Others living nearby joined them as they continued in a time of prayer and praise. God had not abandoned them. Revival had come!

The outpouring quickly spread throughout the region, "creating extraordinary interest." Missionary D.E. Jones prophesied that revival would break out in Phullen, a large village several days away. A teacher was sent to be a carrier of revival to Phullen. When he arrived, he discovered that the revival was already in progress. It apparently had begun about the time of the missionary's prophecy.

Difficult Days

This initial Mizo Outpouring resulted in an increase in church membership and inquirers. It was primarily marked by conviction of sin among church members and adherents. The awakening also helped prepare the church for difficult days that lay ahead.

Pagan village chiefs responded to the threat from the revival by severely persecuting the church. Christians were awakened at midnight and driven into the jungle by angry neighbors. The 1907 persecution was followed by a "revival of paganism" that mocked the Christian revival with its own pagan hymns and festivals. This antirevival, says one report, "spread like wildfire, with demonstrations in every village."

Church leaders despaired as they saw their congregations decline under intense persecution. Life for the believers in the hills grew worse before it grew better. In the winter of 1911–12, the flowering bamboo attracted hordes of rats. The rats devoured the stores of grain and the grain growing in the fields almost overnight. People subsisted on roots. Multitudes died of starvation, while others poured out of the hills to the plains, looking for something to eat.

Missionaries responded with help. Relief offerings were collected in Wales and distributed throughout the Mizo church. Despite the persecution they had experienced, the Mizo Christians chose to share their food ungrudgingly with their hungry pagan neighbors. These acts of kindness demonstrated in the midst of distress brought an end to the pagan revival and created a renewed interest in the Christian gospel.

In 1913, revival fires were rekindled. The Mizo church was once again energized for evangelistic ministry. Six years later, according to one account, "an even greater revival broke out," rapidly sweeping through the region and impacting the neighboring states of Tipperah and Manipur.

At the end of the twentieth century, Mizoram (formerly Lushai) is undoubtedly India's most Christian province. Despite its poverty, it is also the most zealously evangelical region in India. This province, first visited by missionaries only a hundred years ago, now sends out hundreds of its own missionaries to other provinces in India and neighboring nations throughout Asia. Commenting on the effect of the Mizo Outpouring, one observer notes, "The Hill Tribes set forth in indisputable evidence, the power of the gospel to transform a primitive people."

A Summary of the 1904 Revival

The authors judged this revival the greatest because these remarkable accounts from the early twentieth century demonstrate clearly that this awakening shook the world, and many of its influences continued throughout the century. In some ways, the First World War, coming a decade later, probably robbed the 1904 Revival of some of the influences on society it might have otherwise realized. Yet the effects were nevertheless considerable. In Great Britain, for example, it began to shape the morality of a generation. The changed lives of converts resulted in reductions in crime, drunkenness, and gambling, along with increases in honesty, truthfulness, and chastity throughout the nation.

A wave of improved moral behavior in America followed the awakening as well. It produced a revival of righteousness that culminated with the passing of the Eighteenth Amendment to the United States Constitution, which prohibited the sale of alcoholic beverages. Throughout the nation, political reform was effected as corrupt district attorneys, mayors, governors, senators, and assemblymen were replaced with those perceived as honest.

Many young people touched by the revivals went as student volunteer missionaries to foreign fields, where they established schools and hospitals on their various fields. The number of pupils attending Christian schools in India, for example, doubled in the two decades following the revival. Ninety percent of all nurses there were Christians, most trained at mission hospitals. In China, missionaries laid the foundations of that nation's educational and medical systems. The same was true in many nations throughout the African continent.

The Pentecostal Revival begun at Azusa Street continued to grow throughout the century, including within its wake the charismatic renewal in many denominations and "the signs and wonders" movement. It also led to the establishment of many new denominations.

For all these reasons and more, few would dare dispute the conclusion of historian J. Edwin Orr: This revival was indeed "the most extensive evangelical awakening of all time."

CHAPTER TWO

The First Great Awakening, 1727–50

There are some special seasons wherein God doth in a remarkable manner revive religion among His people.

Solomon Stoddard, America's first revivalist

T he First Great Awakening flashed like a bolt of lightning on a dark night across the German skies, crossed the ocean to America, jumped over to England, and from there went on to touch the world. God had said, "I will pour out of My Spirit on all flesh" (Acts 2:17), and in this awakening we see clear evidence of the fulfillment of that promise: The Holy Spirit began falling on the aristocracy of Germany, the poor masses of England, and the rich merchants of Connecticut.

The First Great Awakening: An Overview

Perhaps the earliest recorded outpouring of the Holy Spirit in the First Great Awakening was experienced by a small group of Moravian Christians in Herrnhut, Saxony (Germany), as they gathered to observe the ordinance of the Lord's Supper on a summer evening in 1727. Those who gathered experienced the presence of God so profoundly that the prayer meeting begun a few days later continued twenty-four hours a day for more than a hundred years. Out of that prayer meeting, hundreds of missionaries were sent to carry the gospel to unreached peoples around the world.

The American Colonies

Only a few years later, various outbreaks of revival were experienced throughout the American colonies. The first was in 1734 in Northhampton, Massachusetts, under the preaching of the brilliant Congregationalist pastor and theologian Jonathan Edwards. Within a few short months, awakening had spread across New England.

Four years later, people throughout all the English colonies were stirred to conversion through the preaching of another great evangelist, the Englishman George Whitefield. Benjamin Franklin published Whitefield's fiery sermons for the masses to read, and these publications contributed to the revival as well.

England

The beginnings of the "Evangelical Revival," as this awakening was called in England, are usually traced to a Moravian Watch Night Service at Fetter Lane on December 31, 1739. About three o'clock in the morning, the sixty young men who had gathered to pray experienced what George Whitefield later described as "a Pentecostal season." The Fetter Lane outpouring overwhelmed those who experienced it. They left the chapel that morning empowered by the Holy Spirit to change the world as they knew it.

John and Charles Wesley, ministers in the Church of England, were also present at that meeting. Within months, Whitefield and the Wesleys were preaching in the fields and stirring the hearts of thousands of coal miners thought by many to be beyond the reach of the gospel. John Wesley possessed the organizational skills necessary to harness the energy of revival into an evangelistic movement, which became the Methodist Church.

From the Moravians, the Methodists learned to worship God with a new song. The hymns written during the Great Awakening by Charles Wesley and other Methodists are still widely used in the worship of God by evangelical Christians today.

Native Americans

The awakening that swept Germany, America, and England also had a profound impact on the native peoples of North America. As a young missionary to the Native Americans, David Brainerd was surprised to see these usually stoic people crying out to God for mercy after he preached to them. The highly emotional Indian Revival at Crossweeksung, New Jersey, had a significant and lasting impact on the social fabric of the tribe. Families were strengthened and alcohol use declined.

The Moravian Revival (1727)

No one could anticipate what would transpire in the next few hours as the small group of Moravian Christians gathered in Herrnhut, Germany, to observe the Lord's Supper on Wednesday evening, August 13, 1727. Those present had a growing recognition that all was not right among them. Though they weren't as openly critical of one another as they had been only weeks earlier, their leader challenged them to "quit judging each other."

The Moravians in Herrnhut lived in harmony as a Christian community, but the sweetness of the faith seemed to be missing in their lives. When they assembled that summer evening, however, they experienced the presence of God. As a result, they were changed, "in a single moment into a happy people." The revival went on for a hundred years.

Count Zinzendorf

The Moravian movement had begun with Count Nicholas von Zinzendorf, a young nobleman converted to Christ early in his childhood. At age four, he wrote and signed his own covenant with God: "Dear Savior, do Thou be mine and I will be Thine." When asked later in life about the driving force of his life, Zinzendorf responded, "I have one passion: It is Jesus, Jesus only."

His passion was often expressed in prayer. As a teenager, he established seven prayer groups while studying at the University of Halle. When he graduated at age sixteen, he furthered his education by travelling to various foreign countries.

Zinzendorf had a great love for art, and it was in the Dusseldorf Gallery that he saw the painting that moved him most, a painting of the crucifixion of Jesus. Over the picture was the Latin motto: *Hoc feci pro te; Quid facis pro me?* which means, "This have I done for you; what have you done for me?" As he stood gazing at the picture, Zinzendorf determined to use his resources and influence in the service of God.

Later, Zinzendorf encouraged a small band of religious refugees to establish a community on his estates in Saxony. The Moravian Brethren saw themselves as the spiritual heirs of Bohemian reformer John Hus. For generations, they had wandered from place to place to escape intense persecution. Many had died for their faith. Others had been imprisoned and tortured.

Fleeing to Germany for refuge, the Moravians found it in Saxony. They named their community Herrnhutt, "the Lord's Watch," as a testimony and reminder of God's watch over them.

Their new home greatly improved their physical conditions, but all was not well spiritually. Early in 1727, the community members were deeply divided and critical of one another. Heated public controversies were not uncommon; it seemed they argued about everything: predestination, holiness, baptism. It was doubtful the community would survive much longer.

Zinzendorf himself chose to intervene, visiting the adult members, urging them "to seek out and emphasize the points in which they agreed" rather than emphasizing their differences. On May 12, 1727, they all signed a covenant agreeing to dedicate their lives to the service of the Lord.

A "Baptism of Love"

While it was one thing to stop fighting, it was something completely different to "have fervent love for one another" (1 Pet. 4:8). To address this need, many began praying for a baptism of love. By July, a number of them were meeting together to worship God by singing hymns and calling on God to visit the community. On the fifth of August, the Count and about a dozen others spent the entire night in an emotional prayer meeting. They sensed God was about to do something significant.

On Sunday, August 10, the community experienced a foretaste of what was on the horizon. While Pastor Rothe led the service, he was overwhelmed by the power of God. As he collapsed to the ground, the whole congregation fell in the presence of the Lord. Prayer, singing, and weeping continued until midnight.

It was with this sense of expectation that the community gathered together three days later to share in a communion service. What took place at that service can be described only as an outpouring of the Holy Spirit. According to one Moravian historian, "The Holy Ghost came upon us and in those days great signs and wonders took place in our midst." So great was their hunger for the Scriptures in the days following that service that they gathered daily at 5:00 A.M., 7:30 A.M., and 9:00 P.M. for services. One observer noted, "Self-love and self-will, as well as all disobedience, disappeared, and an overwhelming flood of grace swept us all out into the great ocean of Divine Love."

Many in the community believed the outpouring they were experiencing was the result of increased prayer over the summer. Out of that conviction, twenty-four men and twenty-four women covenanted together to pray continually on August 26. They drew lots and began praying around the clock, each couple praying for an hour.

Others joined in, swelling the ranks of intercessors to seventy-seven. Among the children, a similar emphasis on prayer was begun. The prayer meeting begun on August 27, 1727, outlived any of the people who began it. A century later, one could still find people praying in Hernhutt at any hour of the day or night.

Moravian Missions

Though some church historians think of the celebrated English Baptist missionary William Carey as the father of modern Protestant missions, the Moravian outpouring and hourly intercession that grew out of it gave birth to missions half a century before Carey sailed to India. Within twenty-five years, a hundred missionaries had been sent from Hernhutt to various parts of the world. Carey himself was inspired by mission reports published by Moravian journals, and he challenged British Baptists to follow their example.

One result of the Moravian revival was "a joyful assurance of their pardon and salvation." This was the message they took to all who would listen. It crossed social, economic, and cultural barriers with similar effect. Through this message the Moravian revival had its greatest impact.

Though many of the poor received the Moravians' message gladly, their converts were found in all classes of society. For example, one popular European countess found herself dissatisfied with her affluent life. In the midst of her despair, she met a humble Moravian shoemaker and was puzzled with his cheerfulness.

When she asked him why he was so happy, he responded, "Jesus has forgiven my sins. He forgives me every day and he loves me, and that makes me happy through all the hours." That answer was the beginning of the countess's own spiritual pilgrimage. She discovered for herself "the same joyful faith" and had a profound impact as she shared her newfound faith among the titled families of Europe.

As we shall see when we look more closely at the revival in England, the Moravian outpouring also planted the seeds of the Methodist movement through its influence on that movement's founder, John Wesley. In time, the Methodist movement was to touch millions around the globe.

"The Surprising Work of God" in Northhampton and Beyond (1734)

Like many towns and cities in New England, Northhampton, Massachusetts, was settled by colonists with a deep commitment to the gospel and the Reformed or Calvinist tradition. For these settlers, being active in the life of the church was as much a social as a religious responsibility. The local church in any such town was the center of life in the community. Each colony's founders were predominantly Christians committed to the practical expression of their faith in a new world.

Initially, church members were deeply committed to both Christ and his church, but their children and grandchildren tended not to share their parents' and grandparents' zeal for God. That lack of faith presented a social as well as a religious problem: In these communities, to be cut off from church communion because one was unconverted meant being cut off from society as a whole. In an effort to deal with this dilemma, a novel approach to church membership was developed.

Advocates of the new way called it "the Half-Way Covenant." They argued it was better to have unconverted people in church where they could hear the gospel and be converted, than to cut them off because they were unconverted. Men such as Solomon Stoddard, a widely respected preacher of the gospel, urged their fellow pastors to let morally upright people participate at the Lord's Table even though they were unconverted. While some still opposed the idea, it was hard to convince their brethren to resist the plan once someone of Stoddard's stature endorsed it.

Initially, the Half-Way Covenant seemed to work. Church attendance continued to be part of community life, and the unconverted heard the gospel as often as the pastor cared to preach it. As anticipated, there were from time to time "special harvest seasons" when many who had sat under the gospel ministry were converted to Christ. Stoddard himself had five such seasons during his ministry at the Northhampton, Massachusetts, church he pastored.

When men such as Stoddard pastored churches, the Half-Way Covenant seemed to work well. But not all men in New England pulpits had preaching gifts and abilities equal to his. In many churches, unconverted church members became increasingly influential, and the spiritual emphasis of the ministry suffered.

Jonathan Edwards

Out of respect for their pastor, Stoddard's congregation supported his emphasis on spiritual things. But when Stoddard's grandson, the young Jonathan Edwards, assumed the pulpit, he had difficulties. As a result, the spiritual drift that had been more noticeable elsewhere in New England now became apparent even in Northhampton.

Jonathan Edwards began to see the long-term problems associated with the Half-Way Covenant. He struggled with the decision to bring his church back to the place from which they had fallen. He thought that only those converted to Christ should be members of the church; personal moral uprightness was not enough.

In the fall of 1734, Jonathan Edwards began preaching with a passion to convert the lost who were a part of his Northhampton church. It was not until late in December "that the Spirit of God began extraordinarily to set in and wonderfully to work amongst us," as he later wrote. Within a matter of days, half a dozen church members were converted. This was not a mass movement to Christ; rather, each individual was converted in a unique way, often not knowing what was happening in the lives of others.

While this was the beginning of what Edwards had prayed for, he could not help but be concerned when he heard of the conversion of one young lady in particular. She had a reputation as a woman "who had been one of the greatest company-keepers in the whole town." When she asked to meet with her pastor, he had no idea God was working in her life. Yet as they talked, Edwards himself became convinced that she'd experienced "a glorious work of God's infinite power and sovereign grace" in her life. Apparently, she was truly converted.

Strangely, although Edwards had been preaching for conversions, this conversion caused him some concern. He'd hoped the moral members of the congregation would see their need for Christ and be converted. He feared that news of this young lady's conversion would cause the unconverted members of his church to become even more complacent about their need for Christ.

As it turned out, Edwards' fears were unfounded. It was in fact the conversion of this young lady that fueled the flame of the revival. The change in her life was so significant that soon the whole town was talking about it. The converting power of God was discussed at every level of society.

As in the case of the Samaritan woman of Jesus' day, this young lady's conversion resulted in many other conversions. According to Edwards, "This work of God, as it was carried on and the number of true saints multiplied, soon made a glorious alteration in the town. So that in the spring and summer following, the town seemed to be full of the presence of God. It never was so full of love, nor joy, and yet so full of distress, as it was then."

In every home in Northhampton, people were converted during the revival. Parents rejoiced over the conversion of their children. Individuals with unsaved spouses rejoiced over the conversion of husband or wife.

Christians gathered together to express their newfound joy in the Lord. "Our public assemblies were then beautiful," Edwards recalled. "The congregation was alive in God's service, every one earnestly intent on the public worship, every hearer eager to drink in the words of the minister as they came from his mouth."

As the Spirit of God worked through the preaching of the Scriptures, people responded in various ways. Some wept out of deep sorrow and distress as they became convinced of their sin. Others rejoiced in the joy of their salvation, overwhelmed with a new love for the brethren. Still others agonized in prayer for unconverted friends and loved ones. There was a deep sense of the presence of God in their midst.

Edwards thought that sharing what God was doing in Northhampton would encourage others who longed to see revival in their community. He published a call to prayer encouraging Christians to unite in intercession for revival. He also published other works on revival that described to some degree what God had done in his community.

When describing the revival he'd experienced, Edwards noted "an extraordinary sense of the awful majesty, greatness and holiness of God, so as sometimes to overwhelm soul and body, a sense of the piercing, all seeing eye of God so as to sometimes take away bodily strength." It was not uncommon to see people collapse physically under conviction of sin as they came to see the Lord as the holy God and to recognize his right to judge their sin. As a result, many experienced "an extraordinary view of the infinite terribleness of the wrath of God, together with a sense of the ineffable misery of sinners exposed to this wrath."

But this intense conviction of sin wasn't the only mark of the revival. As people were converted, they developed an intense passion for God. They longed "to be more perfect in humility and adoration." Edwards noted this passion especially in the worship of God: "The person felt a great delight in singing praises to God and Jesus Christ, and longing that this present life may be as it were one continued song of praise to God."

The "surprising work of God in Northhampton," as Edwards called it, soon spread to other communities throughout New England. The movement became known as "the Great Awakening." Edwards was widely recognized as a respected leader in that movement, for his books and preaching called countless people back to God.

George Whitefield

The other great leader of the awakening was the itinerant evangelist George Whitefield. Having arrived from his native England in 1738 for his first preaching tour of the American colonies, Whitefield was soon stirring up crowds of unprecedented size. He insisted on the necessity of repentance, purity of living, and individual conversion through personal experience.

This bold evangelist also thundered forth against unconverted clergymen. At the time, most of the pastors in New England approached religion from a more rationalistic, less experiential perspective. They had been trained in colleges where the curriculum was heavily influenced by Enlightenment thinking. The old emphasis on Bible, theology, and ministerial preparations had been replaced with math, science, law, and medicine. Not surprisingly, then, Whitefield's preaching disturbed many.

In addition, Whitefield attracted listeners to meetings in unusual locations, such as fields, orchards, barns, and riverbanks. One observer said of a typical assembly gathered to hear him: "The riverbanks were black with people and horses." He promoted the separation of the church from political control, "untainted with the affairs of the colonies."

To attract attention to his revival meetings, Whitefield employed loud music and marched through the streets, and his oratorical style was theatrical and powerful. Unlike most of his contemporaries, he spoke extemporaneously—that is, he did not read his sermon from a written text. In all these regards, Whitefield challenged the established way of doing things, raising considerable controversy in the process.

One association of ministers, for example, wrote a letter attacking the itinerants on five points:

1. They claimed it was against the will of God to separate converts from the unconverted.
2. They denied that everyday "saints" could recognize "true ministers."
3. They denied that one need only be a Christian to preach the gospel.
4. They denied that there was any greater presence of God in meetings led by lay preachers.
5. They insisted that God had not disowned the ministry and ordinances of the established churches.

Despite such objections from the religious establishment, however, the awakening blossomed everywhere. God's Spirit would not be corralled.

The Fetter Lane Watch Night Revival (1739)

Only a few years after the outpouring of the Holy Spirit at Herrnhut, the Moravian evangelist Peter Bohler preached the gospel in the colony of Georgia and then went on to plant the Moravian Church in England. At the time, England was desperately in need of revival. In the city of London, for example, one house in six held a "grogshop" where a man could drink gin until he was drunk—and it would cost him only a penny. The rampant use of alcohol led to widespread crime in the street.

In his *Life of Wesley*, biographer John Telford describes a violent group of young men who roamed the streets at this time and called themselves "The Mohocks," noting:

Neither men nor women were safe from these drunken fiends. It was a favorite amusement with them to squeeze their victim's nose flat on his face and bore out his eyes with fingers. Their prisoners were pricked with swords or made to caper by swords thrust into their legs. Women were rolled down Snow Hill in barrels. Those responsible to keep law and order in the city were failing miserably. Criminals were more likely to get away with their crime than be caught, tried and punished. The city was kept in constant terror by those who "set their own rules."

Fetter Lane Chapel

In the midst of these deplorable spiritual conditions, the Moravian congregation of the Fetter Lane Chapel in London sought to live a devout Christian life. Following the custom of the early church and their Moravian brethren in Germany, they were known for celebrating the "love feast" as a prelude to the observance of the Lord's Supper. It was a time of sharing together around a common meal.

According to Moravian custom, New Year's Eve was the occasion for one of these feasts, followed by an opportunity to begin the new year in prayer and praise to God. On December 31, 1738, the Fetter Lane Moravians faithfully made their way to church for this annual "Watch Night" service, as they called it. As the sixty young men belonging to this particular Moravian Society made their way to the meeting, none could imagine the profound effect that night would have on the world.

The great size of the crowd in attendance at the little chapel that evening couldn't hinder the deep commitment of these believers to this distinctive expression of worship. Neither could the ethnic differences between the German and English people who were present prevent them from having fellowship together. In fact, the sixty people at Fetter Lane knew each other well.

Surprisingly few details are known about the meeting that night. The love feast was observed and no doubt enjoyed by those who had gathered. Most likely a passage from the Scriptures or some religious book was read publicly in the meeting. Perhaps one or more in the group exhorted the others from the Scriptures. These activities were common in Moravian meetings, but that night all of them were but a shadow of the one event that the great evangelist Whitefield would later describe as "a Pentecostal season indeed."

As the evening passed and the morning of the first day of the New Year began, the group began praying. As they continued praying together, "the power of God came mightily upon" the group about three in the morning. Responses to this outpouring of the Holy Spirit were varied. Some fell to the ground, awestruck and overwhelmed with the very presence of God. Others were filled with "exceeding joy" as they experienced the presence of God. All were caught by surprise, but when they recovered somewhat, they united their voices to sing a hymn: "We praise Thee, O God, we acknowledge Thee to be the Lord." The Evangelical Revival, as it came to be called in England, had begun.

Seeds of the Methodist Movement

Just a few months before, Peter Bohler had met the Anglican clergyman John Wesley and talked with him on board a ship travelling from Georgia to England. That voyage was a time of deep introspection for Wesley. He'd travelled to Georgia believing God would greatly use him to preach the gospel to the Native Americans, but his ministry experience in the colony was a failure. Returning to England, Wesley had written, "I went to America to convert the heathen. But who will convert my own soul?"

Bohler was part of God's answer to that question. During the transatlantic voyage, a vicious storm arose at sea. Wesley was terrified, but he heard Bohler and the Moravian families on board singing hymns. Wesley was impressed with their composure and ability to continue praying and worshiping God in the face of imminent disaster.

That experience drew the Anglican pastor into a relationship with this group that lasted several years. Indeed, it was in a Moravian chapel on Aldersgate Street in London, just seven months before that fateful Watch Night service, that Wesley heard, understood, and applied the message of the gospel to his own life and received personal salvation. He later wrote about his conversion that night, claiming that as he had listened to the public reading of the introduction to Luther's *Commentary on Romans*, he had felt his heart "strangely warmed."

Wesley was so impressed with the Moravians that he encouraged many of his associates to cast their lot with them. Earlier, as a student at Oxford University, he'd been part of a "Holy Club," a student group that read Christian classics and did charitable work in the community. Most of those involved in that Holy Club were in fact at the meeting at Fetter Lane that evening. John's brother Charles, who had experienced a conversion similar to his own only a few days earlier, was numbered among that group, as was their close friend George Whitefield, who had just returned from ministry in America.

The Fetter Lane Watch Night Revival impacted the entire nation through the Wesleys and Whitefield. Nevertheless, as the group spread out and began preaching, the response of the established church was often cool. Even Whitefield, who often drew thousands to his meetings, found churches were closing their pulpits to him.

The following February, however, the twenty-five-year-old evangelist discovered an innovative way to reach the masses outside the established churches. While visiting his hometown of Bristol, Whitefield learned of opposition to his missions work in America. "If he will convert heathens, why does he not go to the colliers of Kingswood?" his critics asked. Kingswood was a rough coal-mining town near Bristol without a single church.

Inasmuch as the churches of Bristol were reluctant to let him preach in their pulpits, Whitefield chose to answer the challenge of his critics with action. On Saturday, February 17, he began preaching to about 200

Kingswood colliers (coal miners) in the fields near Bristol. Within a month, about 20,000 were braving the weather to hear him preach. Thousands were converted.

Whitefield sensed the need to move on and preach elsewhere, but he had difficulty finding someone to take over the ministry he'd begun in Bristol. He invited his friend John Wesley to join him. Wesley agreed to visit his old friend, but he was still unsure of the wisdom of Whitefield's approach to preaching.

When Wesley arrived on Sunday, March 31, he recorded his negative impressions in his journal: "I could scarcely reconcile myself at first to this strange way of preaching in the fields ... having been all my life so tenacious of every point relating to decency and order, that I should have thought the saving of souls almost a sin if it had not been done in a church." Yet, ironically, while preaching the next evening on the Sermon on the Mount in a small Moravian chapel on Nicholas Street in Bristol, Wesley realized that Jesus himself had preached in the open air.

About four o'clock the next afternoon, with that insight in mind, Wesley "submitted to be more vile, and proclaimed in the highways the glad tidings of salvation, speaking from a little eminence in a ground adjoining to the city, to almost three thousand people." For the next fifty years, Wesley would continue to be an open-air preacher.

Whitefield's open-air preaching was only one of the changes in English church life that came out of the revival. Although Wesley himself later broke with the Moravians, he used Moravian strategies of evangelism and discipleship training to establish Methodist societies across England. Throughout his life, he travelled widely, preached often, and wrote many books on a wide variety of subjects. Many leaders influenced by the Methodist Church became the leading social reformers of that era. Wesley's brother Charles wrote many of the hymns that became favorites of the Moravians, Methodists, and Christians of other denominations.

George Whitefield continued preaching the gospel for many years to large crowds on either side of the Atlantic, becoming the first of a long line of transatlantic evangelists. His example would later be copied by revivalists D.L. Moody, "Gipsy" Smith, and Billy Graham. Both England and America were forever changed with the message of the gospel taken to the nations by the men of Fetter Lane and their disciples.

The Crossweeksung Indian Revival (1745)

The young missionary had been preaching long enough to know that what was happening all around him among his Native American listeners was not normal. Reflecting on the events of the day in his journal, twenty-seven-year-old David Brainerd wrote:

> It seemed to me there was now an exact fulfillment of that prophecy, Zechariah 12:10, 11, 12; for there was now "a great mourning, like the mourning of Hadadrimmon"; and each seemed to "mourn apart." Me thought this had a near resemblance to the day of God's power, mentioned in Joshua 10:14. I must say I never saw any day like it in all respects.

Brainerd concluded: "It was a day wherein I am persuaded the Lord did much to destroy the kingdom of darkness among this people today."

Brainerd's Background

David Brainerd, born in the town of Haddam, Connecticut, was the third of five sons in a family of nine children. For many years his grandfather had pastored the village church, so it wasn't surprising that four of the five Brainerd boys trained for ministry. Only the oldest followed in his father's career as a Justice of the Peace and political leader in the community. The idea of finding a career in ministry was so natural in the Brainerd home that David was already engaged in theological studies before coming to the personal assurance of his own salvation on July 12, 1739.

Brainerd was expelled from school for behavior the college administration felt inappropriate for a student training for ministry, but he didn't allow the experience to prevent him from pursuing his studies privately. He went to live with a pastor and completed his training while assisting that pastor and three other area pastors in their ministry. On July 29, 1742, the young man was examined by the Association of Ministers of the Eastern District of Fairfield County, Connecticut, and licensed to preach the gospel.

While Brainerd performed some ministry among his own people, his real burden was for the Native Americans scattered throughout the forests of New England. Over the years, he'd often fasted and prayed that "God would bring in great numbers of them to Jesus Christ." Because he longed so much to be involved in reaching them, an invitation to be interviewed for ministry among them was quickly accepted.

Mission to Native Americans

Only a few months after his ordination, Brainerd was appointed a missionary to the Native Americans living at the forks of the Delaware River and along the Susquehanna River in Pennsylvania. Because winter had already set in, it was April 1, 1743, before he actually made the journey to his field of service.

Brainerd faithfully preached the gospel to all with whom he came in contact, both native and settler. Some were responsive to the message of the gospel and were converted to Christ, but there was no great turning to Christ as he had hoped. Still, he remained faithful to his calling, travelling often to preach to only a handful of interested people. Whenever he heard of another tribe, he made an effort to find them and share his message of hope. It was this zeal for the lost that led him to the small settlements of Native Americans in Crossweeksung, New Jersey.

When Brainerd arrived, he discovered that the natives were widely scattered. His first meeting in June included only a few women and children. They seemed interested in his message and invited friends in a ten-to-fifteen-mile radius to come hear him, but it was August 3 before he could return to the settlement.

As Brainerd preached among them daily, a growing interest in his message quickly became evident. Then, on the afternoon of August 8, something happened. According to Brainerd, "There was much visible concern among them while I was discoursing publicly; but afterwards when I spoke to one and another more particularly, whom I perceived under much concern, the power of God seemed to descend upon the assembly like a rushing mighty wind, and with an astonishing energy bore down all before it."

The young missionary stood amazed at what he was seeing. While he had longed for a significant work of God among the people with whom he worked, he hadn't expected what he was seeing all about him. The Holy Spirit had come like a mighty flowing river, sweeping away all in its path.

Throughout the meeting place and the surrounding grounds, people were bowed down in prayer crying out to God, "*Guttummaukalummeh wechaumeh kmeleh Ndah!"* Their prayer was simple and direct: "Have mercy on me, and help me to give you my heart."

Their concern was so great that they confessed their sins aloud, apparently unaware of others praying beside them. There was no other way to explain what was happening: God was at work among them.

The revival among the Native Americans at Crossweeksung, New Jersey, had a profound influence on the community. In his own evaluation of the movement, Brainerd noted strengthened families and the absence of drunkenness among those touched by the revival as the most obvious results. Their lives now seemed to be governed by a profound concern for honesty and justice, with many of them paying long-forgotten debts. Their deep sorrow in conviction was replaced with the fullness of joy as they walked with God in the days following.

A Summary of the 1727 Revival

The First Great Awakening lasted about fifty years worldwide (though only ten years in the American colonies) and had a profound impact on both the church and society. Within twenty-five years of the beginning of this revival in Hernhutt, the Moravians had sent out more than a hundred missionaries. Their example inspired William Carey to challenge British Baptists to consider sending missionaries to the unreached peoples of Asia. While later revivals recruited candidates for missions, the First Great Awakening restored the concept of missions to the evangelical churches.

As profound as was the impact of the First Great Awakening on the church, it had an even greater impact on the societies touched by it. It was the First Great Awakening in New England that shaped the moral character of the thirteen colonies that were to become the United States of America. When a French sociologist later toured America to determine the secret of her strength, he concluded, "America is great because America is good." But America had not been so good prior to the awakening.

Given the close relationship of church and state in colonial New England, the ministry of Whitefield and other like-minded evangelists had deep political ramifications as well. When the revival emerged in the 1740s, the churches of New England were supported by property taxes and the church controlled community life. Any change in the religious establishment was thus seen as a threat to the political establishment. Ministers were ordained into a local church for life, and any challenge to their ministry had the potential to erode their status and power within the local community.

The First Great Awakening had tremendous political effects. Following Whitefield's encouragement of itinerant preaching, many evangelists ended up establishing new churches without government affiliation. These churches involved lay people in ministry, but more importantly, they gave lay people a voice in the affairs of their churches. It wasn't long before lay people were wanting a voice also in the affairs of their government and society in general. These churches competed with the tax-supported churches for members.

When the political establishment in Connecticut recognized this threat, the colonial assembly passed a law banning itinerant preaching in 1742. As a result, some itinerants went to jail. The revival continued to spread, however, unchecked by the laws of men.

Thus the First Great Awakening did more than convert the masses. It allowed a new type of preacher to minister for God in both the separate and the traditional churches. The control of the established churches by the ministers was broken, allowing lay expression, lay ministry, and lay involvement. This development—opening the churches to democracy—did more than anything else to lay a foundation for the American Revolution. If Americans could be involved in governing their churches, why not their country? As is often the case, a spiritual awakening led to other kinds of awakening as well.

CHAPTER THREE

The Second Great Awakening, 1780–1810

It is by revivals of religion that the Church of God makes its most visible advance. When all things seem becalmed, when no breath stirs the air, when the sea is like lead and the sky is low and grey, when all worship seems to have ended but the worship of matter, then it is that the Spirit of God is poured upon the Church, then it is that the Christianity of the apostles and martyrs, not that of the philosophers and liberals, keeps rising ... from the catacombs of oblivion, and appears young and fresh in the midst of the obsolete things of yesterday and the day before.

Sir William Robertson Nicoll

A t the end of the eighteenth century, America had just thrown off the yoke of England and was beginning to govern itself. The Methodist and Baptist churches, new self-governing bodies themselves, were growing rapidly. On the other hand, the French Revolution had resulted in the widespread adoption of secularism by many nominal Christians.

On both sides of the Atlantic, the Enlightenment religion known as deism was spreading. Deists denied the reality of God's revelation or intervention in history, rejecting any notion of the supernatural. Deism, in fact, became so popular in Europe and America that the French infidel Voltaire boasted that Christianity itself would be forgotten within three decades.

Because the erosion of the faith was such a great concern, one after another Christian denomination began to call the faithful to prayer. In England, the first Monday evening of each month was set aside for prayer. Two items were high on the prayer list. First, the churches prayed for a revival that would restore many who had lapsed into secularism. Second, they prayed for an extension of God's kingdom into the unreached nations around the world.

The Second Great Awakening: An Overview

Within a decade, the movement of prayer in Great Britain was duplicated in the United States and many other nations. The story of the Second Great Awakening that followed is thus a story of God's bringing revival to praying saints and giving birth to a renewed missionary vision in the church. The outpouring of the Spirit that fell in these meetings impacted the evangelical church for half a century.

The British Isles

Even with the death of John Wesley in 1791, Methodists continued to embrace the new awakening that was similar to the revival that had given them their spiritual birth. Baptists and Congregationalists also reported revival in their churches, as did evangelicals within the Anglican Church. Revival among Anglicans in the London upper-class suburb of Clapham empowered some of the most influential members of British society— William Wilberforce, John Howard, and Elizabeth Fry—who produced some significant social reforms.

About the same time, the Welsh began reporting the blessing of God in their midst. Churches were packed with people seeking God, and thousands gathered in open-air meetings to hear the gospel preached. Here, as in England, Baptists, Congregationalists, and Methodists reported significant church growth during the revival. In addition, a new denomination, Welsh Presbyterians, was established among the converts of that awakening.

Many cities in Scotland also reported phenomenal awakenings. The Haldane brothers, James and Robert, preached to large crowds in major cities, and pastors such as Thomas Chalmers won many in their region for Christ. While the established Church of Scotland, a Presbyterian body, initially opposed the revival, before long Presbyterians themselves also reported the blessing of God in their churches.

The Irish Rebellion of 1798 reflected the pain of a disenfranchised majority in Ireland, yet, despite the social unrest, both Methodists and evangelicals within the Church of Ireland experienced revival. While Presbyterians in the north were consumed with a doctrinal controversy, societies were established throughout the country for the purpose of evangelizing the nation and encouraging the cause of revival in the churches.

Continental Europe

In the early nineteenth century, the revival begun in Britain crossed the English Channel to touch various European nations. Revivals in Scandinavia actually began prior to 1800 and resembled the early awakening under Wesley and Whitefield in England. The movement was largely advanced by laymen such as Hans Nielsen Hauge (Norway) and Paavo Ruotsalainen (Finland), but various national evangelists also had a significant role, including British Methodist George Scott, who won many Swedes to Christ.

In the rest of Europe, the revival was delayed by the Napoleonic Wars. The visit of Robert Haldane to Geneva, Switzerland, however, began what came to be called "Geneva's Second Reformation." His ministry among students had a lasting impact not only in Switzerland but also throughout France and the Netherlands.

The awakening in Germany that followed the defeat of Napoleon produced scores of evangelists, missionaries, and social reformers. According to historian J. Edwin Orr, "Next to British evangelical pioneers, the German revivalists achieved the most lasting social reforms. Close collaboration between British and German revivalists existed in home and foreign mission projects."

North America

In North America, the limited revivals in the 1780s produced the leaders of the wider awakening in the decades following. Sporadic revivals began breaking out in New England in 1792. The Baptist pastor Isaac Backus of Connecticut and others began organizing "concerts of prayer," following the model established in Britain.

By 1798, New England was experiencing a general awakening. Congregations were crowded to capacity. A deep conviction was common in many services, resulting in significant conversions. Virtually every New England state was affected, as were all the evangelical denominations.

The revival spread south to the mid-Atlantic states, then west across the Alleghenies. In its early phase in the Northeast, the awakening had taken the form of a deep movement of God in individual lives, with little emotional extravagance. All that changed on the western frontier.

When the Cane Ridge (Kentucky) Revival began in 1800, conviction was often accompanied by weeping, shouting, fainting, or the "jerks." Crowds met in fields and forests because there were no churches big enough to accommodate them. The "camp meeting," a familiar American revival tradition, was born at Cane Ridge.

The awakening in Virginia, the Carolinas, and Georgia crossed racial and denominational lines. As many as ten or fifteen thousand would gather in forest clearings at camp meetings for the preaching of the Scriptures. Both black slaves and white slave owners from every church background came together to be moved by the Spirit of God.

North of New England, the Maritime Provinces of British North America (Canada) experienced the "New Light Revival." Evangelist Henry Alline and others impacted Baptist and Congregational churches with the revival message. Methodists conducted camp meetings and established new churches throughout Upper Canada. The revival later touched Presbyterians in the same region.

College Revivals

Infidelity was growing rapidly on American college campuses before the coming of revival, but the collegiate awakenings of that era are among the most dramatic stories of the awakening. Timothy Dwight, president of Yale, was the great champion of intellectual evangelical Christianity. Student revival movements swept across American college campuses, producing pastors, teachers, and missionaries for new ministries born out of the revival.

South Africa

Finally, a revival in the Dutch colony of Cape Town, South Africa, touched that city of 30,000 people, producing missionaries who took the gospel to the native peoples of South Africa. That development was followed by similar revival in 1809 among British army regiments. These Methodist "soldier-evangelists" preached the gospel widely in South Africa.

Cornwall's Christmas Revival (1781)

In 1781, the faithful prayer warriors in Cornwall, England, chose to begin their Christmas celebration in prayer. They gathered as early as 3:00 A.M. at St. Just Church to sing hymns and pray to God. Then, as one account puts it, "the Lord of the universe stepped in and took over."

The Christmas prayer meeting continued for six hours. Even then, the intercessors ended the meeting only temporarily to be with their families on Christmas Day. Later that evening, they gathered once again at the church, and the revival continued.

Cornwall's Christmas Revival extended into January and February. By March, prayer meetings were continuing until midnight. This awakening by the Holy Spirit was largely a prayer movement.

A Prayer Revival

No significant preachers were involved in this revival. In fact, most of the gatherings were simply assemblies for prayer rather than evangelistic meetings. In 1784, eighty-three-year-old John Wesley visited the area and immediately recognized the unique movement of God in the community. His journal entry includes the note: "This country is all on fire and the flame is spreading from village to village."

The revival spread from Cornwall, crossing denominational lines. Whitefield's chapel on Tottenham Court Road was enlarged to seat 5,000 people, making it the largest church in the world at the time. Baptists in North Hampton, in Leicester, and throughout the Midlands set aside regular nights to pray for revival. Both Methodists and Anglicans joined the Baptists in such gatherings; soon converts were coming to Christ in these prayer meetings.

Why would the unsaved attend a prayer meeting for revival? Different people had different reasons. Some reported being drawn to the churches by dreams and visions. Others actually came intending to disrupt the meetings or to have a good laugh at Christians engaged in prayer.

Regardless of why they came, God worked in their hearts when they arrived. Many came under intense conviction of sin and found themselves "thrown to the ground under the power of the Holy Spirit." Sometimes the conviction experienced by those attending services resulted in noise and confusion. More often, the meetings were overcome with a sense of stillness and solemnity.

The revival that began on Christmas morning in Cornwall, England, was among the first expressions of revival in the Second Great Awakening. It actually preceded the larger awakening by several years. Like other revivals of that era, it resulted in significant church growth as people who had abandoned the church were won to Christ. What began in Cornwall soon spread throughout the British Isles, North America, and various other nations.

Methodist Circuit Riders (circa 1800)

The Second Great Awakening was spread as much by Methodist circuit-riding preachers as by anyone in America. There were fewer than a thousand Methodists in the new nation in 1782; thirty years later, there were a quarter million. At the end of the Revolutionary War, the Congregationalists were the largest church in the United States, yet thirty years later the Methodists were ten times larger than that denomination.

Of the 550 Yale College students who graduated between 1702 and 1794, 71 percent were ordained into ministry for a particular local church and stayed in that location for life. The typical Methodist itinerant preacher, on the other hand, traveled 200 to 500 miles in a monthly circuit on horseback, had thirty to fifty preaching locations plus classes—and received only $64 a year. The circuit riders slept in homes, at inns, or in the open field. In time, they turned their preaching points into churches and planted their denomination everywhere in the United States.

Francis Asbury, the first bishop of the Methodist Church in America and the human impetus for Methodist growth, crossed the Allegheny Mountains sixty times, visited every state, preached 17,000 sermons, and stayed in 10,000 homes.

Methodist preachers were typically not college-educated, but they were called by God from occupations such as common laborers, farmers, shoemakers, carpenters, shopkeepers, or blacksmiths. (Asbury, in fact, had been a blacksmith before being called to ministry.) Because of their background, they had an affinity with their parishioners. They never read their sermons, as the Anglicans or Congregationalists did, but instead exhorted the people passionately from the Bible, using anecdotes, illustrations, and analogies from everyday life.

They learned how to preach passionately by listening to passionate preaching. Yet it was not their oratory that won their audiences. It was their power.

Asbury told his Methodist preachers, "Feel for power, feel for power." Thomas Ware told them, "People love the preacher who makes them feel." No wonder they were called the "holy knock 'em down" preachers.

Circuit rider John A. Grande travelled the South and was known as "the wild man." Grande once recalled: "I would sing a song, or pray or exhort a few minutes," then "the fire would break out among the people and the slain of the Lord everywhere were many." Crowds followed him from one preaching point to another, "singing and shouting along the way." At one meeting, so many people fell, they "lay in such heaps that it was feared they would suffocate."

By the end of the Revolutionary War, only sixty Methodist chapels had been built, but the circuit-riding preachers used cabins, inns, schools—any place to preach the gospel. With time, each preaching point built a chapel, giving stability and influence to the Methodist movement. By the mid-1800s, it had become the largest Protestant denomination in America.

The Cane Ridge Revival (1800)

The Cane Ridge Revival actually began in a communion service at the Red River Church near the Tennessee-Kentucky border. Reverend James McGready was administering the ecumenical service, preaching a Friday-to-Monday meeting. Nothing unusual happened until Monday. Then a woman at the far end of the house gave vent to her feelings in loud cries and shouts. When dismissed, the congregation showed no disposition to leave, but many of them remained, silently weeping, in every part of the house. The ensuing revival was described this way:

William McGee [a fellow pastor] soon felt such a power come over him that he, not seeming to know what he did, left his seat and sat down on the floor, trembling under a consciousness of the power of God. John McGee [his brother] felt an irresistible urge to preach and the people were eager to hear him. He began, and again the woman shouted and would not be silent.

The methods and spirit of that meeting were repeated in other meetings. Pastor Barton W. Stone soon "learned how to do it" and organized the Cane Ridge ecumenical communion service. The zeal of that meeting has never been forgotten:

It was his [the Methodist preacher's] duty to disregard the usual orderly habits of the denomination, and [the preacher] passed along the aisle shouting and exhorting vehemently. The clamor and confusion were increased tenfold: the flame was blown to its height: screams for mercy were mingled with shouts of ecstasy, and a universal agitation pervaded the whole multitude, who were bowed before it as a field of grain waves before the wind.

Such "agitation" was to become a hallmark of the Cane Ridge Revival.

God on the Frontier
At the end of the Revolutionary War, only 40,000 settlers were located in the hills of western North Carolina, Tennessee, Kentucky, and the area called the Appalachian Region. But within fifty years more than a million people moved West, seeking free lands, a new life, and freedom. These people needed structure and civilization, but most of all they needed God.

The Methodist circuit preachers organized themselves into societies and brought the frontier to God. Eventually, the camp meeting became popular there. It offered a break from hard, backbreaking work, monotonous days, and lonely separation from civilization. One observer described a typical camp meeting this way:

The glare of the blazing camp-fires falling on a dense assemblage of heads simultaneously bowed in adoration and reflected back from long ranges of tents upon every side; hundreds of candles and lamps suspended among the trees, together with numerous torches flashing to and fro, throwing an uncertain light upon the tremulous foliage, and giving an appearance of dim and indefinite extent to the depth of the forest; the solemn chanting of hymns swelling and falling on the night wind; the impassioned exhortations; the earnest prayers; the sobs, shrieks, or shouts, bursting from persons under intense agitation of mind; the sudden spasms which seized upon scores, and unexpectedly dashed them to the ground—all conspired to invest the scene with terrific interest, and to work up the feelings to the highest pitch of excitement.... Add to this, the lateness of the hour to which the exercises were protracted, sometimes till two in the morning, or longer; the eagerness of curiosity stimulated for so long a time previous; the reverent enthusiasm which ascribed the strange contortions witnessed, to the mysterious agency of God; the fervent and sanguine temperament of some of the preachers; and lastly, the boiling zeal of the Methodists, who could not refrain from shouting aloud during the sermon, and shaking hands all round afterwards.

According to a pastor at the scene, "the number of persons who fell" was "the astounding number of about three thousand."

The preaching at the Cane Ridge camp meeting and other places was intense, hot, and moving. An eyewitness remembered:

As the meetings progressed and the excitement grew more intense, and the crowd rushed from preacher to preacher, singing, shouting, laughing, calling upon men to repent, men and women fell upon the ground unable to help themselves, and in such numbers that it was impossible for the multitude to move about, especially at night, when the excitement was the greatest, without trampling them, and so those who fell were gathered up and carried to the meeting house, where the "spiritually slain," as they called them, were laid upon the floor. Some of them lay quiet, unable to move or speak; some could talk, but were unable to move; some would shriek as though in greatest agony, and bound about "like a live fish out of water."

No doubt the more "respectable" folks who heard such an account were scandalized, but those who took part were convinced that God was at work.

"Shouting"

The Cane Ridge Revival introduced the element of shouting to revival meetings, so that many were called "shouting Methodists." So many of their new songs had the word "shout" in the words that it became a common religious expression. When someone died, for example, the Methodists said, "He went off shouting."

Shouting was not simply noise, nor was it loud preaching; yet when a minister was preaching, some would shout from the audience. Shouting wasn't exhorting, nor praying, nor was it a united cheer of many believers. Shouting was an individual response. Loud praying was "shouting," as when a congregation all prayed loudly at the same time, when, for example, they attempted to "pray down" a sinner, so he would get converted.

Shouting was praising or rejoicing in God. It was accompanied with clapping of the hands. Shouting became a revivalistic phenomenon; added to it was shuffling of the feet, which was then followed by running around and an occasional leap. Some shouters would "run the aisle." A circular march by the congregation was called a "ring shout."

Other Revival Activities

The Cane Ridge Revival popularized other revival activities as well:

Singing was attended with a great blessing. At every meeting, before the minister began to preach, the congregation was melodiously entertained with numbers singing delightfully, while all the congregation seemed in lively exercises.

Shaking hands while singing furthered the work. The ministers ... go through the congregation and shake hands with the people while singing. And several ... declared that this was the first means of their conviction.

Giving the people an invitation to come up to be prayed for was also blessed. The ministers usually, at the close of preaching, would tell the congregation that if there were any persons who felt themselves lost and condemned, under the guilt and burden of their sins, that [they could] come near the stage and kneel down.... Apparently under strong conviction, [people] would come and fall down before the Lord at the feet of the ministers and crave an interest in their prayers, sometimes twenty or thirty at a time.

Above a hundred persons ... came forward, uttering howlings and groans, and on the word being given, "Let us pray," they all fell on their knees. But this posture was soon chanced for others that permitted greater scope for the convulsive movement of their limbs, and they were soon lying on the ground in an indescribable confusion of heads and legs.... As if their hoarse and overstrained voices failed to make noise enough, they soon began to clap their hands violently.

Those who were subjected to the "jerks" acknowledged that it was "laid upon them" as a chastisement for disobedience, or a stimulus to incite them to some duty.... The quickest method of warding off the jerks and other disagreeable exercises was to engage in the "voluntary dance."

Shouting and heartfelt singing, hand shaking and clapping, altar calls and dancing, "jerks" and "falling in the Spirit"—all these extraordinary responses to God's presence soon seemed ordinary in the "agitations" of the Cane Ridge Revival.

Peter Cartwright (circa 1800)

Peter Cartwright, a rugged Methodist itinerant preacher, was ideally suited to evangelize the rugged terrain of Kentucky in the early 1800s. His large, square shoulders and considerable strength were sometimes used to subdue the "rabble-rousers" in his meetings, and on many occasions he thrashed the worst rowdies that disturbed his preaching. His creed was to "love everybody and fear nobody," which means that he saw nothing wrong with boxing a troublemaker so long as it was done in love and not revenge. Cartwright was converted in the "overflow" of the Cane Ridge Revival, then gave impetus to its further spread, becoming identified as one of its leaders.

The Cartwright family moved from Amherst, Virginia, to Kentucky in 1785 to an area called Rogue's Harbor. The frontier spot had no school, no newspaper, and very little civilization. All the farmers were self-sufficient, eating what they grew and wearing what they wove from cotton or made from the skins of animals they killed. Cartwright described his early life: "I was a naturally wild, wicked boy and delighted in horse racing, card playing and dancing. My father restrained me little, though my mother often talked to me, wept over me, and prayed for me."

One day an itinerant Methodist preacher came through the encampment, staying at the Cartwright home and giving young Peter his first orientation to religion. When a camp meeting was held in his neighborhood, Cartwright said, "Scores of sinners fell under the preaching, like men slain in a mighty battle; Christians shouted for joy." But Cartwright was not moved to conversion; in fact, he believed he couldn't be saved because he was a reprobate bound for hell.

Cartwright's Conversion

Shortly after the camp meeting, he returned to a home filled with drinking and dancing. He felt guilty when he got there, arose from his bed, and walked the floor, crying out to God. His mother was awakened by his prayers. Cartwright later recalled:

> All of a sudden my blood rushed to my head, my heart palpitated and in a few minutes I turned blind; an awful impression rested on my mind that death had come and I was unprepared to die. I fell on my knees and began to ask God to have mercy on me.

Nevertheless, Cartwright failed to find salvation that evening.

For the next three months, the young man searched long and fervently for God. Conviction of sin was so great he was incapable of going about his chores; he couldn't seem to find pardon for his sins. When he heard about the great camp meeting, he attended and went forward with multitudes of weeping "seekers" to bow and earnestly pray for mercy.

It was there in his soul-struggle that Cartwright heard a voice saying, "Thy sins are all forgiven thee." Cartwright later described his reaction:

> Divine light flashed all around me, unspeakable joy sprang up into my soul. I rose to my feet, opened my eyes, and it really seemed as if I were

in heaven.... I have never for one moment doubted that the Lord did, then and there, forgive my sins and give me religion.

The following year Cartwright was given an "exhorter's license" by the Methodist Church, recognizing the fact that he was already travelling and preaching to small groups.

The next year, the presiding Methodist elder gave him permission to form a circuit of churches in a new region of Kentucky. Cartwright protested, claiming that he was uneducated and an immature Christian. But at length, Cartwright accepted the challenge and told God that he would go preach in a house, and if one soul were converted, it was evidence that he was called to evangelism.

That evening the greatest professing infidel in the area was present to hear him preach. Cartwright read for his text, "Trust ye in the Lord for ever, for in the Lord Jehovah, is everlasting strength" (Isa. 26:4). The infidel was soundly converted, joined the church, and became a leader in the church meeting in that house.

At age nineteen Cartwright was preaching with great unction and power, and his sermons were attended by marvelous manifestations of the Holy Spirit. "Often people were stricken down under an overwhelming conviction of sin," he observed. On one occasion, "the people fell in every direction, right and left, front and rear. It was supposed that not less than three hundred fell like dead men in mighty battle ... loud wailings went up to heaven from sinners for mercy, and a general shout from Christians, so that noise was heard from afar off."

Despite these overwhelming emotional displays, Cartwright had no sympathy for fleshly excitements and always kept people in line with an iron hand. At the same time, however, he didn't want to quench any genuine work or manifestations of the Holy Spirit.

A Bold Preacher

Cartwright was a bold preacher of the gospel to unsaved people. One Saturday night he took lodging in an inn, and after the evening meal sat on the sidelines watching the people dance. A beautiful young lady came over, curtsied in front of him, and asked for a dance. Cartwright took the lady by the hand and led her to the middle of the floor, then announced to all in a loud voice: "I do not undertake any matter of importance without first asking the blessing of God upon it." Then he commanded the lady, "Let us kneel down and pray."

Cartwright pulled her to her knees, then prayed loud and long, refusing to release her. Under the power of his prayers, some watching began to kneel, others ran out of the building, and a few sat still, unable to move. After the prayers, he preached a sermon, and knelt down to pray again.

Cartwright continued praying and preaching until it was time to go to bed. The following day he preached a sermon, organized a Methodist society to meet in the inn, and took thirty-two into the new church. The landlord of the inn became the leader of the church.

Some criticized the emotional expressions known as "jerks" that were manifested in Cartwright's meetings, but they were manifested in all the great Cumberland revival meetings. Some said the "jerks" were purely nervous reactions caused by suggestion when others were seen jerking. Others said it was a manifestation of the Holy Spirit.

Cartwright himself had the ability to sense when people were imitating the "jerks," and he dealt with them strictly. He even told the story of one man who, claiming to have the "jerks" but wanting to get rid of them, went to get a bottle of whiskey to "drink them off." As the man attempted to raise the bottle, a "jerk" more severe than any before broke his neck and he died.

The Yale College Revival (1802)

The First Great Awakening came to an end when Puritan theology was replaced with rationalistic and humanistic thinking. Since the colleges of America trained the clergy, it wasn't surprising that the chilling effect of humanistic thinking eventually deadened the churches. Books promoting the philosophy of the Enlightenment were widely distributed.

Thomas Paine's *Age of Reason*, for example, which openly mocked biblical revelation, was sold to students for only a few pennies. When students didn't buy them, copies were distributed free. Dr. Timothy Dwight, who became president of Yale College in 1795, described such literature as "the dregs of humanity, vomited" on the youth.

As students increasingly embraced rationalism, the effect on the moral life of American colleges was disastrous. Students formed societies named in honor of French philosophers. Colleges originally founded for Christian purposes became centers of skepticism.

At some schools, radical students took control of the entire campus. Mock communion services were conducted in college chapels. One college president was forced to resign. On another campus, a group of students attempted to blow up a building.

As Christians became aware of what was happening on college campuses, their reactions were mixed. Many pious church members who lacked formal education were intimidated by those with formal degrees, so they did nothing. Others only prayed earnestly for those sons who had been sent off to the colleges to prepare for ministry. Few could have anticipated God's solution to meet the challenge of the hour: God prepared an erudite mind that burned with passion to bring revival to the colleges.

Timothy Dwight

Dr. Timothy Dwight was among the best educated and most widely respected ministers of that day. As the grandson of Jonathan Edwards, he was familiar with the stories of the Great Awakening. But more than just a man with knowledge, Timothy Dwight had caught something of his grandfather's passion for revival. As an intellectual, he refused to believe the pursuit of knowledge was in any way hindered by faith in God. When he became president of Yale College in 1795, he chose to use his unique gifts to address head-on the problems of the college campus.

Recognizing the passion with which his students engaged in debate, Dwight challenged their thinking in a series of lectures that confronted aspects of the philosophy they had begun to embrace. Among his lecture topics were "The Nature and Danger of Infidel Philosophy" and "Is the Bible the Word of God?" In another lecture series, Dwight discussed the various principles of deism and materialism.

In a forum that had for so long been sympathetic only to rationalism, the college president's lectures convinced students that Christianity was intellectually credible. While many chose not to embrace the faith of their president, the student body came to respect him deeply and even to admire him. He preached the gospel of their forefathers in the language of their professors.

Dwight's initial ministry led to a limited moral reform on the Yale campus, but it also prepared the school for a more significant change. During a student revival in 1802, a third of the student body professed conversion. It was the first of several Yale College revivals under his leadership.

Other Campus Revivals

As with college revivals throughout history, news of the movement at Yale sparked similar revivals on other campuses. Dartmouth, Williams, and Amherst colleges all experienced a similar outpouring of the Holy Spirit, resulting in the conversion of hundreds of students. The "Infidel Movement" that some years earlier had gripped American colleges came to a quick end as students experienced God in a way that shattered their unbelief.

As Christians came to realize that higher education was not inconsistent with faith in God, numerous new colleges were established to prepare teachers and preachers to serve various communities in the emerging nation.

The Bridgewater Revival of New England (1816)

Throughout his ministry during America's Second Great Awakening, evangelist Asahel Nettleton travelled to many New England churches, bringing them revival. After the revival was technically over, he became pastor of the Congregational church in Bridgewater, Connecticut. It was not his preaching but his absence from the pulpit that ignited revival in his town.

The Puritan view of the state as the protector of the church still governed politics in New England. As a result, the Connecticut State Assembly routinely set aside various days throughout the year for special religious activities. One of those days was the "Annual State Fast" conducted each spring, when churches conducted special services. The Bridgewater church looked forward to the fast day as a time to show off their new, celebrated minister.

Nettleton knew he was coming to a problem church that needed to get right with God before it could have a significant impact on its community.

For several years, members of the Congregational church had been nurturing strife and animosity. As Nettleton began his ministry in the church, he chose to address those issues that hindered the harmony of the church. He spoke plainly and pointedly about the importance of loving one another and living in unity as a means of advancing the cause of Christ.

Unfortunately, his preaching appeared to have little effect. The church seemed content to enjoy the prestige associated with having him as pastor, without heeding his revivalistic preaching. They seemed to think the coming of a revivalist would solve their problems and bring revival without their first resolving problems that hindered the blessing of God.

Throughout his ministry, Nettleton strongly opposed anything that looked like sensationalism in the pulpit, but his actions in Bridgewater demonstrated his own flair for the dramatic. If his preaching could not bring revival, perhaps God could use his silence. Without informing the church of his intentions, Nettleton left town. The church first learned of his absence as they sat waiting for him to preach at the special fast day service.

The "thundering silence of the vacant pulpit" had a profound impact. Some of the people were disappointed, while others were irritated. But when they reflected on what had happened, attitudes began to change.

Many began to search their own hearts, wondering whether their steadfast refusal to apply their pastor's messages had driven him away. Smitten with the unusual rebuke of the pastor, they organized a day of prayer and confession to deal with the problems they had so long avoided. It became a day of "deep repentance and humiliation before God."

While the church didn't know where their pastor had gone, he was only about ten miles away, visiting with a friend in the ministry. Nettleton persuaded this friend, Bennet Tyler, to preach in his place the following Sunday in Bridgewater. Afterward, Tyler reported that there had been a dramatic change in the character of the church, with the result that many sought salvation.

When Nettleton returned to the Bridgewater pulpit, the church experienced revival blessing. Excitement soon spread to other towns. Many recognized their need to reform and began attending services.

Nettleton's faithful preaching, addressing specific spiritual needs, was effectively used by God to bring revival to Bridgewater, Connecticut, and surrounding towns. But it was a silent pulpit and an absent preacher that God used to begin his work of grace in that church and community.

Geneva's "Second Reformation" (1816)

James Alexander Haldane and his brother Robert were well-known revivalists in their native Scotland in the early 1800s, but their greatest work was accomplished in Geneva, Switzerland, with much smaller crowds. The latter work was greater because in the long run it had a much wider and longer influence in reviving God's people. The brothers attracted large crowds to hear the preaching of the gospel in Scotland, but these weren't crusades in the usual sense of the word. Although the two brothers never formally organized their converts into churches, their assemblies were for all intents and purposes the megachurches of that day.

Most preachers would long to have such influence in their preaching, but in the midst of an effective ministry, Robert Haldane left the place of his influence. Just as Philip left the thriving revival in Samaria to preach the gospel to one Ethiopian eunuch (see Acts 8:4-8, 25-40), so Robert Haldane left his revivalistic ministry in Scotland to investigate the possibilities of ministry on the European continent. In doing so, he became the instrument God used to achieve "Geneva's Second Reformation."

While the two brothers had earned their reputation as evangelists, the content of their preaching extended far beyond giving the basic plan of salvation as evangelists typically do today. Robert Haldane, especially, was more of a theologian and often discussed in his sermons aspects of salvation more commonly reserved today for theological lectures. In fact, his sermons on the Book of Romans were later published as a textbook commentary that was widely used to train pastors in both French and English.

Haldane's Visit to the Continent

Robert Haldane began his continental visit in France in 1816. He'd been to that nation three times before as a tourist, but now returned with a growing burden for ministry. Previously, the European political scene would have hindered such ministry efforts, but with the end of the great Napoleonic Wars in Europe, he recognized a window of opportunity that might not open again.

Haldane's journey was not without problems. He knew no one in France and began his trip without making specific arrangements for ministry. He wasn't even sure how long he would be away from Scotland. When someone asked, he hesitantly replied, "Possibly only six weeks." His "six-week" mission ultimately lasted three years.

Arriving in Paris, Haldane encountered a significant disappointment. He made contact with an employee of the American embassy, an evangelical Christian, who had lived in Europe for some time and was familiar with the ministry of the Haldane brothers in Scotland. The American informed Haldane that "there were only two pastors in Europe who shared his views of revival," but neither lived in France. The two pastors who might work with him both served churches in Geneva. The Scottish preacher thus concluded that Geneva would be the next stop on his journey.

When Haldane arrived in Geneva, he learned that one of the two pastors was no longer in town. The other was preaching the gospel faithfully and didn't need the Scottish preacher's assistance. They had warm fellowship together, but the door to ministry was apparently closed.

Meanwhile, a small prayer meeting in the nearby village of Montauban had been asking God for spiritual leadership since their founder, Madame Krudener, had left. The group members considered Haldane the answer to their prayer. Convinced he wouldn't have a ministry in Geneva, he decided to leave the city to minister among the prayer group. Before he left, however, a pastor agreed to take him to visit a local tourist attraction.

The evening before the tour, the pastor came down with a severe headache but arranged for a young divinity student at the local college to accompany Haldane. During the tour, the Scottish preacher and the student began discussing theology. Haldane wrote in his journal:

I found him profoundly ignorant, although in a state of mind that showed he was willing to receive information. He returned with me to the inn, and remained till late at night. Next morning he came with another student, equally in darkness with himself. I questioned them respecting their personal hope of salvation, and the foundation of that hope.... After some conversation, they became convinced of their ignorance of the Scriptures, and of the way of salvation, and exceedingly desirous of information. I therefore postponed my intended departure from Geneva.

After listening to Haldane for a day, the student told a friend, "Here is a man who knows the Bible like Calvin!"

At the time, the Reformed churches of Switzerland were in decline. In 1810, several young men had united under the banner *"La Société des Amis"* ("The Society of Friends") as an evangelical response to the apparent spiritual apostasy in their church. Opposition by the clergy, most of whom adhered to Arian heresy, had been so strong that the group had disbanded in 1814. Some of the more committed members had left the Reformed Church and joined the Moravians.

The commitment to the Scriptures of Swiss reformers such as Zwingli and Calvin was almost nonexistent in Haldane's day. It was not uncommon for ministerial students to complete their course of training and never actually read the Bible through even once. One student testified, "During the four years I attended the theological teachers of Geneva, I did not, as part of my studies, read one single chapter of the Word of God, except a few Psalms and chapters I needed to read to learn Hebrew, and I did not receive one single lesson of exegesis of the Old or New Testament."

"Le Berceau"

When Haldane decided to winter at Geneva, he moved to a suite of apartments located at 19 Promenade St. Antoine. In the generation following Haldane's death, that address was still being called *"le berceau"* (the birthplace) of "Geneva's Second Reformation." The reform began quietly there and never grew into a large meeting.

Revival was centered in classes of twenty to thirty divinity students at a time. It was a quiet awakening in which the Holy Spirit deeply moved in the lives of young men who became carriers of revival throughout Switzerland and the French-speaking world. Students training in the seminary attended their classes, then hurried over to Haldane's home to be taught the Bible and theology by the Scottish preacher.

The university faculty was disturbed by the evangelist's interference in the education of ministerial candidates, but there was little they could do to stop it. Haldane wasn't part of the faculty, so he couldn't be dismissed. When the faculty of the university named him in their lectures and criticized his views, it often served only to alert to his presence more students who hadn't yet heard of him, thus adding new members to his Bible study. When the faculty sought to discourage students on an individual basis from going to his home, many claimed they had learned so much from Haldane that, if forced, they would sooner withdraw from the divinity school than break with Haldane.

Over the winter of 1816–17, Haldane continued training a new generation of leadership for the Reformed Churches of Switzerland. Although his following was small compared to those who had gathered to hear him preach in his native Scotland, his influence throughout the French-speaking world was extensive. As those who had met in *le berceau* completed their formal training, they went out to churches throughout the nations to preach and teach, not what they'd learned in school, but what they'd discovered in Haldane's Bible study group.

These pastors stood in stark contrast to those who had preceded them, and their coming often sparked revival in the churches they served. Several students became involved in a Swiss mission to the French-speaking residents of Lower Canada (now Quebec) and carried the torch of revival to North America. In fact, some of the earliest reported revivals in the later Laymen's Prayer Revival took place in the churches of Quebec established by Haldane's students.

In many revivals, large crowds gather to hear the gospel preached, just as the Haldane brothers had attracted in Scotland. Revivals, however, can't be poured into a mold; God's work in human life has varying expressions. In Geneva, Robert Haldane carried revival to a small group of students, and through a quiet ministry so different from what he'd experienced back in his native land, his students became carriers of revival to the world.

A Summary of the 1800 Revival

There is debate among historians over when the Second Great Awakening began. Some indicate it began with Charles Finney in 1830. However, there was a tremendous movement of the Spirit beginning in 1800 that can't be overlooked.

The Second Great Awakening provided the catalyst for a number of developments in the church apart from political government, and this revival influenced the wider society. One significant outcome was the birth of many great evangelistic organizations. These included in England the British and Foreign Bible Society, the Religious Tract Society, the Baptist Missionary Society, the London Missionary Society, and the Church Missionary Society. In America, Bible, Sunday school, tract, and missionary societies were formed to spread the gospel.

The Sunday school movement in particular gained tremendous momentum in the Second Great Awakening. Robert Raikes began the first Sunday school in Glouchester in 1780, and the movement spread like wildfire. When, four years later, John Wesley visited Leeds, England, he found twenty-six schools operating, with 2,000 scholars taught by forty-five teachers.

In 1784, the Society for the Support and Encouragement of Sunday Schools throughout British Dominions was founded and reported that there were 250,000 registered in Sunday school. By 1830, the fiftieth anniversary of the Sunday school, 1,250,000 were registered in Sunday school—one-fourth of the English population. The regular teaching of the Bible became the foundation of revival.

During the Second Great Awakening the modern missionary movement was also born. Baptist missionary William Carey took the gospel from England to India. His fellow Baptist Adoniram Judson took the same message from America to Burma. British evangelicals sent chaplains to their prison colonies in Australia. Samuel Marsden, one of those chaplains, became the first preacher of the gospel to the Maoris of New Zealand.

In America, the revival transformed an entire society. By the 1820s, evangelical Christianity had become, as one historian notes, "one of the most dynamic and important cultural forces in American life." Just as the First

Great Awakening had shaped the character of an emerging nation, so the Second Great Awakening renewed that character and energized the church for the unique challenges of the century just begun.

CHAPTER FOUR

The General Awakening,
1830–40

No church that values its own standards can afford to depreciate revivals of religion. The whole history of the Christian Church from its foundation until now is the history of revivals. It should always be borne in mind that real revival is something infinitely higher than a mere gale of religious excitement sweeping over the churches. A genuine revival is a manifestation of supernatural and Divine power.

Australian Christian World editorial, 1888

The Second Great Awakening continued in America until approximately 1810, but many of its results were interrupted by the War of 1812. In the fifteen years following the conclusion of that conflict, however, various local manifestations of revivals continued to be reported in North America, Britain, and the mission fields of India, South Africa, Indonesia, and Polynesia. Some historians, in fact, stretch the notion of the Second Great Awakening to include the work of the great revivalist Charles Finney in the 1820s and beyond. We join historian J. Edwin Orr, however, in identifying his influence as a different movement, called by many the General Awakening.

The Second Great Awakening had been unique among the great historic revivals, in that it had not been followed by a significant decline in the church and society. There was no time for that, for quite unexpectedly, the world experienced another outpouring of the Holy Spirit in 1830.

The General Awakening: An Overview

Charles Grandison Finney was a New York lawyer known for his antagonism to evangelical Christianity prior to his dramatic conversion in 1821. Almost immediately after his encounter with God, he began preaching the gospel, using his skills as an attorney to drive home the evangelistic message. Many came under conviction of sin and saving faith in Christ in his early meetings, which were conducted throughout rural New England.

In 1830, the now-popular itinerant evangelist took his ministry to upstate New York. In Rochester he held his first campaign in a major city. It would prove to be his most successful campaign.

The revival of 1830 wasn't limited to Finney's ministry, however. While he was preaching in Rochester, others were experiencing revival, from Maine to Texas. Across America that year, an estimated 100,000 converts were added to the church.

The United Kingdom

While America experienced revival, the Holy Spirit was also poured out in Great Britain during this decade. Local revivals of great intensity were reported by various Methodist groups in England, especially. American evangelist James Caughey saw "many thousands" come to faith in Christ during a series of campaigns throughout the nation. Among his converts was a young man named William Booth, destined to found the Salvation Army in a later revival. The revival might have had an even greater impact on the Church of England had it not been for the Tractarian movement, which opposed the evangelism of the revivals in favor of a more sacramental approach to the faith.

Revival was also experienced in other parts of the United Kingdom. Awakening began in South Wales, later spreading to North Wales. In Scotland, the number of local revivals reported in the 1830s increased, including an extraordinary movement of God at Kilsyth under the ministry of William C. Burns.

In Ireland, the impact of revival on the churches was so great that bishops of the Church of Ireland described it as "a second reformation." At Dublin, evangelicals from various denominations gathered regularly for "the breaking of bread." This was the beginning of the Christian Brethren denomination, which divided not long after its founding. John Nelson Darby became the leader of the "Closed Brethren," and George Mueller led the "Open Brethren."

Continental Europe

The British Methodist evangelist George Scott began his work in Sweden during the Second Great Awakening, but experienced significant revival in his ministry during the 1830s. Carl Olof Rosenius, a native Swede, continued Scott's work after the Englishman left, and he continued to experience awakenings into the 1840s. By that time the revival had begun in Norway, and within the decade revivals were being reported throughout Scandinavia.

Elsewhere in Europe, the disciples of James Haldane during the Second Great Awakening became the carriers of revival throughout Europe, especially in Switzerland, France, and Holland. Various revivals were also reported in Germany despite opposition from the Lutheran Church.

Africa, Asia, and the Pacific

Missionaries touched by the revival in sending countries became carriers of the revival to foreign fields. American missionary Titus Coan experienced a great turning to God among the native people of Hawaii. About the same time, significant awakenings were reported among the people of various Polynesian kingdoms. By the 1840s, revivals were developing in various parts of Australia as well.

Awakenings were reported in the 1830s in Grahamstown, South Africa, that resulted in the gospel being taken to the native peoples of South Africa. Robert Moffat, the father of Protestant African missions, was effective in reaching many for Christ in Botswanaland. In Asia, missionaries reported revivals and awakenings on various fields from the Middle East through China, including a movement among the Karens in Burma under the ministry of Baptist missionaries in that land.

Finney's Rochester Revival (1830)

For much of his early life, preaching the gospel was the last thing on the mind of Charles Gradison Finney, a New York lawyer and confirmed atheist. Because of his brilliance and hardheaded approach to life, many people in town doubted that his conversion was even possible.

Finney was born in Warren, Connecticut, on August 29, 1792, but his family migrated west to the frontier town of Hanover in Oneida County, New York, when he was only two years old. As a student in the local academy, he did well and developed both musical and athletic abilities. From 1808 through 1812, Finney taught in the district school at Henderson.

Finney wasn't content to teach, however; he wanted to practice law. After several years of independent study and training, Finney joined the law office of Judge Benjamin Wright in Adams, New York. In 1818, he was formally admitted to the bar.

The young lawyer seemed to have found his role in life. His logical mind and oratorical skills proved valuable as he argued cases before the bar. Even when outside the courtroom, he would take up any cause and present a convincing argument.

From Atheist to Revivalist

Finney was well known in Adams as one who also argued against the existence of God. That's why people were surprised and suspicious when Finney announced he'd experienced a dramatic religious conversion on October 10, 1821, and intended to abandon his law practice to preach the gospel. In 1824 Finney was ordained by the Presbyterian Church; a dozen years later, the lawyer-turned-evangelist aligned himself with the Congregational Church.

Throughout his ministry, Finney used his skills as a lawyer to argue God's case before his audiences. Unlike the pastors of many of the churches where he preached, he strongly emphasized human accountability before God. As people were called upon to renew their obedience to the Lord, Finney's ministry was often marked by revival.

One of the most remarkable revivals in his ministry occurred during his six months of ministry in Rochester, New York, in 1830. When the invitation to preach in Rochester reached the evangelist, he had several other invitations. He began making inquiries about the city, but the initial reports were not promising.

The Third Presbyterian Church, which had invited him to come, was currently without a pastor and needed a supply preacher. An elder in that church was involved in a major dispute with the pastor of the First Presbyterian Church. The pastor of the Second Presbyterian Church was alienating the congregation with his preaching.

It wasn't the sort of situation in which Finney would choose to preach, yet he couldn't get the request off his mind. He consulted with several praying friends in Utica, New York, telling them about several open doors to ministry, including the Rochester situation. After several prayer sessions together, his friends agreed Finney should turn down the Rochester invitation and travel east to accept the more promising invitation in the larger cities. Finney agreed and decided to leave the next day.

That evening, however, Finney began rethinking his decision. As he went to rest, a question came to his mind, "What are the reasons that deter you from going to Rochester?" Finney had no difficulty listing good reasons why he should turn down the Rochester invitation. "Ah! But are these good reasons?" a voice seemed to ask. "Certainly you are needed at Rochester all the more because of these difficulties. Do you shun the field because there are so many things that need to be corrected, because there is so much that is wrong? If all was right, you would not be needed."

As Finney recognized his motives for turning down the Rochester invitation, he was embarrassed. Before he went to sleep that night, he made up his mind to go where he was needed most. Early the next morning, he informed his wife of the change in plan and later that day began the journey to Rochester.

When he arrived in the city the next morning, he and his wife were taken to the home of an elder who provided hospitality. The next day, the evangelist met with the pastor of First Presbyterian Church and established a working relationship with the church leader.

The "New Measures"

We should note that by this time Finney was already a focus of controversy, in part because of his use of "new measures," or new techniques, in evangelism. Some of his critics charged that his methods were manipulative; others simply objected that things had never been done that way before. Ever the pragmatist, Finney typically justified his strategies by pointing to their success in obtaining conversions.

One of the "new measures" in revival that Finney introduced was the public invitation, or "altar call." Though people under conviction had typically rushed forward in meetings during the Cane Ridge Revival a generation before, that pattern had emerged spontaneously. Finney, on the other hand, issued an explicit invitation to come down in response to the gospel, a move that was quite effective in bringing about the desired result. Because of this and other innovative techniques, Finney has been called "the Father of modern revivalism" and is generally considered the prototype of American evangelists.

Not long after Finney began his ministry in Rochester, the wife of a respected lawyer in town was converted. As he preached the gospel, others soon became anxious about their salvation. Sometimes that anxiety was manifested physically as people squirmed in their seats or began weeping in the pew.

Finney found such responses distracting, both to himself and to those gathered to hear him preach. To solve the problem, he introduced in Rochester yet another of the "new measures": the "anxious seat."

The evangelist arranged to have several pews near the front of the church emptied. Then he urged people who felt they needed to get right with God while he was preaching to make their way to these pews to occupy the "anxious seat," so they wouldn't disturb others around them. As a result, many people began moving to the anxious seats during his messages, a much larger response than he'd anticipated.

Results of the Revival

The anxious seat proved to be an effective tool to reach the professionals in the community. Finney noted, "Very soon the work took effect, extensively, among the lawyers in that city." There had always been a large number of the leading lawyers of the state resident at Rochester. Finney began attracting them. They grew quite anxious about the state of their souls and came freely to the meetings of inquiry. Numbers of them then came forward to the anxious seat and publicly gave their hearts to God. By the end of the Rochester Revival, every doctor, lawyer, and businessman in town was converted.

Because the rift between the First and Third Presbyterian Churches had been healed early in the revival, a spirit of kindness and fellowship began characterizing church relations in town. When the pastor of the First Church asked Finney to preach for him, the crowd was so large that it created stress on a building already in need of repairs. During the meeting, one of the timbers came through the roof and broke a window. In the panic that followed, several people were injured, but none seriously. When the church leaders investigated and realized they could no longer use the building for services, the Second Presbyterian Church offered their facilities. Three churches that had once been at odds with one another were now working together. Soon, churches of other denominations in town joined them in a common effort to reach people for Christ.

As the revival progressed, many were overcome with conviction. One morning, the principal of a local high school found his students in such a state of anxiety that they couldn't carry on their studies. He sent one of his teachers to Finney, asking for help.

When she explained the situation, the evangelist returned to the school with her. By the end of the day, the principal and most of the students had been converted. Forty of the students who were converted that day later entered the ministry, many as foreign missionaries.

In the course of six months, 1,200 people joined the churches of the Rochester Presbytery. Soon, news of the Rochester Revival travelled east to New England. According to Finney, "The very fame of it was an efficient instrument in the hands of the Spirit of God in promoting the greatest revival of religion throughout the land, that this country had then ever witnessed."

According to one estimate, news of the Rochester Revival sparked revival fires in 1,500 towns and villages throughout New England. Years later, the respected preacher Lyman Beecher stated, "That was the greatest work of

God, and the greatest revival of religion, that the world has ever seen, in so short a time." He estimated that 100,000 had been converted and added to the churches in a single year through the revivals sparked by news of the Rochester awakening.

The Hawaiian Revival (1836)

Having experienced revival under the ministries of both Asahel Nettleton and Charles Finney, American missionary Titus Coan longed to see a similar outpouring of the Holy Spirit in his own work in Hawaii. He arrived on the island in 1834 and quickly began studying the native languages. By 1836 he was fluent enough to carry on a conversation and preach with effectiveness.

Coan spent most of his time training the ninety students studying to be schoolteachers in his training college. Other missionaries provided leadership for a boys' boarding school and Christian day school on the compound. Despite the concentration of ministry in the community, the church in Hilo had only twenty-three members, all living in the Christian compound itself.

Nevertheless, Coan's vision was bigger than Hilo, and he prayed for the conversion of all Hawaii. He decided to take the gospel to people where they lived, giving his students an extended Christmas vacation, and on November 29, 1836, he began a ministry tour of the island. Officially, Coan was on an inspection tour of about two dozen schools for which he was responsible. Accompanied only by two or three natives to act as guides and porters, he began walking toward the western coast of the island.

Each time he came to a village, Coan would stop to preach and exhort those who would listen. As he'd hoped, crowds of people gathered in each village to hear the gospel. Coan preached as often as he could, usually three to five times a day. Once he'd shared his message with those who would listen, he moved on to the next village.

Soon the missionary came to the western boundaries of Puna, an area with which he was a little more familiar. When he'd previously visited the area, he'd not been fluent in the native language. This time, he was better prepared.

The people gathered in large crowds, eager to hear him preach from the Scriptures. Many wept quietly as they listened to the message of the gospel. Whenever Coan concluded his message, the people would refuse to leave.

Later he recalled: "When I supposed they would return to their homes and give me rest, they remained and crowded around me so earnestly that I had no time to eat, and in places where I spent my nights they filled the house to its entire capacity, leaving scores outside who could not enter." By ten or eleven o'clock at night, Coan would urge the people to return home and sleep. By the time he rose with the sound of a cock crowing the next morning, the house and area around the house would again be filled with those eager to hear more.

One Saturday evening, the preacher found himself near a line of four villages, each about a half mile down the coast from the previous one. Each village asked him to preach the next day. At sunrise, he began preaching in the first village. When he concluded his message, he travelled to the next village to do the same.

Many who heard him followed him. By afternoon, he was preaching to a large crowd composed of residents from four different villages. "Many were pricked in their hearts," he reported, "and were inquiring what they should do to be saved."

When he finally reached the larger villages of Puna, the size of the crowds multiplied. The blind, the maimed, the aged, and invalids were carried by healthy friends to the meetings. In two days Coan preached ten times in Puna's largest city. "There was great joy and much weeping in the assembly," he reported. God worked in an amazing way among the people.

The high priest of the volcano was among the converts in Puna. Standing more than six feet tall, his presence was felt in any group. His notoriety preceded him: In addition to the idol worship, drunkenness, and adultery associated with his pagan practice, he had engaged in thievery and even murder. He was someone used to getting his own way—he'd been known to kill a man for simply hesitating to obey him. Yet following this pagan priest's conversion, he quickly gained a reputation for being an honest man with an earnest zeal for God.

His sister was the high priestess of the volcano and even more proud and stubborn than her brother. She grew hostile to the gospel her brother embraced, but soon found she couldn't resist its power. She too yielded to God and became a faithful member of the church.

When Coan returned home to Hilo on December 29, he immediately noticed an increased interest in the Scriptures in the compound. While previous meetings had drawn only a few, now the meeting place began to fill. Those who had heard him preach the gospel in Kau and Puna now travelled to Hilo to hear more.

Throughout the next two years, Hilo became crowded with strangers. Often, whole families came to hear him preach. On several occasions a whole village made the journey together.

The population of Hilo increased to an estimated 10,000 as villagers came to learn more. The formerly empty village church was now stretched to the limits. People packed into the two-hundred-by-eighty-five-foot building, leaving hundreds outside. "The Word fell with power," Coan reported, "and sometimes as the feeling deepened, the vast audience was moved and swayed like a forest in a mighty wind."

Without even consulting the missionaries, the people travelled three to five miles into the jungle to cut down large trees for building a new church. They hauled the massive trees by hand over hills, through jungle and mud, and across streams, until they finally arrived back in town. Only then did they explain their plan to Coan. They would build a second, larger house of worship where the missionary could preach to them in the morning while others met for prayer in the smaller church building. Then, in the afternoon, Coan would preach to the others in the new building while those who had attended in the morning gathered for prayer in the older building.

Several thousand men and women worked together for about three weeks to finish building the new church. An enthusiastic crowd of about 2,000 filled the structure as it was dedicated. To economize on space, neither building had floors or seats. Instead, the ground was beaten hard and covered with fresh grass each week. In addition, "ushers" helped pack people into the building, standing shoulder to shoulder. Only then was the command given to "sit down," which they did in unison.

The revival at Hilo spread across the waves to other islands. Waimea, Hamakua, Kohala, Kona, and the other islands of the Hawaiian group were deeply moved by the gospel. Initially, some looked critically upon the movement. Many who worked among the Hawaiians considered them "so debased in mind and heart that they could not receive any true conception of the true God, or of spiritual things." Strangely, even some missionaries believed it was impossible to expect evangelical conversions among the Hawaiians.

As the movement continued, however, the presuppositions of the critics were shattered. Hawaiians were indeed coming to the faith in large numbers. Christianity was shattering the power of pagan religion, and thousands were finding freedom in Christ.

Coan himself was convinced the movement was of God, not unlike revivals he'd experienced in New England. "I had seen great and powerful awakenings under the preaching of Nettleton and Finney," he wrote. "And like doctrines, prayers, and efforts seemed to produce like fruits among this people."

Occasionally, Coan witnessed physical manifestations not unlike those he'd seen in New England revivals. People would begin to tremble as he explained the gospel, then fall helplessly to the floor. While he was preaching on "Repentance Toward God and Faith in the Lord Jesus" to a large crowd gathered in an open field, a man who had been listening intently suddenly burst out in prayer, "Lord, have mercy on me, I am dead in my sins." Coan described what happened next:

His weeping was so loud, and his trembling so great, that the whole congregation was moved as by a common sympathy. Many wept aloud, and many commenced praying together. The scene was such as I had never before witnessed. I stood dumb in the midst of this weeping, wailing, praying multitude, not being able to make myself heard for about twenty minutes. When the noise was hushed, I continued my address with words of caution, lest they should feel that this kind of demonstration atoned for their sins, and rendered them acceptable before God. I assured them that all the Lord required was godly sorrow for the past, present faith in Christ, and henceforth faithful, filial, and cheerful obedience.

At that point, concluded Coan, "calm came over the multitude, and we felt that the Lord was there."

On another occasion, a young man attended a meeting intending to disrupt it. He attempted to make others laugh during prayer. Instead, the young man himself fell unconscious and had to be carried out of the building. It was several hours before he regained consciousness. Immediately he confessed his sin, and before long he'd become a member of the church he'd attempted to disrupt.

About a year into the revival, tragedy hit the area. On the evening of November 7, 1837, a tidal wave struck the island as Christians gathered for an evening prayer service. About 200 people living on the beach at the time were swept out to sea. While many were rescued, thirteen drowned. Those who survived lost most of their worldly possessions.

In the days following the tidal wave, the crowds at church increased. People thought of the wave as the voice of God calling them to be ready. Even British sailors involved in the rescue began attending services.

When the captain responded to the gospel, he returned to the ship and called his officers and crew together. He informed them that they could no longer drink alcohol or use foul language on board. In addition, he announced a ban on chasing whales on Sunday and established new church services each Sunday on board.

While there were thousands of conversions in 1836 and 1837, church membership didn't grow until 1838 and 1839. The delay was due to the missionaries rather than the converts. When a person professed saving faith in Christ, Coan made a note of it, together with the date. He would then look up the convert three, six, nine, and twelve months later. If the person gave evidence that the conversion was real, he or she would then be invited to prepare for church membership.

While the missionaries employed this strategy to assure themselves that a genuine conversion had taken place, waiting a year before allowing a convert to study for church membership delayed church growth. Even so, on the first Sunday of July, 1838, the first converts of the revival were baptized and welcomed into the church. From Coan's list of about 3,000 converts, 1,705 Hawaiians had completed the process of church membership established by the missionaries.

Even then, the large number of new members was only a part of the crowd that should have been admitted. "The selection was made," Coan explained, "not because a thousand and more of others were to be rejected, or that a large proportion of them did not appear as well as those received, but because the numbers were too large for our faith, and might stagger the faith of others. The admission of many was deferred for the more full development of their character, while they were to be watched over, guided, and fed as sheep of the Great Shepherd."

The Hilo church adopted the Bible as its "Confession of Faith." When individuals became members of the church, they placed their hand on the Bible and promised "to abstain from all that is forbidden and to obey all that is written therein." The missionaries also urged church members to abstain from the use of tobacco and alcohol. Many natives struggled to break addictions to these substances, yet during the Hawaiian revival, "multitudes pulled up all their tobacco plants and cast them into the sea or into pits, and thousands of pipes were broken upon the rocks or burned, and thousands of habitual smokers abandoned the habit at once and forever."

The Kilsyth Anniversary Revival (1839)

When Reverend William Chalmers Burns returned to his home church in Kilsyth, Scotland, for a visit, he had no intention of preaching. He'd simply returned to see family and old friends. He knew the communion season would be a good time to visit because many acquaintances who lived in other places would also be in town. He was content to sit under the preaching of his father and uncle and enjoy a break from his own ministry in Dundee, Scotland. But God had other plans.

Early in life, God had given Burns a broken heart for the lost and dying world around him. Kilsyth was a quiet little town, and Burns was seventeen years old when his mother first brought him to the big city of Glasgow. While they were shopping, the two became separated unintentionally. Concerned for her son, his mother retraced her steps and found him in an alley with tears streaming down his face.

"Willie, my boy," she asked, "what ails you? Are you ill?"

"Oh, mother, mother!" he replied. "The thud of these Christless feet on the way to Hell breaks my heart." Such was the heartbeat of the young man

God would use to bring revival to Scotland and China.

A century earlier, Kilsyth had experienced a "glorious awakening" under the ministry of a pastor named James Robe. According to one witness, as the hundredth anniversary of that revival approached, "the Lord was beginning to move in a striking manner." In an attempt to move church members to begin praying for revival and the salvation of others in the community, Dr. William Burns Sr. (William's father) chose to celebrate the anniversary by preaching from Robe's grave.

"God is not dead!" he cried out. "The gospel has lost none of its power!" He knew Christians would have to examine themselves and make significant lifestyle adjustments if revival were to come to their community once again.

"It is we Christians who have lost our power with God," he explained. "God is able right now to give us the same times of blessing that he gave this church one hundred years ago and even greater!" Then he asked his people a probing question: "Are you willing to let God search your hearts to see that there are no sins which grieve God and keep back the blessing?"

The message had its desired effect on those who gathered that day. Many began seeking the Lord in a spirit of repentance and humiliation. A quickening of "dry bones" had begun, as when the "sound of marching in the tops of the mulberry trees" is heard (see 1 Chron. 14:15), as church members throughout the parish began to prepare for the revival they hoped God would send.

The younger Burns hadn't been in town long before being approached by his uncle, who, with Burns' father, served on the pastoral team of the church. He perceived that his nephew was anointed by the Holy Spirit to preach the gospel and asked him to take his place in the pulpit at one of the services planned for that weekend. William agreed, and ended up preaching both Saturday and Sunday.

The effect of his message on those gathered was profound, so much so that his father and uncle asked him to preach again at the Tuesday marketplace meeting. William had planned to return that afternoon to Dundee on horseback, but he agreed to remain and preach the meeting.

For several weeks, William had spent much of the night in prayer, calling on God for revival. Monday evening, the same spirit of prayer gripped many of the Christians of Kilsyth. Throughout the parish, they watched and prayed for yet another outpouring of the Holy Spirit in their church. If God was indeed able to send another revival as he had a century earlier, that was indeed what they wanted.

As the dawn arrived on Tuesday, so did the rain. Because of the heavy downpour, which gave no indication of letting up, the decision was made to move the market meeting into the church itself. The vast crowd who had gathered for the public meeting crammed into the church. The building filled up with working-class men and women dressed in their working clothes. The unusual congregation that morning included those with the worst reputations in the district.

The service began with the singing of a psalm. As Burns read the words they were singing, one verse in particular grabbed his attention: "You will arise and have mercy on Zion; For the time to favor her, Yes, the set time, has come" (Ps. 102:13). *Perhaps today,* Burns thought, as he began to believe that God might answer his prayers for revival even in that service.

Burns' sermon was typical of the kind of expository and evangelical preaching of that day. He began by describing the people referred to in the verse as God's elect, those given to Christ by the Father. Then he reminded listeners of the Father's promise to Emmanuel regarding this group, that "your people shall be volunteers" (Ps. 110:3).

Burns explained that they would be willing to (1) be saved by Christ's righteousness alone, (2) take on his yoke, and (3) bear his cross. He then described the time of the promise, that is, the day of Emmanuel's power, as the day (1) of his exaltation at the Father's right hand, (2) of the free preaching of the Divine Word, (3) when Christ crucified was the center and sum of all doctrine taught, and (4) of the outpouring of the Holy Spirit.

As he drew to the end of his sermon, Burns felt suddenly impressed to retell some of the stories of great revivals and awakenings that formed part of the heritage of Scottish evangelicals. There was no shortage of stories to tell, as the evangelical church in Scotland had experienced many outpourings of the Holy Spirit since the Reformation. Among the stories he told was that of John Livingstone and the revival that came to the Kirk (Church) of Shotts.

Those listening had often heard this story, because it was part of their local history. Yet even as they heard it one more time, the crowd was deeply moved. Suddenly they began to realize that God was about to do something in their midst. Once again, God was using a young man to call his church back from cold and callous apathy and to rekindle a revival flame in their lives.

"During the whole time that I was speaking, the people listened with the most solemn attention," he recalled later. "At last their feelings became too strong and broke forth in weeping and wailing, tears and groans, intermingled with shouts of glory and praise from some of the people of God. The appearance of a great part of the people gave me a vivid picture of the state of the ungodly in the day of Christ's coming to judgment.

"Some were screaming out in agony. Strong men fell to the ground as if they were dead. Such was the general commotion even after repeating for some time the most free and urgent invitations of the Lord to sinners."

What was scheduled as his last meeting in Kilsyth became the beginning of a season of revival that kept him there for some time. During that time, it wasn't uncommon for him to spend his nights agonizing in prayer for the lost and ungodly who attended the meetings. Time after time, waves of the glory of God swept over the crowd as he preached.

Describing one meeting, Burns wrote, "At the conclusion of a solemn address to some anxious souls suddenly the power of God seemed to descend, and all were bathed in tears. It was like a pent-up flood breaking forth. Tears were streaming from the eyes of many and some fell on the ground crying for mercy.... The whole town was moved. The ungodly raged, but the Word of God grew mightily and prevailed."

J. Edwin Orr once observed: "There have been instances in the history of the Church when the telling and retelling of the wonderful works of God have been used to rekindle the expectations of the faithful intercessors and prepare the way for another awakening." As Burns told the original story of revival, God used it to stir the hearts of those gathered in Kilsyth, so that the retelling of the story by carriers of revival around Scotland sparked revival fire throughout the land. God used the young preacher to turn Scotland upside down for Christ.

As Burns' popularity as a revivalist in Scotland peaked, he shocked those around him with the announcement that he was off "to preach the gospel to those who had never heard the precious name of Jesus!" He then went to China as a missionary.

In what seemed to be a chance meeting between Burns and J. Hudson Taylor (God arranges such meetings), each man had a significant impact on the other's life. From Taylor, Burns learned of the great need for missionaries in China. Concerning Burns, Taylor later wrote, "Never had I had such a spiritual father as Mr. Burns." For seven months, the two men served together as kindred spirits seeking to reach the Chinese with the gospel.

As did other pioneer missionaries of the China Inland Mission, Burns endured much hardship in taking the gospel to remote Chinese villages, but that didn't discourage him. Before he'd left Scotland, he'd told his friends, "I am ready to burn out for God. I am ready to endure any hardship, if by any means I might save some. The longing of my heart is to make known my glorious Redeemer to those who have never heard."

The people of Scotland remained interested in Burns' ministry in China long after he left his native country. Often they would ask about him when they met people who had been to China. On one occasion, a missionary returning home from China was asked if he knew William Burns. "Know him?" the missionary replied. "All China knows him to be the holiest man alive!"

The following entry in Burns' journal shows why God used him:

Many who do come into the secret place, and who are God's children, enter it and leave it just as they entered, without ever so much as realizing the presence of God. And there are some believers who, even when they do obtain a blessing, and get a little quickening of soul, leave the secret place without seeking more. They go to their chamber, and there get into the secret place, but then, as soon as they have got near to him, they think they have been peculiarly blessed, and leave their chamber, and go back into the world. Oh, how is it that the Lord's own people have so little perseverance? How is it that when they do enter into their place of prayer to be alone, they are so easily persuaded to be turned away empty?

"Instead of wrestling with God to pour out his Spirit," Burns concluded, "they retire from the secret place without the answer, and submit to it as being God's will."

Though used by God to bring revival to Scotland, Burns' real passion always remained the evangelization of the lost. On one occasion, he explained his life purpose in this statement: "The longing of my heart would be to go once around the world before I die, and preach one gospel invitation in the ear of every creature."

That longing took him through Scotland, China, Ireland, and Canada, preaching to all who would listen. Everywhere he went, lives were transformed by the power of the gospel. The revival in Kilsyth touched the world through the unscheduled preacher who agreed to fill in for a meeting, and the Holy Spirit who was poured out on the people when Burns preached.

A Summary of the 1830 Revival

One of the most important legacies of the General Awakening was the system of "new measures" introduced by Charles Finney. His *Lectures on Revival* have been used by generations of preachers as a handbook for encouraging revival and successful evangelism. He approached revival from an Arminian perspective: that is, he believed that if people properly prepared themselves using "new measures," God would send revival. This was in contrast to the Calvinistic perspective of the First Great Awakening that revival was a sovereign manifestation of God.

In addition to Finney's new methods, the Methodists refined their use of camp meetings—a strategy that had grown out of the Second Great Awakening—as the key to reaching people for Christ. Methodist bishop Francis Asbury instructed his Methodist preachers, "We must attend to camp meetings; they make our harvest time."

By perfecting new methods of evangelism and revival—Methodists got their name from their methods—the Methodist Episcopal Church grew rapidly during the awakening of the 1830s, doubling its membership by 1840. Baptists also experienced significant growth during the General Awakening, establishing churches pastored by local farmers in rural communities. A network of Baptist associations developed a Home Mission outreach in 1832.

Transatlantic Cooperation
Another significant result of the General Awakening was a new season of international collaboration among Christians. After the revivals of the 1830s

and 1840s, a cooperative spirit characterized evangelical churches on both sides of the Atlantic. In 1846, for example, an Evangelical Alliance was formed by church leaders in Britain and America.

This union of sorts was built around a common doctrinal statement that became the basis of the "faith missions" movement born in a later revival. The following eight articles of faith were, in fact, held by most Protestants throughout the nineteenth century:

1. The divine inspiration, authority, and sufficiency of the Holy Scriptures, and the right and duty of private judgment in the interpretation thereof.
2. The unity of the Godhead, and the Trinity of Persons therein.
3. The utter depravity of human nature, in consequence of the Fall.
4. The incarnation of the Son of God, his work of atonement for sinners of mankind, and his mediatorial intercession and reign.
5. The justification of the sinner by faith alone.
6. The work of the Holy Spirit in the conversion and sanctification of the sinner.
7. The resurrection of the body, the judgment of the world by the Lord Jesus Christ, the eternal blessedness of the righteous, and the eternal punishment of the wicked.
8. The divine institution of the Christian ministry and the obligation and perpetuity of the ordinances of baptism and the Lord's Supper.

With these articles of faith as a foundation, evangelical Christians from a number of denominations were able to find common ground for action.

Sunday Schools

Finally, the great Sunday school movement that swept England during the Second Great Awakening swept the United States during the General Awakening and left lasting fruit throughout the young nation. The American Sunday School Union, founded in 1816 in Philadelphia, received great impetus in 1829 when its president, Francis Scott Key (author of the American national anthem), challenged its annual convention with a vision of the "Mississippi Valley Enterprise." He reported that there were four million unconverted souls between Pittsburgh and Denver.

Key called for eighty Sunday school missionaries to go establish a Sunday school in every hamlet, to reach the Midwest for Christ. He asked for a budget of $17,000 to get the job done. Over the next fifty years, the Mississippi Valley Enterprise founded 61,299 Sunday schools, with 407,242 teachers instructing 2,650,784 pupils, using more than a million books placed in Sunday school libraries. A total of $2,133,364—a remarkable sum in those days—was ultimately invested in this project.

Most of those Sunday schools became Methodist and Baptist churches. To this day, they account for the conservative bent of America's Midwest. The greatest influence of the General Awakening was thus on individuals and churches as they continued to grow and spread into new areas that were being populated.

Sunday school missionary John McCullough took up an offering for a Sunday school library in Cumberland, Kentucky, in 1836. The small offering didn't add up to the $10.00 needed to buy one hundred books to start a library. A young girl named Rebecca Thomas, who was present for the collection, handed him a small gold ring as he left.

"My mother gave me this ring and I prize it very much," she said. "Buy Sunday school books with it."

McCullough reluctantly accepted the ring, but a Christian gentleman gave him a ten-dollar gold piece, saying, "Return the ring and purchase the books."

When the missionary tried to return the ring to Rebecca, she hung her head. "I gave the ring to Jesus," she said, "so other boys and girls could learn to read. It wouldn't be right to take it back."

In the days to come, McCullough told the story and showed the ring hundreds of times. Over $14,000 was raised. Rebecca's gift reflects an important spiritual reality of the Sunday school movement, captured in the Scripture verse: "A little one shall become a thousand, and a small one a strong nation" (Isa. 60:22).

CHAPTER FIVE

The Laymen's Prayer Revival, 1857–61

There has never been a spiritual awakening in any country or locality that did not begin in united prayer.

A.T. Pierson

The rapid growth of the church during the Second Great Awakening, followed by continual growth in the General Awakening of the 1830s and early 1840s, led many evangelical Christians to believe the kingdom of God was about to be established on earth by means of revival itself.

In such an age of expectation, a Baptist layman and veteran of the War of 1812 gained a large following among evangelical ministers and congregations alike. Captain William Miller announced that Jesus himself would return as promised on April 23, 1843. His conclusions were based on his own unique approach to the study of the prophetic Scripture, which focused on the mystical meaning of numbers in Daniel and Revelation. Followers of Miller were so convinced that many gave away their property and prepared special "ascension robes" for the occasion.

When April 24 came without incident, Miller concluded the Lord would return at the time he calculated as the end of the Jewish year, rather than at its beginning. The new date was set at March 22, 1844. Once again, the date arrived and passed without incident. A series of other dates were set, all of which proved, of course, to be equally unreliable.

The Need for Revival

The failure of Miller's extrabiblical theology had a predictably damaging effect on the credibility of Christianity throughout American society. Meanwhile, an economic boom took place as well, in part because of the U.S. victory in the Mexican-American War (1845) and the discovery of gold in California (1849). Since economic prosperity often distracts people from more spiritual concerns, this boom, combined with Miller's highly publicized failure, led to significant decline in church attendance.

In Canada, political events had similar effects. The War of 1812, followed by the Rebellion of 1837, heightened tensions between Americans and Canadians, who remained British subjects. Canada experienced a broad reaction against evangelical churches with close ties to American churches south of the border. As a result, the awakening among Canadian evangelicals, especially Baptists and Methodists, came to an end sooner than did that in the United States.

While Britain and much of Europe had experienced the blessing of God during the revival of the 1830s, a reaction among confessional Reformed Christians had soon brought that result to an end. Thus the General Awakening of the 1830s failed to have as significant an impact among European Christians as it had in America. By the 1850s, then, both Europe and North America were ripe for revival.

The Fulton Street Prayer Meeting

By the 1850s, the United States had come to a spiritual, political, and economic low point. Agitation over the slavery issue had bred much political unrest, and civil war seemed imminent. Then, in 1857, a financial panic hit. Banks failed, railroads were bankrupted, factories closed, and unemployment increased. Many Christians realized the need for prayer in such dire situations.

In 1857 Jeremiah Lanphier, a Dutch Reformed home missionary, began a lay prayer meeting in the Fulton Street Church of New York City, which began with only six in attendance. Within a few short months, however, the little prayer meeting sparked an awakening that eventually spread across America and around the world. This revival period takes its name from that meeting. There was no leading preacher through whom God brought revival, nor were there great crusades. Instead, this was a movement of lay people who simply prayed, and in response, God worked in their lives and communities in remarkable ways.

Dwight L. Moody

In 1859 a Chicago shoe salesman named Dwight L. Moody was elected president of the Illinois Sunday School Association. At the annual meeting in Springfield, Illinois, he said, "This meeting is dead; we'll pray until God meets us." Those assembled prayed all night. Again the next morning Moody canceled the meeting until God visited them.

That prayer meeting became known as the "Illinois Band," and it represented a remarkable group of laymen whose goal was to bring Christ to the world. Moody became an evangelist whose campaigns shook America and England. H.J. Heinz, another member of the band, was fast becoming famous for his condiments, but he said firmly, "I want to be known as a Sunday school man, not a catsup man."

A third group member began the project known as the International Uniform Sunday School Lesson. His aim was to have the whole world study the same scriptural texts, at the same time, on the same Sunday. As he put it: "Then we'll answer Jesus' prayer that the world be one."

A fourth member of the band began the *Sunday School Times,* which eventually became the largest circulating magazine in the world, surpassing even the *London Times.* John Wannamaker, owner of the famous Wannamaker Department Store in Philadelphia, was yet another member. He accepted the position of postmaster of the U.S. Post Office only when the president agreed to allow him to return home each weekend because of a prior commitment: He was superintendent of the world's largest Sunday school, at the Immanuel Church, with approximately 3,000 scholars.

In 1873 Moody preached throughout Britain and Scotland with amazing results. During twenty weeks of meetings in London, a total of two and a half million people attended his campaigns. Upon his return to America in 1875, he experienced similar success in campaigns in major American cities. His most successful campaign was conducted at the World's Exposition in Chicago in 1893. There, he surrounded himself with a team of successful evangelists who continued preaching long after his death in 1899.

Hamilton's Wesleyan Methodist Revival (1857)

In the summer of 1854, the Methodist physician and lay preacher Dr. Walter Palmer and his wife, Phoebe, accepted the invitation of Wesleyan Methodist churches in Upper Canada (now Ontario, Canada) to conduct camp meetings. Methodists had established churches in most communities in the region, and the summer gatherings were times of great celebration. Conducting camp meetings was nothing new for the Palmers. In their native New York State they were widely respected as lay leaders in their denomination and had often preached together in churches and at special functions.

The ministry trip north in 1854 was the Palmers' first experience in what was still British North America. What happened that summer ensured it would not be their last. They found Canadians especially responsive in their meetings. On a farm east of the village of Napanee, Ontario, 500 people were converted to Christ during a four-day camp meeting. As the Palmers departed for home, they knew they would return.

They were, in fact, invited to return once more to conduct camp meetings in the summer of 1857. Because of the success of the previous ministry trip, plans were made for an extended ministry. Previously, most of their work had been restricted to the eastern part of the province of Ontario. This time, they would also travel farther west, as far west as the city of Toronto and villages around the provincial capital. Once again, the summer's ministry was marked with great success.

While both Dr. and Mrs. Palmer were scheduled to speak, in practice it was the latter who did most of the preaching. Dr. Palmer struggled to speak before groups, while his wife seemed to thrive on the experience. Usually, the good doctor would speak briefly first, then turn the meeting over to Phoebe.

Those who gathered were not disappointed. Crowds were generally larger than expected. The last of the camp meetings ended in early October (about the end of the harvest season) in the village of Oakville, just west of Toronto. The Palmers reported crowds of 5,000 attending meetings during the week, swelling to 20,000 on weekends.

After a busy and productive summer, the doctor and his wife looked forward to returning home to New York. The easiest route home was to take a coach to Hamilton, Ontario, then transfer to a train that would take them directly to Buffalo. They planned to send their bags ahead to Hamilton and catch a later coach. At the train station, they would be reunited with their luggage and complete the journey home.

While the plan was good, it didn't account for incompetence. As it was, when the Palmers arrived in Hamilton, the baggage did not.

They wouldn't leave without their luggage, so the Palmers made arrangements to spend the night in Hamilton. It wasn't long before a local Methodist pastor learned of their arrival. Quickly he contacted them. There were four Wesleyan Methodist churches in town, and if the Palmers would consent to speak, he would open his church building for the meetings.

The fifty or sixty people who gathered that Friday evening, October 9, in the church basement was a much smaller crowd than those to whom the Palmers had preached in the Oakville camp meeting. Still, the people seemed unusually attentive. Phoebe committed herself to speaking again the next evening, then challenged those gathered to share their faith with unsaved coworkers and bring them to the gathering.

The following night, attendance at the meeting more than doubled. From humble beginnings in a church basement, a revival began that would change the city. Before the Palmers concluded their meetings six weeks later, the mayor himself was seen kneeling at the Methodist altar, calling out to God for salvation. Ironically, this citywide movement of God never enjoyed the support of other Hamilton churches, although the four Wesleyan Methodist churches in town who took part in it experienced significant growth.

News of Hamilton's Wesleyan Methodist Revival was first reported on October 28 in *The Christian Guardian*, an American Wesleyan Methodist weekly. The editor of the paper was a personal friend of the Palmers and often reported on their ministry. Under the headline "A Revival After Apostolic Times," the paper noted: "We are happy to inform the lovers of Zion that a most glorious revival is now going on in Hamilton. A note from the Rev. S.D. Rice informs us that within the last two weeks upwards of three hundred persons have been made the subjects of justifying grace, and the work is still progressing with unabated interest and power."

A week later, the widely read New York Methodist publication *Christian*

Advocate and Journal published a prominent headline, "Revival Extraordinary," on its front page. That paper reported: "The work is taking within its range persons of all classes. Men of low degree, and men of high estate for wealth and position: old men and maidens, and even little children, are seen humbly kneeling together pleading for grace. The mayor of the city, with other persons of like position, are not ashamed to be seen bowed at the altar of prayer beside the humble servant."

The revival that had shaken a city now began to shake the world. Hundreds of pastors in America's largest and most evangelistic denomination, the Methodist Episcopal Church, read the reports of the Hamilton revival and began praying for a similar outpouring of the Holy Spirit. It was, according to revival historian J. Edwin Orr, the beginning of the Laymen's Prayer Revival, now poised to sweep the United States.

The Fulton Street Prayer Meeting (1857)

In New York City in 1857, the Fulton Street Church (Dutch Reformed) hired Jeremiah Lanphier as a missionary to those working in the city who were unreached by the church. Not quite sure how to proceed in his new ministry, Lanphier decided to organize a noon hour prayer meeting for businessmen in the neighborhood. He printed an invitation to take part of the lunch hour to gather for prayer in a designated room at the Fulton Street Church. Then he distributed the flyers on the street to as many as would take them. On the appointed day, he set up the room and waited.

Twenty minutes after the prayer meeting was scheduled to begin, no one had arrived. Then a few steps were heard coming up the stairs. By the end of the hour, only six had attended the first noon hour prayer meeting at Fulton Street.

In the weeks following, the numbers attending began to increase. By October, the weekly meeting had turned into a daily prayer meeting attended by many businessmen. By year's end, the crowd had grown to fill three separate rooms in the church.

Similar prayer meetings were organized throughout New York and in other cities across America. By March 1858, front-page stories in the press claimed that 6,000 people were attending noon hour prayer meetings in New York, and another 6,000 in Pittsburgh. In the nation's capital, prayer meetings were conducted five times during the day to accommodate the crowd. As the movement spread from city to city, it became increasingly more common to see a sign posted in various businesses throughout the city: "Will open at the close of the prayer meeting."

Throughout February 1858, Gordon Bennett of the *New York Herald* gave extensive coverage to the prayer meeting revival. Not to be outdone, the *New York Tribune* devoted an entire issue in April 1858 to news of the revival. The news quickly travelled westward by telegraph. This was the first awakening in which the media played an important role in spreading the movement.

In all the major cities of the Eastern seaboard, the lay prayer meetings flourished. Taking up the challenge of Christ, who once asked the apostle Peter, "Could you not watch with Me one hour?" (see Matt. 26:40), most of the prayer meetings were held for exactly one hour, from noon until 1:00 P.M. Many factories began to blow the lunch whistle at 11:55 A.M., allowing workers time to dash quickly to the nearest church (since the revival crossed denominations, they didn't have to attend their own churches) so they could pray for one hour. The whistle then blew again, signalling them to resume work, at 1:05 P.M.

The prayer meetings were organized in the cities by laypeople and were interdenominational. With earlier awakenings, preaching had been the main instrument of revival, but this time prayer was the tool instead. The meetings themselves were very informal—any person might pray, exhort, lead a song, or give a word of testimony, with a five-minute limit placed on each speaker. In spite of the less structured nature of the prayer meetings, they lacked the extreme emotionalism that some had criticized in earlier revivals.

By May 1859, 50,000 people had been converted to Christ through the prayer revival. Newspaper reports throughout New England reported there were no unconverted adults in many towns. In addition to an unknown number of nominal church members won to Christ by the revival, more than a million unchurched Americans were converted to Christ and added to church membership roles. The movement seemed to be God's call to America to repent before the Civil War, in which more Americans were killed than in any other of the nation's wars.

The revival begun on the American continent spread to the Old World, beginning in Ulster, the most northerly province of Ireland, in 1859. About 10 percent of the population professed faith in Christ during the revival. Similar results were experienced as the revival spread to Wales and Scotland. An awakening also began and continued for several years in England. As in America, a million converts were added to church roles during the British awakening.

The Ulster Revival (1859)

In September 1857, the same month Jeremiah Lanphier began the Fulton Street Prayer Meeting in New York City, James McQuilkin, a young Irishman, began a prayer meeting in the village schoolhouse near Kells with three other men. The four young men were concerned for the unsaved in their community and began interceding for them by name at their weekly meeting. By December, the group rejoiced to see the first conversions among those on their prayer list. Many Irish church historians view that prayer meeting as the beginning of the Ulster Revival.

Ulster is the northernmost province in Ireland. While McQuilkin and his friends gathered for prayer, other Christians throughout Ireland were doing the same. Throughout 1858, hundreds of prayer meetings were started and many Irish preachers were speaking about revival in their sermons.

Early in 1859, the Spirit of God began to move in remarkable ways. Sometimes these manifestations of God's convicting power took place in churches, but not always. In the midst of a crowded market in the town of Ballymena, for example, a young man suddenly fell on his knees and cried out to God, "Unclean!" He began praying, "God be merciful to me, a sinner."

The incident in Ballymena quickly became known throughout the town. In response, James McQuilkin and his friends invited Christians to a special prayer meeting at the Ahoghill Presbyterian Church. The crowd that gathered on the evening of March 14 was larger than any had expected.

Because those responsible for the maintenance of the building were concerned that the large crowd might put too much stress on the galleries, they cleared the building as a precaution. The crowd thus had to stand outside in a chilling rain as a layman preached with unusual spiritual power. By the end of the meeting, hundreds were kneeling in the rain in repentance, calling on God in prayer. The meeting was the first of many conducted throughout Ireland in the revival that followed.

According to some estimates, the revival that swept through Ireland in 1859 brought 100,000 converts into the churches. In both large and small meetings, people came under great conviction of sin. Often even physically strong people fell prostrate on the ground, unable to move for several hours. There was deep repentance and lasting change in lives, demonstrating the reality of the revival.

One distinctive feature of the Ulster Revival was the spiritual movement among children and teenagers. It was not uncommon for teenage boys to conduct street meetings among their peers. In these meetings, according to some reports, children would often "swoon, fall down, tremble, shake, and weep."

Adults critical of the movement called it "juvenile sickness," but the children responded, "This is not taking ill. It is the soul taking Christ." At one such meeting, an Irish clergyman counted forty children and eighty parents listening to the preaching of twelve-year-old boys.

The phenomena that sometimes accompanied conviction in the Ulster Revival weren't nearly as dramatic as the social change growing out of the meetings. According to civic records, crime was greatly reduced in 1860, and judges in Ulster found themselves on several occasions with no cases to try. In County Antrim, it was reported that the police had no crimes to investigate and no prisoners in custody.

The Maze horse race typically drew 12,000 gamblers, but their numbers dwindled to 500. A Belfast whiskey distillery was listed for auction because of the decline in business. In Connor, the landlords of the local inns were converted and closed their pubs.

In short, according to some estimations, the Ulster Revival "made a greater impact on Ireland than anything known since Patrick brought Christianity there." One observer described the effect of the revival in terms of "thronged services, unprecedented numbers of communicants, abundant prayer meetings, increased family prayers, unmatched Scripture reading, prosperous Sunday schools, converts remaining steadfast, increased giving, vice abated, and crime reduced."

News of the Ulster Revival had a stirring effect in other parts of the British Isles. Similar revivals broke out in England, Scotland, and Wales. In Wales alone, an estimated 10 percent of the total population was won to Christ during the revival. Similar results were reported in many other communities as the revival swept through England and Scotland. As had been the case in Ireland, lives changed by the revival resulted in a significant decline in crime in many communities.

The Jamaican Revival (1860)

As news of the Laymen's Prayer Revival in America reached the Caribbean island nation of Jamaica, churches began praying for a similar outpouring. "Peep of day" (dawn) prayer meetings were organized across the islands so Christians could gather for prayer before going out into the fields to work. Most of these prayer meetings were organized at plantations and were well attended. As people prayed, anticipation of an imminent revival heightened. By 1860, most Christians believed God would send them revival by year's end, but none anticipated the intensity of the showers of blessing they were about to receive.

The revival began in a Moravian chapel in September 1860, but quickly spread from there throughout the island and across denominational barriers. Reverend Theodor Sonderman was the Moravian missionary serving St. Elizabeth Parish, in the southwest part of Cornwall County. In the course of his regular ministry, he came to the town of Clifton and was told a meeting was already going on.

Within the group, some could be heard weeping for joy. Others appeared to be under deep conviction. Still others stood, looking confused at what they were seeing. The German missionary attempted to calm the excitement of the crowd, but as he prayed his own emotions overpowered him. He decided to leave the meeting to seek the direction of the Holy Spirit.

On Friday, September 28, Sonderman began what he thought would be a typical meeting at nine o'clock. A hymn was sung, followed by the usual opening prayer. As the prayer ended, however, someone else began praying. That prayer was followed immediately by another. Even the children led in prayer.

As one boy poured out his soul to God, "a trembling seized the company." Sonderman watched as tears flowed from the eyes of people crying out for mercy. Even hardened sinners groaned out to God in prayer. Then, when one particular young girl prayed earnestly and fervently, "the Spirit came like a rushing mighty wind."

Strong men began to tremble on their knees, shaken by an invisible power. So many people began weeping under conviction that the missionary became concerned things might quickly "overstep the bounds of order." The meeting broke up three hours after it began so that Sonderman could deal "with those distressed," but many who left the meeting simply reassembled at a local schoolhouse to continue meeting with God. Reflecting on the revival the next morning, Sonderman concluded that he "might as well have attempted to stop the river in its course as to stem the stream of the outpouring of heart."

Prayer meetings quickly sprang up in other communities in nearby districts. The prayer meetings seemed to "generate a supernatural power which won a multitude to reformation of living and frighten others into temporary conformity." Those who had previously been accustomed to curse and swear now called on the name they had abused so long.

From the beginning, the revival was viewed as a movement of God, but some Christians spoke of it with fear and trembling. "Minister, we been praying for revival of religion," some local believers confessed. "And now God poured out his Spirit, we all 'fraid for it."

After four weeks, Sonderman was dealing with 314 inquirers, and the movement was still going strong. The revival had already spilled over into churches of other denominations, including Anglicans, Baptists, Congregationalists, Presbyterians, and Methodists. God was doing something remarkable in Jamaica. What had happened in St. Elizabeth's Parish was about to be repeated throughout the island.

In early November, a minister travelled to Montego Bay to preach a Sunday sermon. The whole town seemed to be talking of the revival. People came to the minister even before he had an opportunity to preach the sermon: Beginning at five o'clock Saturday evening, he received a steady stream of inquirers.

After preaching in Bethel Town, a missionary proposed a dawn prayer meeting for the following morning. On Monday morning, 500 people showed up to pray. A second meeting was announced for that evening, to be led by a local minister, as the missionary was travelling on to another town. At the conclusion of that service, "the Spirit was poured out and the mighty revival movement had commenced in real earnest."

People refused to leave the chapel. The missionary was contacted, and he returned for the Wednesday evening meeting. According to one account, "As many as a hundred hardened sinners [were] prostrated at once. A dozen couples living in sin asked the church to publish the bans for their marriage."

In the absence of a missionary, the local justice of the peace presided over services at the Mount Carey chapel. At the 11:00 A.M. service, 1,200 people crowded into the building. Others stood outside, listening through open windows. In three smaller communities, "there were 3,000 sinners awakened," even though there was no minister preaching. These kinds of reports tended to be typical throughout the island.

Among the Methodists in Montego Bay, revival began in October 1860. The 800 regular members of the local chapel soon welcomed "547 professed converts on trial," an increase of about 70 percent. In early 1863, Kingston Methodists reported the "holy fire was still burning, though the leaders were weary in well-doing." Bible sales jumped during the revival years from an average of 4,700 Bibles per year to 20,700 Bibles sold in 1860 and 1861.

Similar results were experienced among Baptists and Congregationalists during the revival. In Savanna-la-mar in Westmoreland, Baptists gathered in groups of fifty to a hundred, meeting daily in homes to read the Scriptures and pray. Eighty island churches reported 6,000 baptisms and an additional 6,000 waiting to be baptized. The revival ended a twenty-year decline in attendance among Baptists, with a 25 percent increase instead. The Congregational churches planted by the London Missionary Society were so strengthened that the Society withdrew from the field entirely in 1867, to leave the work completely in the hands of the indigenous church.

Missionaries serving the United Presbyterian Church of Scotland described the revival's results as "the most remarkable and encouraging that have ever come from Jamaica." Church membership rose from 4,299 to 5,561, including 1,326 converts admitted to the church in 1860. An additional 1,928 converts were still waiting to join the church. By the end of 1861, another 1,703 converts were waiting to join the twenty-six churches affiliated with the Scottish body.

Like many revivals, this one was characterized at times by unusual behaviors, with people under conviction of sin responding in various ways. According to one account, "convicted sinners were sometimes struck deaf and dumb, but on other occasions they gnashed or screamed or tore clothes." Others reportedly remained speechless for a couple of weeks, while still others "twitched" or lay unconscious for days. Some went without food for days.

These responses among the people weren't so much caused by a fear of hell but rather by a deep sense of their own sinfulness. As the Moravians argued, the excesses of the revival were "no worse than those which occurred in England during the Evangelical Revival"—and the good fruit of the revival was indisputable.

One published report of the revival stated: "Chapels became once more crowded. There was a widespread conviction of sin. Crime diminished. Ethical standards were raised. There was renewed generosity. Old superstitions which had reasserted themselves once more declined in power. As the movement spread, unhealthy excitement and religious hysteria showed themselves in places, but the testimony of almost all observers of whatever denomination was that the Revival did permanent good."

Baptist missionary John Clark listed several reasons why he viewed the revival as a unique work of God: "Very large numbers were giving their names to be published for marriage, and separated couples were leaving paramours and coming together again. Many were seeking admission to church membership, including more young people than had ever been seen in thirty years of service. Backsliders were seeking pardon and readmission. The rum shops were much less frequented and the noise of quarrelsome and tipsy patrons on the roads was no longer heard."

Clark's description of the revival is not unlike that of a Congregational minister who listed his own reasons for believing the revival was genuine: "It closed the rum shops and the gambling houses, reconciled long-separated husbands and wives, restored prodigal children, produced scores of bans to be read for marriage, crowded every place of worship, quickened the zeal of ministers, purified the churches, and brought many sinners to repentance." The minister added yet another evidence that this revival was indeed a work of God: "It also excited the rage of those ungodly people whom it had not humbled."

When the excitement of the revival passed, "the largest part of those awakened continued quietly in their Christian profession." The nation of recently liberated slaves had discovered their real liberty in Christ, and most chose not to return to the bondage from which Christ had set them free. Indeed, many also became themselves messengers of the liberating gospel of Christ beyond the shores of their island. According to Anglican bishop Stephen Neill, "In many cases, members of the African race in the West Indies rendered a notable service in building up the African Church in West Africa." The Jamaican Revival was too big not to be shared with the rest of the world.

Moody's British Campaign (1872)

In 1872 Dwight L. Moody, by then a successful evangelist known throughout the United States, went to England for a vacation. The previous year had been the most emotionally wrenching time of his life. He'd been challenged concerning his own relationship with God, and he'd travelled widely to raise funds to rebuild the church he pastored, which had burned.

As spring turned into summer in 1872, Moody was tired, perhaps even on the edge of ministry burnout. He knew he needed a break from his work, and he wouldn't get it if he remained in America. He thought that if he went to England, where he wasn't as well known, he could rest and learn under the well-known British Bible teachers he so admired.

The cause of Moody's fatigue had begun about ten months earlier. He'd returned to Chicago after a ministry trip to California to find his church flock scattered. It had been a hot, dry summer in 1871, and his people had found other things to do while their spiritual leader was absent.

Moody was impressed by the Lord to begin preaching sermons on the lives of various biblical characters. He knew people would be attracted to his practical preaching about people. What he didn't know was just how successful his sermons would be. By the fall of 1871, he was preaching to some of the largest crowds he'd ever encountered.

Then, throughout September and early October, Moody chose to preach a six-week series of messages tracing the life of Christ from the cradle to the cross. On Sunday evening, October 8, he completed the fifth sermon in the series, preaching on the text, "What then shall I do with Jesus which is called Christ?" At the conclusion of his message that evening, he announced, "I wish you would take this text home with you and turn it over in your minds during the week, and next Sabbath we will come to Calvary and the cross, and we will decide what to do with Jesus of Nazareth."

"What a mistake!" Moody recalled twenty-two years later. That evening, the great Chicago fire brought death and devastation to the city. Many who had been in Moody's meeting earlier were in eternity by dawn.

"I have never dared to give an audience a week to think of their salvation since," he later explained. "But I want to tell you of one lesson I learned that night, which I have never forgotten; and that is, when I preach, to press Christ upon the people then and there, and try to bring them to a decision on the spot. I would rather have that right hand cut off than to give an audience now a week to decide what to do with Jesus." Moody concluded: "I have asked God many times to forgive me for telling people that night to take a week to think it over, and if he spares my life, I will never do it again."

The Chicago fire changed the strategy of evangelism for the next century. Prior to that time, evangelists typically challenged listeners to "pray through" or to agonize over their sin. Salvation was thought of as a process that took time, so Moody preached for a week or two, then gave an invitation for conversion on the last night of a crusade. After the Chicago fire, Moody gave an invitation after each sermon. He preached one particular sermon, "Instantaneous Conversion," to explain how people could be saved immediately by accepting Christ. Other evangelists followed his example, until a century later, Billy Graham epitomized the new position with his use of the title *The Hour of Decision* and other uses of the term "decision."

The Chicago fire affected Moody and his family personally, just as it did many of his parishioners. By one o'clock that morning, the church in which he'd preached just hours before was burned to the ground. Thinking they were safe because they lived on the other side of the Chicago River, the Moodys retired for the evening, only to be awakened an hour later by the sound of an alarm. The fire had jumped the river, and by morning Moody's home was charred wood and ashes.

While the fire wore Moody down emotionally, he found himself drained spiritually as well. Two ladies in his church seemed to sense the problem, so they regularly sat in the front row, praying for him during the service. At the end of the service they would greet the evangelist with the words, "We have been praying for you."

Moody objected, urging the ladies to pray for the unsaved instead. They refused, claiming that they believed he needed "the power of the Spirit." Moody was irritated by their words, but God was soon to demonstrate that what they said was true.

Through the generosity of several businessmen sympathetic to Moody's ministry, a seventy-five-by-one-hundred-foot temporary building was completed by Christmas Eve to replace the one destroyed by the fire. This "North Side Tabernacle," as it was called, could serve only temporarily, however, and Moody knew additional funds were needed to rebuild the church. Reluctantly, he travelled east to raise the needed funds.

Meanwhile, those two faithful, praying ladies were also having an effect on their pastor. Moody needed more than finances. Describing his visit to New York, he later recalled:

My heart was not in the work of begging. I could not appeal. I was crying all the time that God would fill me with His Spirit. Well, one day, in the city of New York—oh, what a day!—I cannot describe it, I seldom refer to it; it is almost too sacred an experience to name. Paul had an experience of which he never spoke for fourteen years. I can only say that God revealed Himself to me, and I had such an experience of His love that I had to ask Him to stay His hand. I went to preaching again. The sermons were not different; I did not present any new truths, and yet hundreds were converted. I would not now be placed back where I was before that blessed experience if you should give me all the world—that would be as the small dust of the balance.

In a small room lent by a friend he'd sought out, Moody had encountered God.

Although the evangelist was spiritually revived through that experience, he still needed physical rest, so when he arrived in England, it was his intention to refrain from preaching. When he attended "the Old Bailey prayer-meeting" in London, however, an old friend there, the Reverend Mr. Lessey, asked him to preach in his church. For the sake of their personal friendship, Moody reluctantly consented to preach the next Sunday.

That Sunday morning, Moody felt he was preaching to one of the coldest congregations he'd ever encountered. Little interest had been shown by the people, and Moody himself felt the exercise had been a complete waste of time. The experience served only to confirm his resolve not to preach in England, but to take time to rest and study instead. He was sorry he'd committed himself to preach in the evening service as well, and he resolved to refuse the next time a friend pressed him to preach.

A lady who heard Moody that morning cared for a bedridden sister who couldn't attend church. For months, the sick sister had been praying for revival in her congregation. When she'd read reports of the ministry of Moody in America, she'd begun to pray that God would send the American preacher to her church. Yet, at the time, she found it inconceivable that God would answer her prayer.

"Who do you think preached this morning?" the bedridden woman was asked by her sister when she returned from the morning service. The ill woman suggested several names of those who had preached in the church previously. Finally, her sister answered her own question: "It was Mr. Moody, from America."

"God has heard my prayers!" the sick woman cried out. She told her sister not to bring lunch or to disturb her if any visitors came to the house. Instead, she would fast and agonize in prayer for the evening service.

At 6:30 that evening, the church gathered once more for the preaching by Moody. This time, Moody felt a difference in the spirit of the meeting. According to his biographer, "It seemed, while he was preaching, as if the very atmosphere was charged with the Spirit of God. There came a hush upon all the people, and a quick response to his words, though he had not been much in prayer that day, and could not understand it."

At the conclusion of the service, Moody called for a response. He'd learned his lesson in Chicago, so he asked all those who wanted to become Christians to stand. Throughout the building, people began standing until it looked as if the whole church were standing.

Moody concluded that his English listeners were having difficulty understanding him. He told those who wanted to become Christians to make their way to "the inquiry-room." They crowded into the room—so many that extra chairs had to be brought in.

Lessey was just as surprised at the response as Moody was. Neither had seen anything like this before. While Moody had often seen people respond to his preaching, he'd never before seen almost the entire congregation respond.

Once again, he asked those who really wanted to be Christians to stand. The entire crowd stood in unison. After he instructed them in the gospel, Moody told them that those who were really serious should return to meet with the pastor the next night. The following morning, Moody left for Dublin, Ireland.

On Tuesday morning, an urgent message arrived for Moody, pleading with him to return. The pastor had opened the church Monday night to deal with inquirers, only to discover that the crowd had increased in size. Recognizing that God was at work in London, Moody returned to the church. For ten days he conducted meetings, and by the end of the campaign, 400 new members had been received into the church.

That unscheduled revival in a north London church was the beginning of Moody's ministry in Britain. It convinced the evangelist that God could use his preaching to reach the British for Christ. It also convinced the British that Moody's revivalism was not just an American phenomenon. By the end of his life, it was said that Moody had planted one foot in America and the other in England, to shake two continents for Christ.

Sunday School Revival

As revivals, the awakening of the churches in America gave continuing strength to the Sunday school movement. Nowhere was that strength more evident than in the efforts of missionary Stephen Paxson in the Midwestern states. Paxson's success was reflected in the introduction he received at the 1872 National Sunday School Convention in Indianapolis: "You will find a broad belt of light through central Illinois and northern Missouri caused by the labors of one pioneer Sunday school missionary."

Born with a speech impediment, Paxson was later nicknamed "stuttering Stephen." He also was crippled and lame for life. Yet, after he was won to Christ in a mission Sunday school, he went out and founded 1,314 new schools with 83,000 students. This is a splendid story of one man who overcame almost insurmountable obstacles to preach Christ and spread revival.

Paxson was a hatter by trade, but he was also the favorite fiddler for Saturday night dances in a small village in rural Illinois. One day his daughter, Mary, begged her father to attend a mission Sunday school to help her win a prize. Because Paxton could read, he was pressed into service to teach a class of boys.

He didn't have to lecture on the Bible; he just had to correct the boys as they read the Scripture and then ask questions printed in the Sunday school book. Paxson was embarrassed that he didn't know the answers, however, so he took the Bible home and devoured its pages. As a result of his study, he received Christ.

Immediately, Paxson showed sincerity in voluntary service. He became a missionary of the American Sunday School Union, taking up the challenge of Francis Scott Key to evangelize the Mississippi Valley. His personal target was Indiana and Illinois.

Paxson was never daunted by bad weather. He often said, "A Sunday school born in a snow storm will never be scared by a white frost." His horse, named Robert Raikes after the founder of the Sunday school movement, never passed by a child, but automatically stopped so Paxson could give out the gospel.

In a book, Paxson wrote the name of each child who accepted Christ through his ministry. When he retired, the book contained more than

83,000 names. When Paxson's horse died, a friend sent a hundred dollars to purchase another horse, "Robert Raikes Jr."

Paxson often returned to the East to raise money for libraries to establish Sunday schools. For ten dollars, he told his listeners, he could buy a wooden box of a hundred books for a school. No group of believers, he insisted, could call themselves a Sunday school without such a library.

The sophisticated audiences alternately wept and laughed at his messages, never heeding his grammatical mistakes. They gave liberally. In doing so, they became a part of founding Sunday schools in log cabins, tobacco barns, taverns, and dance halls.

A Summary of the 1857 Revival

The Laymen's Prayer Revival which began in 1857 deeply influenced America and spiritually prepared the nation for the agony of the Civil War. Across the ocean, the 1859 awakening in Britain raised a host of evangelists, missionaries, and social reformers. The celebrated Baptist preacher Charles Haddon Spurgeon built his famous Tabernacle during the revival; he once preached to more than 20,000 people in the Crystal Palace on a fast day.

Existing mission, Bible, Sunday school, and tract societies in both Britain and America flourished, with new workers revived or converted during the awakening. New societies were formed to promote home missions, establishing Sunday schools and churches throughout both nations. The YMCA, the Salvation Army, the China Inland Mission, the Christian Brethren, and the Christian and Missionary Alliance were just a few of the many ministries and denominations born early in this awakening.

The revival in America and Britain soon spread to other lands as missionaries were sent out to previously unreached peoples. Hudson Taylor and his colaborers took the gospel from the coast of China to the peoples of the interior. At the same time, Japan experienced seven years of revival before rationalistic theology in the pulpit brought it to an end. Toward the end of the century, C.T. Studd left China for Africa and began a missions organization that grew into the World Wide Evangelization Commission. An awakening also began in Uganda, effectively Christianizing the entire country. Andrew Murray became the unwilling leader among revived Christians when revival broke out at a youth meeting conducted in his South African church.

In Latin America, significant revivals were reported among the established churches of the Caribbean. The first permanent Protestant missions to Brazil were launched by converts of the 1858-59 revivals. Both Indonesia and India reported large numbers converting to Christianity.

During the later years of the revival, awakenings were reported throughout Scandinavia. A thirty-year revival began in Germany in 1880, in part the result of Moody's preaching. At the same time, a peasant revival was reported in the Ukraine and an effective evangelism campaign was conducted by two British gentlemen among the Russian upper classes.

Campus and Youth Ministries

Charles Darwin published his *Origins of the Species* in 1859 as the revival began in Britain, but it would take time for his theory to undermine biblical authority in popular thinking. Darwin and many of his associates were hostile to evangelical Christianity, but their influence didn't hinder the revival from making a significant impact on university campuses. Students at both Oxford and Cambridge Universities formed Christian Unions, which became the beginnings of the InterVarsity Christian Fellowship. Similar unions were formed in American colleges. In 1875, the student fellowship at Princeton included several outstanding Christians, including Woodrow Wilson, later president of the United States.

Although he saw himself unfit to preach in academic circles, Moody was convinced to conduct meetings at Cambridge University. Out of the awakening that followed, a new student group calling themselves "the Cambridge Seven" committed themselves to world missions. They travelled to other universities, where they enlisted others to follow their example. Many students followed them to China and other mission fields around the world.

Encouraged by the Cambridge success, Moody organized a student conference at Mount Hermon school in Massachusetts, back in the United States. Two hundred young people responded to the challenge of missions at the conference. By the end of the academic year, 2,000 American students had volunteered for missionary service. The Student Volunteer Movement had begun with a daring goal: to "evangelize the world in our generation."

In Britain, the Keswick Movement for the Deepening of the Spiritual Life grew out of the revival in 1875. In 1881, a local revival in the United States in Maine gave birth to the first Christian Endeavour Society for precollege youth in local churches. Within fifteen years, the movement boasted more than two million members in 40,000 local churches. Several denominations organized a similar ministry among their own youth. In many ways, the Laymen's Prayer Revival still bears fruit down to our own day through the continuing ministry of countless organizations that are dedicated to reaching out to young people around the world.

CHAPTER SIX

The World War II Revival, 1935-1950

> Whenever God intends great mercy for his people, he first sets them praying.
>
> Matthew Henry

S ome great revivals seem to be associated with a war. The Laymen's Prayer Revival, for example, prepared many Americans spiritually for the trials of the Civil War. The World War II Revival has taken its name from the second great conflict of the twentieth century, but the dangers of war weren't the only factor that gave impetus to the revival.

The Background of the Revival

The global collapse of colonialism began after World War I, when the political face of Europe was changed and great empires were losing their ability to control their colonial conquests. It was not that Britain, the Netherlands, Spain, and Portugal could no longer control the emerging nations that they had ruled for 400 years. Rather, a new spirit of independence was sweeping the world.

The people of every nation wanted to rule themselves. In the past, the missionary had gone hand in hand with foreign traders, soldiers, and diplomats, but now native churches sought national religious leaders and wanted to rule their own congregations. The rule of Western civilization began to give way to indigenous leadership. Western political ways were thrown out, and the native way of doing things began to reemerge.

When the foreign politicians left, foreign businessmen arrived selling soft drinks, sleek cars, and a multitude of Western products. Quickly, the clothes, tastes, and practices of foreign nations became Westernized. What colonization couldn't do from the top down, commerce did from the bottom up—transforming the thinking of entire cultures.

World War II brought a vast multiplication of new inventions and products to help win the conflict: drugs, plastics, prepackaged goods, new technologies in communication and transportation. After 1945, these products were used to make life easier. Every new nation sought to develop national radio, television, and highway systems, and they all joined the United Nations.

Meanwhile, shorter working hours, better and easier working conditions, conveniences, and newly discovered wealth diverted people's thoughts from God. The church found it hard to keep abreast with the population explosion, and in many places found itself in a minority situation. Christians desperately needed revival.

The mushroom cloud of August 6, 1945, ended the war, and shortly thereafter a split developed between the First World (the United States and its allies) and the Second World (Russian Communists and their allies). So-called Third World countries became the focal point of humanitarian aid and development.

The church had for many years borne a great portion of the burden of such assistance; in 1963, for example, UNESCO reported to the United Nations that 85 percent of all schoolchildren in Africa were in Christian schools. World affairs were becoming in many ways more secular, however, and what the church had done for the world tended to be forgotten. The United Nations and other nonreligious organizations became the primary catalyst for international humanitarian efforts.

In academic circles, the growth of rationalism—that is, thinking apart from divine revelation—and evolutionism—a form of science that denies God's creation of the world—led to the influence of liberal theology throughout Christendom. The denial of biblical authority made its entrance first into the seminaries of the larger denominations, but eventually it trickled down to the churches. The result: a denial of the supernatural, including a repudiation of revival and its emotionalism.

For all these reasons, many in the church, though not actually deists, came to live as if they were. They treated God as though he dwelt in heaven with no access to modern life. The spiritual need was great, and the stage was set for revival, not only in America but in other nations as well.

The New Zealand Revival (1936)

Ngaruawahia was the gathering place each Easter for New Zealand Christians concerned about the deeper Christian life. In the spring of 1936, many anticipated that this might be the year when God would bring revival to their group. Much of that anticipation was created by the invitation of revival historian J. Edwin Orr to speak at the Easter conference.

Several revivals had occurred during Orr's ministry in other places. By the beginning of April of that year, many intercessors were praying for revival in New Zealand as well. Even before Orr got off the boat in Auckland, he began meeting people who assured him they were praying for him. "I was greatly struck," he later recalled, "by the atmosphere of expectancy which prevailed, especially among the young people. There was no end of enthusiasm."

The forerunner of revival began on April 8, the last day of classes at the Bible Training Institute in Auckland. Orr and several other Christian leaders had been invited to preach to the students. When Orr concluded his message on revival, he invited students to pray.

Revival actually began as students confessed various sins in prayer. The next speaker decided not to preach, so they could continue the prayer. Orr sensed that God was about to do something significant during his visit to New Zealand.

Next Orr preached a message directed at Christians in a tent meeting in the Mount Eden district of New Zealand. As he spoke, "the Lord began to work in their hearts." A young man stood to request prayer for deliverance from sin. He was followed by another, then another. Then one of the leaders of the group rose to speak.

"You all think that I am a deeply spiritual Christian," he began. "I know that I have that reputation, but I want to tell you that inside I am like a sepulchre."

His confession changed the tone of the meeting. Some in the group began to weep. Others broke down as they tried to speak. Two or three began to pray at once. A young man began to sing:

> Calvary covers it all,
> My life with its guilt and shame.
> My sin and despair
> Jesus took on Him there
> And Calvary covers it all.

As the meeting came to an end, no one seemed willing to leave. "Many of us have been praying for revival," commented a local pastor. "Revival has started."

The convention at Ngaruawahia began the next day with all the usual formalities. Throughout the day, there was a growing expectancy that revival was coming, but nothing seemed to happen. After the final meeting Friday evening, Orr was approached by a young man telling him a dozen of his peers in Tent #29 were concerned about revival and would like to meet with him.

After the evangelist discussed hindrances to revival with those gathered, he asked, "Do you really believe that God is going to give us revival?"

The dozen young men who were gathered responded in unison, "Amen."

"Yes," Orr prodded, "but do you believe that he will start the revival here in this tent tonight?" After a moment of silence, one young man answered quietly, "If we pay the price."

Orr suggested the group put God to the test by praying together for revival, to "see if God keeps his Word." As several in the group began to kneel, one young man spoke up.

"Don't!" he cried out. "Before we pray to God for revival, I want to get something off my mind." He turned toward another in the tent and said, "I want to confess openly that I have been criticizing you behind your back. Will you forgive me? I think I ought to get right with you first."

The friend answered, "It's my fault, too. I have been doing the same thing behind your back. May God forgive us both."

As the group knelt, conviction swept over them. Secret sins, pride, criticism, and unbelief were all confessed honestly before God. Each of the twelve got right with God, and the meeting was ended. Orr made his way to his hotel room, while those in the group went through the camp, sharing what God had done in their lives.

Despite the lateness of the hour, Orr had difficulty getting to sleep in his hotel room. He decided to go for a walk. He walked back toward the camp and was surprised to see a dozen prayer meetings going on throughout the camp.

When he got back to his hotel, he discovered that he'd been locked out, so he walked back to camp to find a place to spend the night. As he passed the main tent, he heard unusual sounds.

There he discovered "a deep revival" had begun. Two young men from Tent #29 who were leading the meeting didn't know what to do. Recognizing the situation, they called for Orr to assume control.

"O God, take the hatred out of my heart," someone prayed. "Knock the pride out of me, so that I may have the grace to go shake hands with him and ask his forgiveness." As he concluded his prayer, the man got up, crossed the room, and held out his hand toward a former enemy. They shook hands as tears rolled down the faces of others gathered in the meeting. Then a wave of praise swept through the tent, and the group stood to sing.

A young man turned on the public address system and announced, "Praise the Lord—revival has begun in the camp." The announcement drew others to the tent. They continued to sing past midnight.

The next morning, Orr quickly learned that not everyone was happy about the noisy meeting of the night before. In an attempt to deal with criticism, he addressed the morning meeting briefly. He had the sixty stand who had experienced revival the previous evening.

"We have come to Ngaruawahia for revival," he explained. "Revival has begun. Take heed that you do not hinder the work of the Spirit. Mark my words, you may see revival sweep the camp tonight."

His words were to prove prophetic. Orr stepped up to the pulpit Saturday evening, preaching for an hour as a holy hush of conviction came over the crowd. When an invitation was given, twenty young people responded to confess sin. Many in tears knelt at the front. Throughout the tent, people began to break down in tears.

In all, more than 500 gathered in seventeen after-meetings scattered throughout the camp. About 300 older people who remained in the main tent also experienced revival that evening. Later that night, a thousand people returned to the main tent for a praise service that lasted another hour.

J. Oswald Sanders, head of the China Inland Mission, and one of the leaders involved that evening, later wrote, "Those of us who were responsible for the conduct of the camp had the great joy of sitting back and seeing God work in a sovereign way. We were as men that dreamed."

Those who had come to Ngaruawahia for "times of refreshing from the presence of the Lord" had not been disappointed. They returned to their homes, churches, and communities as changed people. Before the weekend ended, hundreds of young people committed their lives to foreign missions. During the revival in New Zealand, J. Edwin Orr wrote the words of the gospel chorus that became the theme of his next great revival a few years later in Australia:

> Search me, O God, and know my heart today,
> Try me, O Savior, and know my thoughts, I pray.
> See if there be any wicked way in me,
> Cleanse me from every sin and set me free.

The New Hebrides Awakening (1949)

Church attendance was in decline after World War II. Not a church in the Hebrides Islands off the coast of Scotland could boast of having a single young person attending Sunday services. Instead, the youth of Scotland flocked to "the dance, the picture-show and the drinking-houses." Although the region had experienced many revivals in its past, the postwar years weren't encouraging for those committed to the progress of their faith.

Peggy Smith, an eighty-four-year-old blind prayer warrior, and her sister Christine, ailing with severe arthritis that left her in pain most of the time, were the human instruments responsible for revival. The two sisters were no longer able to attend services in the Parish of Barvis, but their humble cottage just outside of town had become a sanctuary of prayer for revival. As the two sisters prayed together, blind Peggy had a vision of the churches crowded with youth, and sent for her minister.

The Reverend James Murray MacKay visited the two shut-ins and listened intently to the account of the vision. His own wife had had a similar dream only a few weeks earlier. Neither the pastor nor his wife had told anyone of the dream, but Peggy's vision confirmed it. The pastor knew what he had to do next.

Reverend MacKay called his leaders to prayer. For three months, they prayed two nights each week among bales of straw in a local barn. They asked God to send revival.

After several months, a young deacon rose in the meeting one evening and began reading from the Scripture: "Who may ascend into the hill of the Lord? Or who may stand in His holy place? He who has clean hands and a pure heart" (Ps. 24:3-4). He paused, closed his Bible, and began to speak.

"It seems to me so much humbug," he said, "to be waiting and to be praying, when we ourselves are not rightly related to God." Then, lifting his hands toward heaven, he prayed, "O God, are my hands clean? Is my heart pure?"

The words had barely come out of his mouth when he went to his knees and fell into a trance. Some observers mark that night as the beginning of the New Hebrides Awakening.

Even so, Pastor MacKay knew he needed help. He considered inviting Duncan Campbell, an experienced Scottish revivalist, to preach in his parish. Then MacKay received word that Peggy Smith wanted to see him again.

God had told her in prayer, she informed him, to have Pastor MacKay invite Duncan Campbell to preach. "God is sending revival to our parish," she insisted, "and he has chosen Mr. Campbell as his instrument."

So MacKay invited Campbell for ten days of meetings. This evangelist, who had been raised in the Highlands of Scotland and spoke fluent Gaelic, had a burden for the Gaelic-speaking people of the Highlands and the islands. Yet, even though he was willing to minister in Lewis, he had other commitments. Campbell thus declined the invitation but agreed to come a year later if the invitation were still open.

MacKay wasn't sure what to think when he received Campbell's response. He believed that God was about to send revival to the area, and wanted

Campbell to be a part of it, but as a Calvinist he also believed strongly that God would work his work on his own schedule, quite apart from the involvement of Campbell or anyone else. The difficult task that now faced him was communicating the bad news to Peggy.

"That's what man says," Peggy replied when the pastor told her Campbell's response. "God has said otherwise! Write him again! He will be here within a fortnight!"

Unaware of these events in the town of Lewis, Campbell was beginning to wonder whether he'd done the right thing in turning down the invitation to preach. He felt strongly impressed by God to accept the invitation he'd rejected, but the decision had already been made.

About the time Peggy Smith and her sister began praying for revival, God began preparing Duncan Campbell for the revival. At home he was preparing a sermon in his study when a granddaughter asked him, "Why doesn't God do the things today that you talk about in your sermons?"

The child's question brought deep conviction on Campbell. He shut the study door and fell on his face before God, praying, "Lord, if you'll do it again, I'll go anywhere to have revival."

A little time later he sat in the front row getting ready to preach at the famed Keswick Bible Conference. It was the opportunity of a lifetime, a place Campbell had always dreamed of preaching.

Nevertheless, the Holy Spirit told him to leave immediately and go to the New Hebrides Islands to accept the invitation he had previously turned down. Turning to the moderator, Campbell excused himself, saying, "Something has come up; I must leave immediately." He left the building and went to catch the next boat to New Hebrides.

As Campbell stepped off the boat, he didn't look well. Crossing from the mainland to the island on a choppy winter sea had left him sick. The church elders who met him wondered whether he'd be able to preach that night. Yet preach he did, drawing from the parable of the ten virgins (see Matt. 25:1-13), challenging Christians concerning their responsibility toward those who were "asleep in sin."

"There's fire here," thought one of the elders. So instead of going home that evening, he walked across the moor to pray by a peat-bank.

The next night, according to one report, "a solemn hush came over the church as Campbell preached." After the benediction, the people left. As Campbell stepped out of the pulpit to leave as well, a young deacon raised his hand, moving it in a circle. "Mr. Campbell," he began, "God is hovering over us. He is going to break through. I can hear already the rumbling of heaven's chariot-wheels."

At that moment, the door opened and the clerk of the session (the church elders) beckoned to Campbell, calling, "Come and see what's happening!" When he went outside, he discovered that the entire congregation had remained outside the church. Others had joined them as well, drawn from their homes to the church by some irresistible force they couldn't explain. The faces of more than 600 people in the churchyard were marked by deep distress.

Suddenly, a cry from within the church pierced the silence. One young man, agonizing in prayer, had felt such intense anguish that he fell into a trance and lay prostrate on the floor. The crowd streamed back into the church, filling the building beyond its capacity.

A witness later recalled: "The awful presence of God brought a wave of conviction of sin that caused even mature Christians to feel their sinfulness, bringing groans of distress and prayers of repentance from the unconverted. Strong men were bowed down under the weight of sin, and cries for mercy were mingled with shouts of joy from others who had passed into life. A mother was standing with her arms around her son, tears of joy streaming down her face, thanking God for his salvation."

"Oh, praise the Lord!" she cried out. "You've come at last."

Peggy and Christine Smith, though still at home, also shared in the revival that night. "We had a consciousness of God that created a confidence in our souls which refused to accept defeat," Peggy explained the next day. She told how she and her sister "struggled through the hours of the night, refusing to quit praying." They reasoned: "Had God promised and would he not fulfill?" So far as the Smith sisters were concerned, the New Hebrides Awakening was a "covenant engagement," God's faithful keeping of a promise.

The revival spread quickly to neighboring districts, "travelling faster than the speed of gossip," according to one observer. Campbell received a message one night that a nearby church was crowded at one o'clock in the morning and wanted him to come. He arrived to find a full church and crowds of people outside. Two hours later, a group of more than 300 people were still praying in a nearby field. Unable to get into the church, they had begun their own prayer meeting.

In the village of Arnol, people were generally indifferent and opposed to the revival. Nevertheless, a prayer meeting was organized there. Shortly before midnight one night, one of the men present stood to pray. As he prayed, the room in which they met shook as "wave after wave of divine power swept through the house, and in a matter of minutes following this heaven-sent visitation, men and women were on their faces in distress of soul."

The New Hebrides Awakening had a significant impact on life throughout the island. In one village, "the power of God swept through the town and there was hardly a house in that village that didn't have someone saved in it that night." On Sundays, the rural roads of these remote islands were crowded with people walking to church. Drinking houses, which were common before the revival, remained closed for a generation following it.

The Los Angeles Crusade (1949)

A few months after the events in Scotland, God was setting in place the preparations for revival in America. Evangelist Billy Graham had accepted the invitation to preach a Los Angeles crusade, but first he was to speak at an annual briefing for Christian colleges held at Forest Home, a Christian retreat in the San Bernardino Mountains outside Los Angeles. At that conference, he spoke several times with Henrietta Mears, the director of Christian education at First Presbyterian Church in Hollywood, California. A dynamic Christian, Mears had led the growth of that church's Sunday school from 175 students to more than 4,500 in only a few years.

Mears talked with Graham about his commitment to Christ. At the same conference, J. Edwin Orr challenged Graham to consider the possibility that God might spark a national revival through the latter's preaching at Los Angeles.

But Graham was struggling with his faith after conversations with a longtime friend and evangelist, Chuck Templeton. Templeton had attended Princeton University in the Ph.D. program and accepted the "new" theology of German theologian Karl Barth, questioning the inspiration and authority of God's Word. Chuck criticized Graham, saying, "Billy, you're fifty years out of date. People no longer accept the Bible as inspired. Your language is out of date. You're going to have to learn new jargon if you're going to be successful in your ministry."

One night, Graham walked under the full moon in the hills, where he dropped to his knees, opened his Bible, and prayed in commitment, "O Lord, there are many things in this book I do not understand ... there are seeming contradictions.... I can't answer the philosophical and psychological questions Chuck and others are raising.... Father, I'm going to accept this as Thy Word by faith.... I will believe this is Thy inspired Word." Graham called this a life-changing event. His faith newly secured in the Word of God, he would ever after pepper his sermons with the phrase "the Bible says."

With a renewed vision of revival, Graham left the retreat center spiritually ready for Los Angeles. J. Edwin Orr continued to offer him support, attending many of Graham's later crusades as a prayer warrior and preaching to sponsoring pastors on revival.

Graham approached the Los Angeles Crusade with an invitation from a group of businessmen representing a loosely organized association of 200 churches called "Christ for Greater Los Angeles." He later wrote in his best-selling book *Just As I Am:* "I burned with a sense of urgency ... that if revival could break out in Los Angeles ... it would have repercussions around the world."

Because of this conviction, Graham had insisted that the committee meet three requirements before he could accept the invitation. They had to broaden support for the crusade to include all churches and denominations, raise the budget from $7,000 to $25,000, and erect a tent for 5,000, rather than for 2,500 as they had proposed.

Given these terms, many had criticized Graham for being "a self-promoting money-grabber." Yet Graham had maintained faith that God would do a new and greater work than before: At that time, most evangelists would have been considered successful if fifty people were converted and more than 2,000 attended. The committee had finally agreed to his conditions, and the campaign was set to begin in the last week of September and to run for three weeks.

As the crusade began, Henrietta Mears had Graham present a series of Bible studies to Hollywood stars and songwriters in her home off Hollywood Boulevard. Also attending was Stuart Hamblin, a West Coast radio legend whose popular show was heard up and down the Pacific Coast for two hours every afternoon. Hamblin quipped that he could fill the tent if he endorsed the crusade. J. Edwin Orr moderated these Bible studies, again pressing the need for revival.

Graham conducted a news conference with the local media before the crusade began, a strategy he'd never taken before. The next day there was nothing in the paper except for a paid announcement about the crusade. Stuart Hamblin interviewed Billy on his radio show and told his audience, "Go down to Billy's tent and hear the preaching," adding, "I'll be there."

That night Hamblin attended, but he angrily stomped out in disagreement with the message, though in reality he was under conviction. This episode was repeated two or three more times. Finally, Hamblin and his wife, Suzie, came to Graham's hotel at 4:30 in the morning, where Hamblin gave his heart to Christ. Later, Hamblin would write the well-known songs "It Is No Secret (What God Can Do)" and "This Ole House."

Graham had been praying about extending the crusade, and the conversion of Stuart Hamblin was his sign from God to continue. When he arrived at the tent that night, reporters were crawling all over the place. William Randolph Hearst, owner of two newspapers in Los Angeles and a string of newspapers across the country, had been quoted as saying, "Puff Graham" [that is, "make this story big"].

Some in the media claimed that was the cause for the success of the crusade. In response, Graham said the credit belonged to the work of God in the hearts of the multitudes, not Hearst. While the organizational committee had expected fifty conversions in three weeks, that many were being converted every evening.

The newspapers ran the story because something unusual was happening. Stories ran in Detroit, New York, and Chicago as well. *Time Magazine* reported:

Bland, trumpet-lunged North Carolinian, William Franklin Graham, Jr., a Southern Baptist minister ... dominates his huge audience from the moment he strides on stage to the strains of *Send a Great Revival in My Soul.* His lapel microphone, which gives added volume to his deep cavernous voice, allows him to pace the platform as he talks, rising to his toes to drive home a point, clenching his fist, stabbing his finger at the sky, and straining to get his words to the furthermost corners of the tent.

The headlines announced, "OLD-TIME RELIGION SWEEPS LOS ANGELES."

The next sensational conversion was that of Jim Vaus, a wiretapper for the Mob, who worked for Mickey Cohen, a high-profile local Mob boss. That event not surprisingly hit the headlines. When Graham visited Cohen's home to present the gospel to him, Cohen rejected the appeal, yet even Graham's visit there made headlines.

The Associated Press put out a daily press release on the events of the crusade that was printed in almost every newspaper in America. The meetings went on for seventy-two nights, and thousands were converted, 82 percent of whom had never made a profession of faith.

The Los Angeles Crusade kicked off fifty years of crusades by Billy Graham. Millions made professions of faith. Every major city in America held a Billy Graham campaign, and he preached around the world as well. More than one million in a single audience heard him in person in Seoul, South Korea. The conditions were ripe for a work of God after World War II, and Billy Graham was the man God used to bring, as the title of his book described it, *Revival in Our Time.*

A Summary of the World War II Revival

Billy Graham's crusade in Los Angeles led to much bigger things than the planners had envisioned, and it helped to spark revival around the world. We should also note that just as secular media attention was focused on Graham, the evangelist in turn used mass media to evangelize the nation. He founded *Decision,* a nationwide newspaper, and a radio and television broadcast called

The Hour of Decision. In addition, he implemented the most comprehensive organizational structure ever used to reach a city for Christ.

The broader evangelical movement that Graham represented also gained considerable ground during this period. For example, when mainline Sunday school literature came under the influence of liberalism, many independent Sunday school publishers arose to offer an alternative. They sold to independent churches and eventually to some denominations as well. In time, even a few of the larger denominations were using more of the independent material than their own denominational material.

To meet the need of new leaders for these movements, dozens of new Christian liberal arts and Bible colleges were born and grew rapidly in reaction to the growth of liberalism. At the same time, new evangelical churches and evangelical denominations were founded. The National Association of Evangelicals was established in 1945. Interdenominational agencies such as Youth for Christ, the Navigators, and Campus Crusade for Christ began their ministries. Whole new missionary agencies appeared—evangelical, fundamental, and pentecostal—and they made a considerable impact on worldwide outreach. Over 100,000 servicemen who saw the nations of the world during World War II were converted and trained, and returned to spread the gospel around the world in one of the greatest missionary outreaches ever.

CHAPTER SEVEN

The Baby Boomer Revival, 1965–70

We may or may not be entering a new "age of the Spirit" as some more sanguine observers hope. But we are definitely in a period of renewed religious vitality, another "great awakening" if you will, with all the promise and peril religious revivals always bring with them, but this time on a world scale.

Harvey Cox

As men returned home from the battlefields of World War II, they were filled with hope for a golden future. Nazi tyranny, Italian fascism, and Japanese imperialism had been defeated in a conflict that had formed strong new alliances. Nations had begun working together in a new United Nations despite their political and ideological differences. As with World War I, they believed that World War II was "the war to end all wars."

The world was not a perfect place, but it was much better than it had been during the war years and the Depression that had preceded it. People were employed and buying new homes, and the largest generation in U.S. history was born—a population explosion called the "baby boom." As the 1950s gave way to the 1960s, there seemed to be no end to prosperity. The new, unusually young president John F. Kennedy and his elegant young wife Jacqueline reigned over, as some viewed it, a fairy tale season in national life. "Camelot," said the press, had come to the White House.

A Shattered Fairy Tale

Then one day in Dallas, the golden world of Camelot suddenly came crashing down. A major American network interrupted a soap opera to announce that the popular president had been shot by an unknown assassin while visiting Texas. By the weekend, Lee Harvey Oswald had been arrested and charged with the assassination.

Oswald himself was assassinated before the case could come to court, leaving a shattered generation with lingering questions about the political system. Within a few years, other leaders who had captured the imagination of the world met similar fates. Bobby Kennedy was assassinated on the eve of the California primary, just as he seemed poised to grasp the presidential office formerly held by his brother. Baptist preacher Martin Luther King Jr. was shot at a Memphis motel after achieving several significant breakthroughs in the civil rights movement.

Idealistic Baby Boomers were coming of age as their leaders fell victim to violence. At the same time, America found itself engaged in an unpopular war in South Vietnam. As draft notices arrived in American homes, many young men feared that they, too, would fall as victims of violence. A strong anti-war movement developed and began to grow. The war was viewed by many of the young as part of "the Establishment"—an establishment they now rejected.

The new generation began embracing a new value system that was contrary to the traditional Puritan ethic of America. Popular songs of the day expressed new values with regard to drugs, sex, and rock and roll. Harvard professor Timothy Leary encouraged students to use LSD and other illegal drugs to stretch their minds into psychedelic experiences. In San Francisco, a sexual revolution was under way among hippies who had adopted a simple and promiscuous lifestyle, as they preached their message to all who would listen: "Make love, not war." When a new, mop-haired British band appeared on the popular *Ed Sullivan Show,* "Beatlemania" swept the nation.

Church attendance began declining in the 1960s as North America abandoned the faith of its fathers and humanism and hedonism increased. The actions of the U.S. Supreme Court removed officially sanctioned Bible reading and prayer from public schools. For the first time in history, abortion was legalized. Homosexuality would soon come out of the closet.

Television, only two decades old, began shaping the culture of America. It was said that Ed Sullivan kept more people out of church on a Sunday evening than the devil himself. The lead singer of the Beatles boasted that they were more popular among American youth than Jesus Christ.

As had happened before, churches in decline began praying more intently for divine intervention. Only a matter of years earlier, their buildings had been full as families brought their children to Sunday school. Now a generation was drunk with wealth, materialism, and technological advances.

The masses had less time for God. Children were raised outside the church. The public schools were in the process of removing all Christian influences.

The Charismatic Movement

Faith was by no means dead, but it was taking some surprising forms. Many Pentecostal churches were initially skeptical when they began hearing of "charismatic phenomena" appearing in mainline denominations. In 1960 the testimony of an Anglican minister that he, too, spoke in tongues gave birth to the charismatic movement, a movement within established denominations reporting phenomena similar to those experienced at Asuza Street.

As the movement grew, various parachurch movements came into existence promoting the pentecostal message among lay people, such as the Full Gospel Christian Businessmen's Association. Charismatic mission organizations, such as Youth With a Mission and Operation Mobilization, were flourishing. Soon reports appeared of nuns and priests speaking in tongues, and the Catholic charismatic movement was born.

The East Timor Indonesian Revival

As Christians in North America began debating the issue of spiritual gifts in the church, news of an unusual movement of God in Asia was reported in major Christian publications. Contradictory stories about a revival in Indonesia claimed that evangelistic teams were experiencing various miraculous phenomena as they carried the gospel to villages throughout East Timor. Books and articles were written describing the movement from various perspectives, but all agreed that God was indeed at work among the people of Indonesia. Accounts of the Indonesian Revival encouraged many Christians in North America to pray for a similar outpouring of the Holy Spirit in their communities.

The "Jesus People"

As has often been the case throughout history, when the revival came it was first noticed among the youth. Two popular Broadway musicals, *Godspell* and *Jesus Christ Superstar,* reflected the music industry's attempt to profit from the religious trends of the day. While Christians had prayed for the youth of their nation, many weren't sure what to make of the revival movement that had begun among California hippies.

Time, the weekly news magazine, put a portrait of Jesus Christ on its cover and announced to its readers that a "Jesus Revolution" was gripping youth across the nation. The "Jesus People," sometimes called "Jesus Freaks," embraced Christ as Savior but didn't abandon aspects of their subculture, including communal living. Instead, they formed "Jesus communes" and began writing and singing contemporary Christian music in the new coffeehouses that opened in most American cities and towns. Maranatha, a publisher of such music, came out of the California Jesus People, and its praise and worship music eventually found its way into many American churches.

The generation that had rejected the establishment continued to do so as Christians. As the movement matured and participants became more involved in churches, most became part of the newer denominations such as the Vineyard and Calvary Chapel movements.

The Asbury College Revival

On a cold and windy February morning in 1970, students made their way to the regular chapel service on the campus of Asbury College in Wilmore, Kentucky. Various student prayer groups had been meeting on campus to pray for revival. That morning, their prayers were answered.

The fifty-minute chapel service ended up lasting more than a week. The Asbury College Revival, as it came to be called, quickly spread to various local churches in the community. As news of the revival was reported in both the secular and evangelical press, teams from the school were invited to other communities and schools to share what had happened.

In most cases, reports of the Asbury Revival sparked similar movements in other meetings. In the years following, several evangelical colleges reported a similar outpouring of the Holy Spirit on their campuses.

The Saskatoon Revival

In the heart of Canada's Bible Belt, the pastors of Saskatoon, Saskatchewan, had been meeting for more than a year in weekly prayer meetings, asking God to send revival to their communities. Several had been encouraged in their expectation of revival by the testimony of Duncan Campbell, leader of the New Hebrides Revival, that he had had a vision of a fire beginning in Saskatoon that would spread around the world.

When Bill McCleod, pastor of Ebenezer Baptist Church, invited evangelists Ralph and Lou Sutera to his church for special meetings, Christians were challenged to reconcile fractured relationships. As they did so, revival came to the church and quickly spread throughout the community. The week of special meetings stretched into almost two months of services.

By the end of the campaign, Christians from various churches were gathering together in a 2,000-seat civic auditorium, the only meeting place in town able to accommodate all those who were attending the meetings. As had the revival at Asbury College, the revival in Saskatoon quickly spread to other communities. Those involved became carriers of revival across western Canada by sharing what God was doing in their own communities.

The Jesus People Revival (1965)

News of the Jesus People Revival broke across the country when full-page photographs appeared in *Time, Life, Newsweek,* and *Look* magazine. One memorable picture showed the glistening, tan body of a long-haired hippie emerging from the waters of the Pacific, smiling because he'd just been baptized after receiving Christ as Savior. Chuck Smith, pastor of a Pentecostal church, was leading a southern California movement to win the counterculture youth who were flocking to the beaches of southern California.

These young people had rebelled against their families and the influence of a Puritan culture. They wanted their freedom. Yet even though many had concluded that the American political system was the locus of evil in the world, their personal experience soon proved otherwise. They began to discover that evil lurks in each person's intrinsic nature. They became addicted to drugs, alcohol, free sex, communal living, and Eastern religions.

One day Chuck Smith and his wife sat in a coffee shop watching a California beach that was populated with youthful bodies "as far as the eye could see." Determined to do something to help these young people, they led a few to Christ and took them into their home to disciple them. Because the youth were committed to communal living, they invited others to join them.

Eventually, the church acquired a Christian communal house where those converted could live and be discipled. No more drugs and free sex: The houses taught them discipline, soul-winning, and ministry. The first hours of every morning were given to Bible study, the afternoons to beach evangelism, and the evenings to rallies and evangelistic Bible studies.

Chuck Smith's congregation grew. They moved from an old church building to a rented Lutheran church to an abandoned school to ten acres, where they pitched a tent that seated 2,000. Next, they moved to a shopping center; then an auditorium was built that would seat 2,200. So many came, however, that they still had to sit on the floors, and the multitude spilled outside.

The church was winning more than 200 to Christ each week. In a normal month, about 900 were baptized in the Pacific Ocean, with crowds of over 3,000 spectators. The highly visible occasion was used to preach the gospel and win more to Christ. Eventually, Smith's congregation grew to fill four separate services each Sunday and became one of the twenty largest churches in the world.

The Jesus People revolution was more than a California phenomenon. Another group recruited from countercultural ranks, calling themselves the Jesus People, left Seattle, Washington, and traveled to Milwaukee, Wisconsin, to begin Jesus People Milwaukee. There were also the Jesus People Chicago, and yet another group, Jesus People USA. Jesus People revivals began spreading throughout Michigan, Illinois, and Wisconsin, and finally to Florida.

What kind of youth became part of the Jesus People revival? Every kind: college students and high school dropouts, church kids and kids with no church background, youth with relatively "straight" backgrounds and youth who had tasted the poisonous elements of the sixties culture—drugs, alcohol, "free" sex, the occult. But they all came to know Christ as Savior, and churches who were willing to reach out to them welcomed them with "coffeehouses" and other ministries that made them feel at home.

When attendance at Chuck Smith's Calvary Chapel reached more than 10,000 per week, those young people he trained were sent out to start other Calvary chapels, first in California, then up and down the Pacific Coast, and finally to New York, Florida, and elsewhere. Today the largest church in the northeastern United States is Calvary Chapel of Philadelphia, with more than 10,000 in attendance, pastored by Joe Focht (who was reached on the beaches of California as a youth and trained by Chuck Smith). Now there are more than 600 Calvary Chapels, and most of them are large churches, each pastored by a "hippie convert." According to these church planters, they never intended to start small churches; each set out instead to do a great work for God.

The Independent Baptist Revival (1969)

In 1968 Elmer Towns, Sunday school editor for *Christian Life Magazine*, visited Canton Baptist Temple in Canton, Ohio, to write a story on its gigantic Sunday school. He was overwhelmed with the size of the church—over 4,000 in weekly attendance—and its massive Saturday morning soul-winning outreach through bus ministry. When he preached on a Sunday morning, a vast number of people walked the aisle to receive Christ and submit to baptism. He knew he didn't have the gift of evangelism, so he concluded that this was the work of God. Towns continued visiting Independent Baptist churches, and everywhere he found the same work of God.

He reported what he saw in *Christian Life* magazine:

When I walked into an auditorium, I felt the presence of God. When I preached in their pulpit I felt the power of God. When I looked out on the crowds, they didn't look like the typical Sunday church crowd, they looked like the crowd at K-Mart, but they had come to the church expecting to touch God and have God touch them.

Towns concluded: "Each church—although spread over the United States—seemed to be experiencing revival."

Towns decided to do research to find the churches in America with the largest attendance. Since most didn't keep church attendance figures, he decided to identify and publish the attendance of *The Ten Largest Sunday Schools*. He spent one year surveying all denominations, Sunday school associations, and leaders in each state, and published the first list of the hundred largest churches in America.

Towns found that more than sixty of these megachurches were Independent Baptist. When he released the book on the ten largest, seven of these were Independent Baptist. They led the nation in number of baptisms, growth, and size.

Towns followed his heart and associated himself with Reverend Jerry Falwell, pastor of Thomas Road Baptist Church, Lynchburg, Virginia, the ninth on the list with 2,640 in attendance each week. The church grew to over 8,000 in the next few years. Towns became cofounder of Liberty University with Falwell, and more than 10,000 students were registered in the largest enrollment during that time.

These churches were single-minded in their purpose to win the lost and teach them the Bible. Thus they were the cutting-edge leaders for the megachurch movement; they became the role models for size and they taught the churches of America how to grow. In fact, hundreds of pastors from across the country obtained a list of those large Independent Baptist churches, then personally visited them to learn how to grow.

There were only ninety-eight churches in America with an average weekly attendance of more than 1,000 when Towns first published his list of the hundred largest in 1967. Thirty years later, there are over 8,000 such megachurches in America.

Many pastors took part in this revival, but one individual—John R. Rice—went throughout these churches teaching a unique view of the baptism of the Holy Spirit that was the foundation for revival wherever he ministered. He taught that a person could be divinely empowered by the Holy Spirit for extraordinary results in ministry that ushered in great soul-winning and church growth.

What happened to the Independent Baptist Revival? Many pastors turned against Sunday school busing in 1974 when the Arab oil embargo forced gas prices from thirty cents a gallon to $1.30 a gallon. In addition, many pastors looking for sophisticated congregations didn't want to pick up dirty little kids on their buses to bring them into their shiny new church buildings. Other churches turned their efforts to Christian school education and away from revival.

Perhaps most importantly, legalism was the worst influence among the Independent Baptists. They credited their own separation from sin for the coming of revival, and they tried to maintain revival by legalistic separation from the world, not realizing that only the power of the Holy Spirit gives revival.

The Canadian Prairie Revival (1971)

Located in the heart of the Canadian Bible Belt, Saskatoon, Saskatchewan, was among the nation's "most Christian cities," with more churches per capita than any other community in Canada. Yet, despite the strong evangelical influence in the community, something was lacking. Several pastors recognized the problem and began praying for revival. Among those committed to seeing God move in his community was the pastor of the local Baptist General Conference church, Reverend Bill McCleod.

McCleod was a student of revival and had often prayed for revival in his own ministry. When it was announced that Duncan Campbell, leader of the New Hebrides Revival, was preaching at a pastors' conference in a neighboring province, McCleod attended the meeting. His heart was stirred as he listened to the stories of what God had done in Scotland.

"If God could do it in Scotland, why not Canada?" McCleod wondered. His conviction that God would indeed do it in Canada was strengthened when Campbell told him of a vision. The Scotsman claimed he had seen a prairie fire starting in Saskatoon that would spread around the world. Both

Campbell and McCleod agreed revival would come to Saskatoon, and that the revival would have a global impact.

The pastors of various Saskatoon churches gathered weekly to pray for revival in their town. Beyond that prayer meeting, they also encouraged their churches to pray for revival. Further, they preached the Scriptures, calling their churches to a deeper commitment to Christ.

Although there was no significant immediate response, McCleod himself became even more convinced the revival was imminent. He had a unique dream one night in which he believed God was purifying him to be "a vessel of honor" in God's service. As McCleod continued to pray, he heard about the unusual response taking place in the meetings of a pair of evangelists.

Ralph and Lou Sutera were twins serving the Lord together in an itinerant evangelistic ministry. The fact that they were graduates of Bob Jones University in Greenville, South Carolina, sat well with the conservative Baptist church McCleod pastored. Initially, the Suteras' ministry had not been much different from that of a host of other travelling American evangelists. Then, without explanation, God had begun to move in an unusual way in the churches in which the Suteras preached.

Christians who had held grudges against one another for years were reconciling in Sutera meetings, breaking down barriers to both revival and evangelism. Weeklong evangelistic crusades were being stretched into monthlong revival meetings because the churches and evangelistic team were hesitant to conclude meetings in which the Holy Spirit was obviously moving.

McCleod contacted the Sutera twins and invited them to conduct a campaign at his church, Ebenezer Baptist in Saskatoon. The meetings began on Wednesday evening, October 13, 1971. From the beginning, it was obvious this would not be a usual "week of meetings."

God began to speak to longtime members about grudges they held toward other Christians. Two brothers who hadn't spoken to each other in several years responded to the invitation one evening to embrace publicly before the church. Barriers that hindered revival were shattered. By the weekend, a spirit of conviction had gripped the church. Among the first to respond were the twelve counsellors who had been chosen and trained to deal with inquirers.

The revival that came to Ebenezer was too big not to share with others. McCleod called his fellow pastors to tell them what God was doing. Members of the church began sharing what God had done in their lives with other Christians they knew in town. Attendance at the meetings grew rapidly.

When the crowd outgrew the little Baptist church, they moved the meetings to an Anglican church that seated 700 people. The next night that building was full. Then they moved the meetings to an Alliance church that seated 900 people. That building filled in two days. Next the meetings were moved to a United church in town that seated 1,500 people. Before the Sutera Campaign ended, they were meeting in a civic auditorium that could accommodate 2,000 people.

The meetings were conducted every night for seven and a half weeks, usually continuing until ten or eleven in the evening. Following each meeting, many people stayed for an additional gathering to get right with God. The after-meetings, as they were called, were often characterized by humble confessions of sin and the reconciling of fractured relationships. It was not uncommon to find people still in the prayer room at four or five in the morning.

As Christians returned to the Lord, many of their unsaved friends and family members noticed the change and embraced Christ as Savior. Revival had come to the Canadian prairie.

Before long the unchurched in town began to realize something unusual was happening in Saskatoon. Taxi drivers began getting calls to pick people up at church late into the night. They also got calls from people under conviction, asking the drivers to take them to church late at night.

About half of those converted in the revival were young people. The large numbers of converted youth changed the atmosphere in local schools and colleges. Student rebellion and cheating were transformed into a spirit of cooperation as campus Bible studies and prayer groups began forming.

Businessmen in town also noticed the change. People began paying overdue bills that were about to be written off. Others who had cheated restaurants or hotels returned to pay their bills in full. Shoplifters began returning stolen goods they could not afford to buy. Criminals turned themselves in to the police, confessing their crimes.

A new and radical honesty characterized many who were touched by the revival. It was reported that some businesses actually opened new accounts to deposit the "conscience money" they received during the revival.

While some continued to resist the revival, news soon spread to other communities. Denominational leaders from across Canada travelled to Saskatoon to see for themselves what was happening. As they returned home, they became carriers of revival to their own communities.

In addition, groups of laymen and women travelled to other churches to share what God had done in their lives during the Saskatoon Revival. Often, a similar movement began in those churches during the meetings. Reports of related revivals were also received from communities in the United States and Europe.

The prairie fire had begun to spread with a global impact, just as Duncan Campbell had prophesied. But the real impact of the revival would be felt through the long-term ministries of those whose lives had received a "touch of God" in Saskatoon.

Because the revival had begun in his church, McCleod received hundreds of invitations to preach in other communities. It soon became clear that he couldn't continue to pastor a church and also travel extensively. At the same time, after the Saskatoon meetings, Ralph and Lou Sutera found themselves conducting a different kind of local church campaign.

As these men and others began devoting themselves to carrying the message of revival to others, the Canadian Revival Fellowship came into being. The extent of this ministry's influence extends farther than its name suggests. In the decades since Saskatoon, communities across Canada, the United States, and Europe have experienced the blessing of God under the ministry of a team of evangelists who associate themselves with the group.

Another pastor deeply moved by the revival in Saskatoon was Henry Blackaby. Today the revival continues to spread its influence through his books. A couple of years before the revival, Blackaby had accepted a call to pastor a small Baptist church in Saskatoon that had seriously considered closing its doors rather than continue. When Blackaby arrived at Faith Baptist Church, there were only ten people attending services. Under the new pastor's ministry, however, the church experienced some growth and became the hub of a church-planting movement across the Canadian prairie.

This Canadian pastor was deeply committed to ministry in his native land, but when his denomination asked him to provide leadership in calling Southern Baptist churches to prayer for a spiritual awakening, Blackaby agreed to assume the responsibility. He headed up the efforts of revivals for the Home Mission Board of the Southern Baptist Convention, and through his books—including *Experiencing God*—Blackaby has been used by God to bring revival to churches throughout the Southern Baptist Convention and beyond. At least eighty other denominations have begun using his material with similar results.

The Asbury College Revival (1970)

A cold wind blew over the barren Wilmore, Kentucky, campus of Asbury College as nearly a thousand students made their way to Hughes Auditorium that February morning. The 10:00 A.M. chapel service was an integral part of life on this Christian college campus, and students were required to attend three times a week. That morning, Custer Reynolds, the college dean, was scheduled to preach, but he didn't feel impressed to do so. Instead, he asked students to participate in a testimony meeting by sharing what God was doing in their lives.

The practice itself was not unusual, but within the half hour, nothing else would be usual on this college campus. When asked a week later what was happening at Asbury, college president Dennis Kinlaw explained, "You may not understand this, but the only way I know how to account for this is that last Tuesday morning, about twenty of eleven, the Lord Jesus walked into Hughes Auditorium, and he's been there ever since, and you've got the whole community paying tribute to his presence."

Wilmore, Kentucky, a small city of about 4,300 people sixteen miles south of Lexington, is home to Asbury College, an interdenominational Christian college with roots in the Wesleyan Methodist tradition. Revival was part of the proud heritage of the school. Thirty years earlier, a similar revival had swept over the campus, transforming the lives of students. An even earlier revival in 1905 had also had a profound impact on Asbury students, including one of the school's best-known alumni, E. Stanley Jones, a missionary to India. Ironically, though the school sought to encourage revival by scheduling periodic revival meetings, there were no revival meetings scheduled for that day in 1970 when true revival actually came.

A few months earlier, Jones had been on campus talking to the students. He'd been accompanied by J. Edwin Orr, the noted historian of revival who had himself been instrumental in bringing revival to many places around the world. While Orr encouraged people to pray for revival wherever he preached, his real passion was to see revival among students. His study of revival history had convinced him that many of the world's most far-reaching revivals had begun as student revivals. As he'd arrived on the Asbury campus that fall, he'd longed to see America's campuses experiencing revival once again.

Orr had been scheduled to speak on the subject of "Campus Revivals in American History." It was a topic he often addressed when speaking to Christian students in American colleges. He knew his subject well, well enough to depart from his usual text and dwell a little longer on the 1905 Asbury College Revival. As was customary, students were invited to ask the speaker questions following his address.

Recalling that meeting later, Orr remembered one student and his question in particular. "I found your discussion of the Asbury College Revival interesting," the student began. "Was there any real lasting value coming out of that revival?" The student had failed to see any evidence of revival at Asbury College sixty-five years later.

"Oh, yes," Orr responded. "I could describe much that has been accomplished for God by the students touched by that revival, but I may not be the best one to answer that question." At that point, he introduced Jones as someone who had been a student during that revival, then asked him to talk about its effect on him and his fellow students.

After years of ministry in Asia and writing several books, Jones was well known and respected by the student body. In fact, Jones has been described as one of the most influential missionaries of the twentieth century. While Orr had described the revival well, Jones shared his first-person account of what he'd seen, heard, and experienced during the revival. He then described how the things he'd learned and experienced in the revival had led him and many of his fellow students to consider missionary service. Students listened attentively as the history lecture took on a new life of its own.

The meetings with Jones and Orr had a profound influence on some of the students gathered. A group of them organized themselves to hold one another accountable in disciplines such as prayer, Bible study, and practical expressions of ministry. Their goals were not unlike those of the Oxford Holy Club that had had such a profound effect on the Wesleys. Even among students who weren't part of that group, the hunger for revival had been stimulated. Many accepted Orr's challenge to pray that God might once more send revival to America.

The months of praying had begun to shape the attitude of many Asbury students. There was, according to one report, "an air of expectancy on the campus." Many students were individually entering into a deeper relationship with God. Some students were claiming that "a great outpouring of the Holy Spirit was imminent." Some of the faculty and staff had begun to share their sentiment.

The morning revival came, Dean Reynolds began by sharing something of his own experience with God. He then invited others in the student body to do the same. Quickly, across the auditorium, several students rose to their feet. The experiences they shared were recent and real, communicating something of the freshness of their walk with God.

"I'm not believing that I'm standing here telling you what God has done for me," one senior began. "I've wasted my time in college up to now, but Christ has met me and I'm different. Last night the Holy Spirit flooded in and filled my life. Now, for the first time ever, I am excited about being a Christian! I wouldn't want to go back to the emptiness of yesterday for anything."

Other students rose with similar testimonies and confessions. A conscientious professor realized that the fifty-minute chapel service would soon be over and felt that something needed to be done to invite students to respond to what they were hearing. He rose to take the platform and suggested that any student who wanted to pray should feel free to come to the altar. This was in keeping with an evangelical tradition in which individuals kneel at the altar or steps at the platform area to pray when settling issues with God.

One student who was present that day later recalled: "No sooner had the invitation been extended than a mass of students moved forward." Instinctively, the students began singing an often-sung invitation hymn, "Just As I Am." Before long the altar was full.

Throughout the auditorium, students began kneeling at their seats or in the aisles. Some turned the first row of seats into an altar, crying out to God to meet them as he had met so many others. It quickly became apparent to those present that chapel would not end on time that morning. Indeed, that fifty-minute chapel service went on to last 185 hours.

Looking back twenty-one years later, one student recalled, "There was a kind of aura, kind of a glow about the chapel." Remembering the time he spent in Hughes Auditorium that week, he explained, "I always have been reminded of the verse, 'Take your sandals off your feet, for the place where you stand is holy ground' [Exod. 3:5]. You just walked in and sensed that God had indeed sent his Spirit."

The presence of God was obvious to many others who were present as well. In the midst of the revival, one student began taking notes. Jeff Blake explained it this way: "The God of the Universe made his way to a remote spot on earth and I, one of his three billion children on this planet, found myself in the midst of one of his great divine moments in this century. My natural desire was to be a part of this transaction. My second desire was to capture the moment with written words of description and reflection." Blake's account of those days also describes a wide range of emotional expression among the students, from deep sobbing to fullness of joy, as they "prayed through" and got right with God.

The Asbury College Revival was more than a student movement. Faculty knelt at the altar alongside students, settling various issues in their own lives. Initially, not all the faculty was enthused with the coming of revival to their campus, but the revival itself soon changed that.

J.T. Seamand, a professor at Asbury Theological Seminary, was at home eating lunch when he first heard what was happening. His daughter Sandra, a student at the college, arrived home late for lunch, bursting into the room to exclaim, "You simply wouldn't believe what's happening at the college!"

As she explained the revival of the past couple of hours, her prediction proved correct. Seamand couldn't believe what he was hearing. He returned to the campus to see the 1,500-seat auditorium jammed and the revival still going strong. Though he'd been a skeptic of revival, he was no longer.

College president Dennis Kinlaw was also among those initially skeptical of the revival. When it began, he was conducting meetings in western Canada. Shortly thereafter, he received a phone call from Dean Reynolds.

Kinlaw had his reservations. He knew he would be held responsible if things got out of hand. Still, he didn't want to quench the Spirit if the revival was indeed genuine. Two days later he was back on campus. When he arrived very early in the morning, as it was still dark, he was surprised to find the meeting still in progress.

It was 2:00 A.M. when he walked into Hughes Auditorium and sat in the back pew to observe. Before long he was approached by a young lady seeking his counsel. Although no one was aware of her problem, she confessed that she'd been a habitual liar. She'd wronged people on the campus with her actions and wanted to make reparations. Encountering such deep and genuine signs of repentance, soon Kinlaw himself was convinced that this revival was legitimate.

One remarkable feature of the Asbury College Revival was the order of the meetings. Most of those gathered in the auditorium were young college students, yet they were not loud. Each waited his or her turn to speak. Neither were there the demonstrations of religious ecstasy common in some revivals that are part of the Methodist heritage.

Before long others began hearing that something unusual was happening at Asbury. Local newspaper and television stations reported the revival and issued releases on wire services and to their network affiliates. Strangers began coming to Wilmore to worship with the students. College officials canceled classes, and seminary officials did the same when revival broke out on their campus on Thursday.

Soon major American newspapers were carrying stories on the revival. Leading Christian publications also reported the news. People across America and in other parts of the world were aware that revival had come to a college campus in a remote town in America.

As news of the revival spread, both students and faculty were invited to visit other campuses and share what was happening. It seemed as if each of these visits was accompanied by a fresh outbreak of revival on a new campus. By the end of the summer, the Asbury College Revival had spread to an estimated 130 other American colleges. There were additional reports of revival spreading beyond the American borders, some even as far away as South America.

The revival also spread beyond college campuses. Many students were invited to share their experiences in churches across America. For example, when students shared at the Miridian Street Church of God in Anderson, Indiana, "a spontaneous revival that lasted fifty consecutive nights" began. The crowds grew so large that the church moved its services into a nearby school gymnasium. According to newspaper reports at the time, "up to 2,500 people a night flocked to the gym in hopes of being touched by God."

Outbreaks of revival continued intermittently for several weeks following the initial outpouring at Asbury. Eventually, the revival spread across America and into several foreign countries. Those who were part of it agree that what they experienced that week changed their lives and continues with them thirty years later. "There was this sense of the Divine presence that one doesn't have often in his life," Kinlaw later explained. "And when you do have it, you never quite get over it."

The East Timor (Indonesia) Revival (1965)

According to revival historian J. Edwin Orr, "The most controversial and sensational movement in Indonesia in the latter half of the decade of the 1960s was the revival in Timor." This revival was widely reported in books, articles, and lectures in North America, but many of the reports were contradictory or vague. Still, both critics and supporters of that revival agree that God moved in an unusual way to bring awakening to the Timor Evangelical Church and to reach many of the animistic people of that region for Christ.

Statistics suggest that 100,000 people were won to Christ from animism in East Timor from 1965 to 1972. That doesn't include vast numbers of nominal Christians who experienced the reality of new life in Christ during that time.

Prior to the revival, missionaries expressed concern over the condition of the Timor Evangelical Church. Many church members clearly had a very limited understanding of essential Christian doctrine. Promiscuity and drunkenness were common among professing Christians. Magic and sorcery were widely practiced. According to some estimates, perhaps 90 percent of the Christians routinely used the services of local shamans. Many also used charms, part of the fetish worship they had never fully abandoned when they had embraced Christianity.

Twenty years earlier, a limited revival had come to the area while it was still under Japanese occupation. Led by a national pastor, the earlier revival had reported that 40,000 people had been "restored or added to the church fellowship."

In 1964, missionary Johannes Ratuwalu announced that God had given him a healing ministry. With the support of his Reformed Church synod, he began conducting healing campaigns in Kupang and Soe. People were indeed healed, but there was little or no emphasis on evangelism during his meetings. According to local reports, Ratuwalu himself "succumbed to the excesses of pride" as his popularity grew, bringing the movement to a quick end.

Early in 1965, a member of the pastoral team at the Soe church began conducting a series of evangelistic meetings, "to supply what had been lacking in the healing campaign." The preacher, Benjamin Manuain, preached Christ-centered messages calling people to repent of sin and to trust Christ alone for salvation. According to Reverend J.M.E. Daniel, pastor of the Soe church, the evangelistic campaign in January and February marked the beginning of the revival.

A similar campaign was conducted by another church leader in July of that year. Detmar Scheunemann, rector of the Indonesian Bible Institute in Batu, and an evangelistic team of students conducted campaigns in Kupang, Soe, and other places. As did Manuain, the team preached the gospel and called listeners to repent and trust Christ. The campaign was marked by a number of conversions as nominal Christians were liberated from the bondage of witchcraft. The revival that had begun earlier that year now began to have a greater impact.

Daniel's nephew, Nahor Leo, claimed he'd seen a vision in which God had commanded him to surrender all his fetishes to his uncle. That action caused others to follow his example, bringing their charms to their pastor at a communion service. Liberated from spiritual bondage, Leo and others wanted to share the message of the gospel. The revived Christian formed a team of twenty-nine members who travelled to Kupang. Their ministry in that community emphasized repentance and faith, but also included an emphasis on healing and prophesying.

About the same time, a Christian teacher was deeply moved by a message preached by the team from Batu. Hennie Tunliu had a good university education, but she claimed a voice was calling her to serve God in Batu rather than pursue her university studies. As she shared her testimony with the youth at Soe, eighty responded with an open profession of faith.

The visiting team concluded its campaign on September 1, 1965. At that meeting, the team's director prophesied that "local teams would be raised up to evangelize all of Timor." Later, Hennie Tunliu shared her final farewell at the Soe church. She began speaking at eight o'clock in the evening and continued past midnight, urging the youth to "forsake sin, cleanse their lives, and surrender to God." That evening, a hundred responded to her challenge.

Unknown to the Christians, Communists in Indonesia had planned a coup for September 29. While some later reports suggested the revival had come in response to the failed coup, the revival itself was established and spreading prior to the Communist uprising.

Exaggerated miraculous claims by some writers caused many in the West to doubt all accounts of the revival, but Christian leaders from the West who visited the region and talked with church leaders agree that while some reports were fabricated, there can be little doubt that ministry teams in East Timor experienced phenomena in their meetings similar to those described in the Acts of the Apostles. These phenomena included "the rushing wind, the prophesying, the extraordinary prayer, the visions, tongues, and healings." While supernatural phenomena were present in the revival, the emphasis of evangelistic teams in East Timor throughout the revival remained calling people to repentance and faith.

A revival team visited the town of Niki-Niki in early October 1965. During a two-week campaign, 9,000 people professed conversion. Prior to the Niki-Niki campaign, many pastors had been indifferent or even hostile toward the lay revival movement. At Niki-Niki, most began assisting the teams in ministry. Within two years, more than a hundred similar teams had been organized and commissioned to take the gospel to other communities.

Christian leaders gathered in Soe on October 4, 1966, to evaluate the movement. While there were concerns with some extravagances on the part of a few teams, the pastors and theologians agreed the movement was indeed a work of the Spirit of God and gave it "a careful commendation." Pak Octavianus, chairman of the Bible Institute in Batu, visited Timor that month and listened carefully to reports from several revival teams.

Recognizing that certain weaknesses had crept into the lay movement, Octavianus gathered the people together for training. He preached a series of four-hour sermons each afternoon and evening to correct error and encourage workers to continue. The movement continued to impact the people of Timor.

Revival teams were held accountable by the churches that commissioned them and were required to make regular reports to their sponsoring church. In one report dated February 8, 1967, team leader M.F.J. Selan reported that 12,725 people had surrendered their amulets and fetishes, 6,210 had claimed physical healings, 29,457 had repented of sins, 387 families had become members of the church, and 3,435 other individuals had also joined the church.

While the revival primarily reached the poor tribal people of Timor, it also crossed socioeconomic barriers, bringing the gospel to the highest office in the region. When the local rajah, Petrus Octavianus, was won to Christ through the witness of a simple Christian woman, he surrendered his amulets and fetishes to be destroyed and immediately began making restitution for past sin. In a public statement, he announced, "I was glad when I became king and glad when I became a member of the Indonesian parliament; but I was never so glad as yesterday, when I received Jesus Christ as my own personal Savior."

As teams spread out through the region, the revival was "unofficially" carried beyond Timor into the Portuguese territory. Teams also travelled to the nearby islands of Roti, Sabu, Alor, and Flores. Reports of the revival came to the West at a time when many Christians were interested in spiritual gifts. While it became the center of much controversy and debate in some Christian groups, the revival was widely embraced as a work of God and encouraged many Christians to begin praying for a similar outpouring of the Holy Spirit in North America.

There can be little doubt that the revival had a profound impact on the Timor Evangelical Church. World-Wide Evangelization Commission missionary Robert Little returned to Timor in 1969 following his furlough to discover that many of the converts were making significant progress in the Christian life. As the 1960s came to a close, he found the emphasis of the movement had moved from the miraculous to one of personal holiness.

That change in emphasis didn't hinder the outreach of the church in any way. In 1972, a church in Kupang that had struggled to fill its building once a week prior to the revival was conducting three Sunday morning services to accommodate the crowds. Many other churches in that and other cities were conducting two services each week. The spiritual fruit of revival had remained.

A Summary of the Baby Boomer Revival

Unlike other revivals described in this book, the Baby Boomer Revival has had an impact that's hard to measure because it's not over yet. Many who were students in college revivals or touched by the Jesus People revolution now serve as pastors and church leaders worldwide. The Sutera twins and at least two pastors involved in the Saskatoon Revival—Reverend Bill McCleod and Reverend Henry Blackaby—are still actively engaged in promoting revival among God's people today.

Even this book might be viewed as a product of that revival. Author Elmer Towns became a carrier of revival as he published and told the stories of America's fastest-growing and largest churches across the nation. Author Douglas Porter yielded his life to God to preach the gospel during a youth leadership conference marked by an outpouring of the Holy Spirit in 1969.

If the world is on the threshold of yet another worldwide awakening, as many Christians hope and pray, those converted and committed to Christ through the Baby Boomer revival will no doubt provide the spiritual leadership required in such a movement. Perhaps it's still too soon to abandon the idealism of the generation that witnessed the collapse of Camelot.

CHAPTER EIGHT

The Pre-Reformation Revival, 1300–1500

Revival is that sovereign work of God in which He visits His own people, restoring and releasing them into the fullness of His blessing.

Robert Coleman

After Pentecost, the Christian message was preached throughout Europe. Both peasants and kings responded to the message as nation after nation declared itself Christian. As the gospel spread, so did the influence and power of the Christian church.

The church extended its reach until it exerted great power in the areas of social life, education, politics, and economics. Perhaps its increased economic power led to its downfall, but ultimate power corrupts ultimately. After many of the clergy became corrupt, the people in the pews grew cold in the love of God, and many in the established church became corrupted throughout much of the Middle Ages.

A Survey of Medieval Awakenings

A survey of what was done to awaken the church will lead us to the Pre-Reformation Revivals. The historical records of the Middle Ages are less abundant in revivals than in later centuries, but there are some indications that God intermittently poured out his Spirit during this period. While records of local church revivals don't exist, there are records of several movements in the medieval church that have some evidences of revival movements.

Most revivals in that era took the form of movements among the religious orders of monks, nuns, and friars, in which believers sought to separate themselves from a corrupt world in order to pursue holiness. Evangelical sects tended to separate themselves and seek a return to the apostolic Christianity of the early church.

Early Monastic Leaders

Monasticism was an early response to perceived corruption in the church. Initially, becoming a monk was an individual affair, and monks lived a solitary existence. Anthony (ca. 250–356) is usually viewed as the first monk, but Pachomius (292–346) was the first to organize a monastery. He did so in about 320 at Tabennisi, Egypt, with a dozen other monks. Soon, some 7,000 monks were part of his movement in Egypt and Syria.

The best-known leader of Western monasticism was Benedict of Nursia (ca. 480–543). Shocked by the vice he saw openly practiced in Rome, Benedict withdrew to live as a hermit in a cave east of the city. In 529, he began what is now known as the Benedictine Order with the founding of the monastery of Monte Cassino.

The monastery itself continued until it was destroyed during World War II. Benedict's rules of life and discipline became a guide for monks throughout Europe and were in near-universal use there by the time of Charlemagne.

During the seventh and eighth centuries, the monks of Ireland took the gospel from their monasteries on the Emerald Isle throughout northern Europe. Among the best known of the Irish monks was Columba, who established a monastery on the island of Iona, which became the base from which he evangelized the Scots. One of his students, Aidan, followed his example when he established a monastery on the island of Lindisfarne as the base from which he evangelized the people of Northumbria (northern England).

In 909, Duke William of Aquitaine gave a charter to the Benedictine abbot Berno of Baume to establish a new monastery at Cluny in eastern France. Under the terms of the charter, the monastery was to be free of all secular and episcopal control. Berno and his immediate successor, Odo, proved to be capable leaders, causing many Benedictine monasteries to reorganize to be more like the monastery at Cluny. The monks of Cluny were marked by their financial integrity and sexual purity and became the center of much social reform in the region. By the middle of the tenth century, nearly seventy monasteries were under the control of the abbot of Cluny.

The Franciscans

In the early thirteenth century, the Franciscan order was established in Italy by Francis of Assisi, who was converted during an illness. He abandoned his previous pleasure-seeking lifestyle and adopted one marked by poverty, chastity, and obedience. His order was formally established in 1210 and quickly became popular. About 1215 a young woman named Clare established a companion order for women named the Poor Clares.

During his lifetime, Francis preached the gospel across Italy and as far away as Spain and Egypt. Along with the Dominicans, an order of preachers, the Franciscans provided the principal missionary movement of the day.

The Waldensians

About 1176, Peter Waldo, a rich merchant of Lyons, France, was impressed with the claims of Christ as he read a translation of the New Testament. He liquidated his assets, keeping only what he felt was necessary for the care of his family, and established a group known as "the Poor in Spirit." These Waldensians, as they came to be called, sought to preach the gospel as laymen, but were forbidden to do so by the pope except when they were invited to do so by the clergy. When they refused to stop preaching, the Waldensians were formally excommunicated in 1184. They continued to exist as a hidden church until granted liberty centuries later.

The Waldensians believed that people should have the Bible in their own language and that the Scriptures should be the final authority in matters of faith and practice. They went out to preach two by two, following the example of Christ, who sent his disciples out in groups of two. As this lay movement grew, they eventually established their own churches and clergy.

Others sympathetic to the Waldensians were known as "friends," but continued their affiliation with the established church. Where possible, these friends worked as evangelicals within the established church. When they were no longer able to do so, many formally identified with the hidden church.

John Wycliffe

For several years, John Wycliffe carried on a campaign among academics and ecclesiastics in England, calling the church to return to its biblical heritage, but the church began condemning his teachings as heresies and errors. In 1382 Wycliffe's disciples broke with a long-standing tradition of the church and translated the entire Scripture into the English language. It was the first time in a thousand years that the whole Bible had been translated into a European language, though portions of it had often been translated into various vernaculars. Armed now with the Bible in their own language, the poor priests of Wycliffe, called Lollards, took the message of the gospel to villages scattered throughout England.

Wycliffe died two years after the Lollard Revival began in England, but his teachings continued to promote revival in the following generation. Early in the fifteenth century, it was estimated that one of every two men in England embraced the teachings of John Wycliffe. This estimate seems a bit hyperbolic—by that time the term *Lollard* had come to mean anybody dissatisfied with the church. The Lollard movement was subjected to an intense persecution, which included the exhumation of Wycliffe's bones to be burned for heresy. Still his followers multiplied. In 1523, the Renaissance scholar Erasmus described the Lollard movement as "conquered, but not extinguished."

John Hus

Despite the condemnation of Wycliffe's books as heresy, they continued to be widely read, even as far away as Bohemia. As the church burned Wycliffe's books in the streets of Prague, the popular Bohemian preacher John Hus began preaching the same truths from his pulpit. The masses quickly followed Hus, enabling him to make significant social reforms in his nation.

Hus also felt the brunt of ecclesiastical persecution and was martyred for the cause of Christ on his fifty-sixth birthday. The seed sown in Hus' preaching took root, however, giving birth to the Bohemian Brethren. For centuries they continued as an underground church, hidden away in rural villages until they found refuge on the estates of Count Zinzendorf.

Girolamo Savonarola

In one of the more dramatic attempts to revive and reform the Catholic Church in this era, an Italian priest called for reforms in central Italy. Girolamo Savonarola challenged corruption in both the church and state from his pulpit in Florence. He began preaching the same year Martin Luther was born. His ministry was often better received in rural Italian villages than in Florence itself.

When the ruler of Florence tried to silence the bold preacher, he failed. Even his critics recognized that Savonarola possessed an unusual spiritual power. Revival swept through Florence under his ministry, transforming the city and reforming autocratic laws into democracy. In fact, Savonarola wrote the basis for a system of city government that was copied throughout Europe.

But Savonarola's attacks on the corruption of the church would not be ignored. Like Wycliffe and Hus before him, the Italian preacher was condemned. He was hanged in the public square in 1498.

Some might want to place the pre-Reformation revivals farther down the list of the ten greatest revivals ever. But they are placed eighth because of the opposition they faced, the price they paid, and the seed planted that ultimately took root to grow underground. Eventually, the work of God burst through the ground in the ministry of Martin Luther and the Protestant Reformation.

Wycliffe and England's Lollard Revival (1382)

Almost two centuries before Martin Luther posted his ninety-five theses on the Wittenburg Castle church door, the poor priests who followed John Wycliffe were preaching the evangelical message and calling for reforms in the corrupt church throughout the villages of England. Historians looking back call Wycliffe the "morning star of the Reformation" because his teachings were prototypical of those of the later reformers.

Wycliffe was born in Yorkshire about 1330 and trained for the priesthood at Britain's historic Oxford University. In 1372, he became a Doctor of Divinity and joined the Oxford faculty. Two years later, King Edward III appointed him rector of the parish of Lutterworth. In addition to his duties pastoring the Lutterworth church, Wycliffe also exercised a significant degree of influence within Britain's royal court.

Wycliffe served as the clerical advisor from 1376 to 1378 to John of Gaunt, who effectively governed England until his nephew, Richard II, came of age in 1381. In 1377, the king and Parliament of England turned to Wycliffe for advice as to whether it was lawful to withhold traditional payments from Rome. When Wycliffe agreed it was, he alienated himself from church authorities. Pope Gregory XI issued five edicts against him, but none had any serious effect. In 1381, Wycliffe retired from government service to Lutterworth, where he remained during the final years of his life.

While consistently describing himself as a loyal churchman willing to subject himself to the pope, Wycliffe was also openly critical of the various abuses of the church. Wycliffe also held that the Scriptures alone were the ultimate authority in all matters of doctrine and practice. The application of that principle led to a host of differences between Wycliffe and the established church. He claimed that even the pope could not be trusted if his statements were contrary to the clear teachings of Scripture.

For his part, Pope Gregory XI strongly condemned Wycliffe. In 1382, a church council presided over by the archbishop of Canterbury condemned twenty-four specific doctrines of Wycliffe, ten as heresies and fourteen as errors.

While some historians have sought to attribute Britain's Peasant Revolt of 1381 to Wycliffe and his teachings, it's unlikely he had much to do with it. To that time, Wycliffe's writings had been circulated only in academic and ecclesiastical circles, so it's doubtful that many in the general population had any understanding of his views. Probably many were even unaware of his existence. However, all that was about to change.

In 1382, Wycliffe's disciples translated the Bible into English. Prior to Wycliffe, those who wished to read the entire Scriptures had first to learn Latin. As the use of English in church services was not approved by the established church, Wycliffe organized his own itinerant preachers to take his Bible directly to the people of England. The first English sermon preached by a Lollard appears to be that of Nicholas Hereford at St. Frideswide's on Ascension Day, 1382. It was the beginning of a movement that resulted in a turning to God among the common people throughout England.

Wycliffe's "poor priests" endured hardship and took the gospel throughout England's scattered villages. His critics began describing the men as "Lollards." Various explanations have been given for why the term was applied, but probably the term was based on a Dutch word for "mumblers." Others argue that the term was based on the Latin word meaning "tare," a French term describing "hypocrites," or an early English word referring to the "idle." The various suggested roots of this term reveal something of the hostility of the established church toward this movement.

Intense persecution swept through England, directed at those who adhered to Wycliffe's views. The intensity of that opposition endured far beyond Wycliffe's natural life. The English reformer died on December 31, 1384, as a result of a stroke. Forty-four years later, the pope ordered his bones to be exhumed and burned as the remains of a heretic. His ashes were scattered in the Thames River. Yet even as the river carried his ashes to the sea, the order of poor priests he'd founded continued to carry his gospel across the country and the continent of Europe.

The influence of Wycliffe extended beyond his life. In the first thirty years of the fifteenth century, the Lollards continued to spread the message into parts of England that hadn't been reached during Wycliffe's life. After a series of church condemnations of Wycliffe as a heretic, the movement became increasingly lay-led, especially strong in the eastern counties of Britain.

Following the death of Wycliffe, Sir John Oldcastle of Herefordshire continued the movement. Although his "Lollardy" was well known, his position and wealth protected him from official sanction until 1413. At that time he was arrested, tried, and sentenced as a heretic, but he managed to escape from the Tower of London cell in which he was being held. Oldcastle continued to lead the movement from various hiding places until he was finally captured, condemned by Parliament, and executed in 1417. Under Sir John's leadership, many British leaders believed the Lollard movement was becoming stronger than the established church itself.

Despite the intense persecution, the teaching of Wycliffe and the Lollards continued to be held by many Christians throughout Britain and on the European continent. The seeds of the evangelical gospel had been widely sown and had taken root. They would sprout again with the coming of a later reformation.

The Burning of John Hus (1415)

Crowds filled the meadow on the edge of Constance, Bohemia, to witness the execution that had been anticipated for months. The popular Bohemian preacher was tied to a stake with seven moist thongs and a rusty old chain. Broken pieces of wood and straw were piled against his body. Then the marshal gave the condemned man one more chance to recant and preserve his life.

"What errors shall I renounce?" John Hus asked. "I know myself guilty of none. I call God to witness that all I have written and preached has been with the view of rescuing souls from sin and perdition, and therefore most joyfully will I confirm with my blood the truth I have written and preached."

A burning torch ignited the dry straw at the base of the pile. Hus prayed as the flames surrounded him on every side. By the time the fire burned out, the body of Hus had been consumed, but the burning of Hus didn't extinguish the movement he led. As his ashes were scattered in the Rhine, the influence of the martyred leader grew.

Born July 6, 1369, in Husinec, South Bohemia, John Hus was an unlikely candidate for heroism. Not a particularly brilliant student, he persisted in his studies, eventually graduating from Prague University. It was in the pulpit, first as rector of the university and then later at the Bethlehem Chapel, that Hus first attracted attention.

Hus was deeply committed to personal morality and urged others to follow his example. When he addressed the sins of the rich, his preaching became a source of irritation to political leaders. The complaint of an aristocrat to the king prompted the king to urge the archbishop of Prague to warn the popular preacher. The archbishop responded, "Hus is bound by his ordination oath to speak the truth without respect of persons." When Hus later addressed the vices of the clergy, the archbishop found himself complaining to the king, only to be reminded, "Hus is bound by his ordination oath to speak the truth without respect of persons."

Hus' preaching gave Bohemians a controlling influence in the administrative affairs of Prague University, but Hus was more than a social reformer. He began preaching the views of Wycliffe even though the English reformer had been condemned by the Council at Black-Friars, England. The public burning of Wycliffe's books in Prague did not dissuade him. Remaining true to his ordination oath, Hus was soon addressing the sins of the pope.

When John XXIII launched a military campaign against the king of Naples, he financed the campaign with the sale of indulgences. As sales began in Prague, Hus declared his opposition in no uncertain terms. "Let who will proclaim the contrary; let the Pope, or a Bishop, or a Priest say, 'I forgive thee thy sins; I free thee from the pains of hell.' It is all vain, and helps thee nothing," he declared. "God alone, I repeat, can forgive sins through Christ."

Hus' message was as quickly embraced by the people as it was opposed by church authorities. In 1412, Hus conducted a public funeral for three young men beheaded for challenging the sale of indulgences. That action thrust him into leadership of the reform movement and placed his own life in jeopardy. He took refuge in the Castle of Kradonec and continued to encourage reform, preaching to crowds in the fields and writing two significant books.

Hus' first book, *On Traffic in Holy Things*, restated his opposition to the sale of indulgences, suggesting that the pope was guilty of simony. His second book, *The Church*, challenged the popular concept of "the Holy Catholic Church," claiming that the true church was composed exclusively of those predestined to heaven. Hus suggested that the moral failings of many religious leaders in that age, even the pope, might indicate that they were not members of the true church. This second book undermined the authority of the established church, which had already been weakened by the Great Schism between East and West.

Under pressure from Sigismund, king of the Romans and Hungary, Pope John XXIII convened a general church council at Constance in 1414 to restore order to Catholicism in Europe. Over 50,000 religious and civic leaders gathered to bring an end to the Great Schism. Hus attended to present his views, having been promised "safe conduct" and a free hearing by Sigismund.

Hus quickly learned Sigismund's letter of safe conduct would not be honored. John XXIII imprisoned him in a dungeon on an island in the Rhine River. Three and a half months later, Hus was moved to the tower of a castle on Lake Geneva. During his imprisonment, John XXIII was deposed and replaced by Martin V. The change in popes did not alter his fate. His views were examined by the council and condemned.

On July 6, 1415, Hus finally appeared before the council to give his defense, but the decision had already been made. His views had been condemned by the council in Hus' absence. His fifty-sixth birthday was to be the day of his death. When the sentence was pronounced, Hus prayed for his accusers: "Lord Jesus Christ, pardon all my enemies, I pray thee, for the sake of Your great mercy! You know that they have falsely accused me, brought forward false witnesses and false articles against me. Oh, pardon them for Your infinite mercies' sake."

Revival in Florence, Italy (1481)

Girolamo Savonarola began his career as a preacher in 1452, the same year Martin Luther was born. While unknown to many people today, Savonarola was a significant forerunner of the Protestant Reformation that later swept Europe and the world. He was a man of deep piety and protracted prayers, a powerful pulpiteer with a voice like thunder so that people shook with conviction when they heard his sermons.

Savonarola preached that all believers made up the true church, the body of Christ. He was best known for preaching God's judgment and vengeance upon sin. His Bible was covered with notes that came to him as he studied the Scripture, and his sermons were expositions of the Word of God. He had visions of ecstasy, and made many predictions about the future—most of them came true—and many agree that he was the man God used to bring great revival to Florence, Italy.

Savonarola was by no means just an emotional preacher. Early on, he became an earnest student of Aristotle and the great philosophers; then he studied the writings of St. Thomas Aquinas, which challenged his thinking about God. Concerning his visions he said:

They came to me in earliest youth, but it was only at Brescia that I began to proclaim them. Thence, was I sent by the Lord to Florence, which is in the heart of Italy, in order that "the Reformation of Italy might begin."

As a young man, his intense devotion to Jesus Christ became evident. He spent many hours in prayer and fasting and knelt at the church altar for long periods of time.

Savonarola's soul was deeply troubled by the sin, worldliness, and vice that he saw everywhere in Italy, but his concern was not just over such filthy sins. He lashed out as well at luxury, splendor, and wealth that dragged people away from God.

At the age of twenty-three, Savonarola submitted himself to a Dominican priory because St. Thomas Aquinas was a Dominican, but he didn't ask to become a friar. He wanted to be a drudge, to do the lowest forms of servant work in the convent. He spent much of his time fasting, praying, and leading a quiet life. Only later in life did he become a friar.

At twenty-nine, he was sent to the priory of St. Mark's in Florence, considered the most beautiful and cultured city of Italy. Ruled by the de Medici family, Florence had been shaped by the Renaissance as had no other city in Europe. Many of the citizens knew Greek and Latin and read the classics. Savonarola expected the Florentines to lead a more pure and noble life because of their culture and intelligence, but was utterly disappointed in their corrupt life and passion for festivals, entertainments, and worldly displays.

At St. Mark's, he was made instructor of the novices, a task that he would consider his main calling for the rest of his life. When he began preaching, his sermons were filled with a strong sense of approaching judgment and the vengeance of God upon the sins of the city. The cultured people paid little heed to Savonarola. When he travelled to outlying districts, however, his sermons were better received in the small villages, where people were uneducated and more trusting.

Savonarola was sent to Reggio D' Emilia, Italy, and there his preaching was so "white hot" and eloquent that he made a great impression on the people. Returning to Florence with a greater reputation, he began delivering his sermons at the little church of the Murite Convent. Here he began to pray and wait upon God for a direct revelation from heaven.

One day while talking with a nun, he suddenly saw a vision in which heaven opened and all the future calamities of the church passed before his eyes. The vision charged Savonarola to announce God's judgment to the people. From that moment on, he was filled with a new unction in preaching, and his voice denounced sin so effectively that people staggered out from the small church, dazed, bewildered, and speechless. People broke into tears while he preached. Sometimes the congregation couldn't hear his preaching because of the sobbing and weeping of people repenting of sin.

Records tells us that when Savonarola was engaged in prayer, he frequently fell into trances and lost all touch with the world about him. On Christmas Eve, 1446, while seated in the pulpit, he remained unmoved for five hours; the people waited patiently all during this time, for they knew he was receiving a message from God. As he sat in the pulpit, his face appeared illuminated to all the church. There seemed to be a beam of light from his eyes, as though from heaven itself.

In 1484, Savonarola was sent to preach in the region of Lombardi, and when he returned, the citizens of Florence had greater confidence in his mission. His fame continued to spread over all Italy. Returning to Florence, he began teaching the Book of Revelation to the friars in the garden of St. Mark's. But the laymen begged for admittance to his lectures because he preached the Word of God, and his fame was still increasing.

Often people arose during the middle of the night to line up at the front door of his church to make sure they got a seat. Others climbed the iron grating and clung there for hours to see and hear him preach. Because of his fame, Savonarola was transferred to the larger Duomo Cathedral Church of Florence. However, when taking this new charge, he predicted that he would be there only for eight years, which proved to be accurate.

One account described his great popularity this way:

People came along the streets, singing and rejoicing and listening to the sermons with such interest that when they were finished, the people thought he had scarcely begun. Savonarola seemed to be swept onward by a might not his own, and carried his audiences with him. Soon, all of Florence was at the feet of this great preacher.

Lorenzo de Medici, ruler of Florence, tried every way possible to silence the young preacher, but could not.

For his part, Savonarola predicted that within a year, three people would die: Lorenzo, the pope, and the king of Naples. It all came to pass as he predicted.

Two years later the new king of France, Charles VIII, invaded Italy and sacked Naples. As he advanced on Florence, Savonarola cried for the people to repent of their sins in order to save themselves from destruction, and they did. Then Savonarola went out to meet Charles and begged him to spare Florence, which he did. Savonarola also predicted that if Charles didn't leave Florence, he would incur the vengeance of God. Charles left.

During the French invasion, the government of the de Medicis collapsed and the people came to Savonarola wanting to know what kind of government they should adopt. Through his sermons, Savonarola outlined a form of democracy, similar to our representative form of government. He preached that the new government should have a just form of taxation, do away with torture, pass laws against gambling, and institute a court of appeal for those who were tried unjustly. The new laws of Florence became a model for many other cities throughout Europe and eventually influenced the entire world.

The revival in Florence became so great that even the hoodlums gave up singing their filthy songs and began singing hymns. The children went from house to house gathering all types of items people had acquired from carnivals, sinful entertainment, and other kinds of wickedness, bringing them to the piazza to be burned. The sinful articles that were burned formed an octangular pyramid some 60 feet tall and 240 feet in circumference at the base.

Nevertheless, this triumph was short-lived. Pope Alexander IV excommunicated Savonarola for refusing to stop publicizing his prophecies, and the preacher had made many enemies in Florence. The people ultimately turned against him and imprisoned him. Finally he was hanged in the public square in Florence.

A Summary of the Pre-Reformation Revivals

A history of the Christian church includes both a survey of triumphs accomplished by the people of God and a survey of corruption and unbelief when God's people didn't follow the truth. The church was barely born when the greed of Ananias and Sapphira manifested itself, even when God was working miracles among his people.

From the apostles onward, there was a struggle between the forces of corruption and the forces of good, but too often sin won out, and the churches staggered onward. Throughout the Middle Ages, after the dissolution of the Roman Empire and the domination of barbarian peoples, perhaps the brightest lights were in the monasteries.

Outside the Catholic Church, the influence of evangelical sects such as the Waldensians, the Lollards, and the Brethren of the Common Life grew.

A few reformers stood out at the end of the Middle Ages. Their message of light pointed many toward the coming Reformation and, in fact, these reformers laid the foundation for the Protestant Reformation: they included John Wycliffe in England, John Hus in Bohemia, and Girolamo Savonarola in Italy. The greatness of their revival is not measured by what they accomplished, but by what was accomplished by those who followed their example.

CHAPTER NINE

The Protestant Reformation, 1517

A true revival means nothing less than a revolution, casting out the spirit of worldliness, making God's love triumph in the heart.

Andrew Murray

When Europe entered the Dark Ages, the church's five major centers of Christianity were Jerusalem, Antioch, Alexandria, Constantinople, and Rome. By 1500 four of these centers were controlled by Islam, which had conquered North Africa, the Near East, and parts of Eastern Europe. The light of Christianity was dimmed in some of these areas and extinguished in others. Of the ancient Christian centers, only Rome was left. But even the Christianity of the Eternal City was obscured by corruption and political intrigue.

The medieval order held that everyone was governed by God's will. All people had their respective places in the political, economic, social, cultural, and religious worlds. God determined who would be a king or a peasant by birth, and it was the church that ruled them all.

The Renaissance, beginning in Italy, motivated a few individuals to grow intellectually in logic, reason, mathematics, the humanities, and the arts. Intellectual individualism was stirring. Wealth was no longer controlled by feudalistic landowners—that is, the royalty and the church. A new wealth grew in trade centers, creating a middle class of bankers, traders, merchants, industrialists, and some workers' guilds. Thus economic individualism was also stirring.

Martin Luther

Religious individuals had already stirred Europe, reformers such as Wycliffe, Hus, and Savonarola. However, one individual would break upon the scene—protected by political powers—to challenge the religious control of the Catholic Church over the Christian world. Martin Luther wanted freedom of the individual conscience before God, and he boldly proclaimed his position to Rome. Meanwhile, the state rulers saw in Luther an occasion to free themselves from the oppressive economic and political control of Rome.

At the same time, there were other forces concerned not with political power but with knowing God: the Swiss Brethren, the Anabaptist movement in the Netherlands, the Brethren of the Common Life in Germany, and the Pietists in many places. The Huguenot Revival in France could be added to this list, but they were concerned with both knowing God and political power.

Other Reformers

After Luther nailed his ninety-five theses on the castle door in Wittenburg, other reformers appeared on the scene, preaching against the same abuses in the Catholic Church and calling for a newly established church.

In Zurich, Switzerland, Ulrich Zwingli, a young priest, followed the example of Luther, but went further in reform. Luther hadn't changed the church's local form of government because he supported an episcopal form of government ruled by bishops. Zwingli established a Reformed church in Switzerland by making substantial changes in worship, which was not an interest of Luther. Zwingli stripped away every form of the former church's practice that he believed couldn't be supported by Scripture.

John Calvin brought complete church reforms to Geneva, Switzerland, in 1541, organizing the religious life of the city around his concepts (later known as Calvinism) with a view of turning Geneva into a model Christian city (a theocracy) which was to be a "New Jerusalem." One strength of the Catholic Church was in its commitment to feudalism and the agrarian way of life. Zwingli and Calvin were urban leaders, and from the cities they gained strength for the Reformation.

Henry VIII allowed the Protestant Reformation to get a toehold in England by channeling Rome's authority, but not because of his religious commitments. Henry wanted to divorce his wife and to get his hands on the vast wealth of the Catholic Church, which included extensive property, buildings, and labor. He wanted the wealth of England to stay in the country, not to be funneled to Rome. From 1547 to 1558 England shifted back and forth between Catholicism and Protestantism. It was Queen Elizabeth I who finally stabilized England in the Protestant fold.

Before the Protestant Reformation, considerable political power as well as religious authority was concentrated at Rome. The temptation to abuse such power was great, and many church leaders had become morally corrupt. For a new foundation of the church and freedom of the conscience before God, Martin Luther was raised up as a symbolic leader who changed the face of European civilization.

Martin Luther (1517)

Martin Luther didn't intend to become an international reformer in 1517 when he posted ninety-five theses on the door of Wittenburg Castle. Rome was selling indulgences for the forgiveness of sins to finance the lavish building of St. Peter's Basilica in Rome. Luther's theses didn't challenge the entire fabric of the Catholic Church; he simply gave theological reasons for opposing the sale of indulgences.

Luther had a long pilgrimage to true faith. He had a deep sense of guilt and personal condemnation. He studied the apostle Paul's books of Galatians and Romans, realizing the message of grace and forgiveness through simple faith in Jesus Christ—not by the religious demands of the church. He understood justification, that is, that a man was declared righteous before God, not by works or indulgences. But the underlying foundation of this reformation was the appeal to "conscience," not to the leaders of the church. It was the individual's study of Scripture that introduced the Protestant Reformation.

Luther had no idea where his challenge of papal authority would go, but when this unknown German priest stood up to the pope, German rulers took note. It was an opportunity to free themselves of the political and economic burdens of Rome.

Frederick, imperial elector of Germany, gave Luther protection so the pope couldn't touch him. In several debates against papal representatives, Luther triumphed. By 1520 Luther was no longer trying to reform his mother church, Rome; he had totally abandoned it. He called Rome the antichrist and publicly burned a papal edict requiring him to submit to Rome. Luther had most of Germany on his side.

Luther was excommunicated but was more popular than ever. He was still under the protection of Frederick. Emperor Charles V of the Holy Roman Empire called Luther to a council at Worms and gave him a position while there. Because Luther was given an imperial guarantee of safety, he attended.

At this meeting, Luther voiced the well-known phrase, "Here I stand, I can do no other." He based his stand on his conscience and an understanding of Holy Scriptures. Luther left Worms before the council could revoke the guarantee of safety given him. (Earlier, John Hus had been given the same guarantee, but was burned at the stake.)

Before this time, most people didn't have direct access to the Word of God; their Bible was the Latin Vulgate translation. Since few of the people or the priests knew Latin, the light of God's Word was in many ways hidden. Frederick had Luther secluded in a castle, where the reformer translated the Bible into the German language.

Ulrich Zwingli (1522)

In 1552 the Swiss preacher Ulrich Zwingli opposed the traditional fast during Lent because it didn't have a scriptural foundation. The Zurich, Switzerland, civil government supported Zwingli's position. When the Catholic bishop of Constance tried to suppress Zwingli, Zwingli saw it as an opportunity to take control of religious practices in its domain.

Because Zwingli advocated the Scriptures as the sole religious authority, he supported the government of Zurich, claiming that civil government was under the leadership of Christ, as directed by Scripture. The reformation of Zwingli spread to other cities—Basel, Constance, Bern, and Strasbourg—establishing in each a Reformed government, based on the model of Zurich.

Luther did not embrace this position, focusing his reformation more narrowly on personal justification; he wasn't interested in reforming the worship practices of the church, or its government. Luther felt the church should remain under the authority of the bishops, possibly because of his loyalty to the nobles who had supported his break with Rome.

Zwingli had a more humanist background than Luther, and Zwingli sought the Greek and Hebrew origins of the church. He felt that Rome had departed from the original purity of the church and had perverted its nature.

Zwingli thought the celebration of the Lord's Supper was only symbolic, while Luther taught that the real presence of Christ was in the elements. Some in the two parties tried to bring them together, but the gap between their positions was unbridgeable. Lutheranism and the Reformed Church remained permanently separated.

Many rural areas of Switzerland remained loyal to the Catholic Church, while the cities embraced the Reformed Church (a prevalent trend in Europe). The leaders of the rural Swiss cantons bitterly opposed Zwinglian reforms, and war broke out between the two camps. Zwingli was killed in a battle in 1531. If he had lived, the Reformed Church might have made greater strides.

John Calvin (1541)

John Calvin was a young French law clerk who tried to persuade King Francis I to sympathize with the quarrelling Protestant movement in France. As a young man, he wrote and published in 1536 his *Institutes of the Christian Religion*, a theological treatise that would be the foundation of the movement known as Calvinism.

Not only did Calvin fail to convince the king; the treatise identified him as a religious radical. He was forced to flee France for his life, and went to Geneva, Switzerland. The reformer William Farel invited Calvin to help organize a Reformed government in Geneva, but Calvin was too highly disciplined and demanding for the rebellious city of Geneva. In 1538 he and Farel were banned from the city, and he went to the reform-minded city of Strasbourg.

Things changed in Geneva within the next three years, and in 1541

Calvin was invited to return there. Reluctantly he accepted the invitation, but he told the city council it would be on his terms. He reorganized the religious life of the city around ordinances he wrote, with a view to making Geneva a model Christian city. The Reformed city was quite a contrast to the opulent but corrupt city of Rome.

The feudal order of the medieval religious way of life was crumbling. Calvin directed his energies toward building a new urban order of purified Christianity. Eventually, he tried to influence not only religious life but every area of public life. He gave a theological basis to the new European trade cities for governing themselves under the direct authority of God, without the intermediate authority of Rome. Thus Calvin sought to establish a Christian socioeconomic and political way of life and government.

Calvin had no rebellious intent in his teaching; he advocated that each was to be a good citizen, to be submissive to proper government, and to pay taxes. The rulers of the cities went along with Calvin when they saw that the "Protestants" were obedient citizens who were productive in their private lives.

John Knox (1560)

Educated at Glasgow University, John Knox was ordained into the priesthood in 1539. Throughout his life he played many roles: he was a minister at St. Andrew's; he was captured and became a galley slave in French bondage; he was a writer and chaplain to King Edward VI of England. But most importantly, he brought the Reformation to Scotland.

When Mary Tudor came to the English throne, Knox went into exile, primarily in Geneva, where he was taught by John Calvin. He returned briefly to an all-Catholic Scotland in August 1555, and his preaching won many to the Reformed faith. Because of Catholic opposition, he couldn't remain in Scotland; he left after suffering many attempts on his life.

In his absence, the queen proclaimed him an outlaw, and Knox was condemned to death. Because of the Reformation in England and Scotland, the French (motivated by Rome) rushed in soldiers to keep Scotland Catholic. Queen Elizabeth (who disliked Knox) refused to intervene. Still, Knox's preaching kept alive the hope of Protestants in Scotland. Knox wrote the *Book of Common Order,* the *Scot's Confession of Faith,* and the *First Book of Discipline.* In July 1560 the alliance with France was revoked, and the English army came to Scotland to help the Protestants.

When the English army arrived, Knox hoped that the wealth of the Catholic Church would come to the Protestant Church, but that hope was shattered by politicians. Most of the finances went elsewhere.

Knox became sole minister of St. Giles Church in Edinburgh, preaching twice every Sunday and three times during the week, to more than a thousand each time. Knox prayed, "Give me Scotland or I die," and due to his influence Scotland has a strong Reformed heritage to this day.

The Communion Revival at Shotts (1630)

Early in the turbulent 1600s, the Protestant Reformation was just beginning to take root in Scotland. When the hardy Scots quickly embraced the Reformed faith, there weren't enough ordained clergy to go around. As a result, churches gathered together during special seasons to observe certain ordinances of the church. As Christians looked forward to the beginning of summer, they also anticipated the coming of what they called "the Communion Season." Thousands would gather in the village of Shotts to celebrate the Lord's Supper together.

During their days together, there were several preaching services, and the preaching would be shared by several of the ministers present. It was always an honor to be asked to address such a gathering, an honor usually reserved for the older and better-known pastors. But when the people gathered in 1630, there was an exception.

Among those asked to speak was a relatively unknown young man named John Livingstone. No one was more surprised than Livingstone himself when he received this invitation. While he recognized it as an honor, he felt himself unworthy of the trust that had been placed in him.

The young pastor pleaded with his elders to allow him to decline, claiming that he wasn't capable of rising to the challenge. His elders, however, apparently disagreed. Livingstone eventually realized that he wasn't about to change their stubborn Scottish minds. Reluctantly, he consented to prepare and preach the requested sermon.

As the day of his sermon grew closer, the conviction grew stronger in Livingstone that he'd been called on to perform a task well beyond his natural ability. The evening before he was to speak, he couldn't sleep. Instead, he cried out to God in prayer. Yet, the longer he prayed, the stronger became his "overwhelming sense of utter weakness."

By morning, Livingstone was a wreck. As the hour approached when he was to step into the pulpit, he could think of nothing else to do but run, so he did. As he ran through the fields, he looked back and could barely see the church building in the distance. Then something strange happened.

Although he knew he was alone, he heard a voice as if it came from heaven, saying, "Have I been a wilderness to Israel, Or a land of darkness?" (Jer. 2:31). The verse stung deeply. Suddenly he realized that the opportunity to preach had come not by the invitation of the elders but by the appointment of God. He thus turned back to the village to keep his appointment.

During the Communion Season, the crowd always swelled beyond the capacity of the village kirk (church). John Livingstone rose to address the large crowd, reading from Ezekiel: "Therefore say to them, 'Thus says the Lord God: "You eat meat with blood, you lift up your eyes toward your idols, and shed blood. Should you then possess the land? You rely on your sword, you commit abominations, and you defile one another's wives. Should you then possess the land?"''" (Ezek. 33:25-26).

The young preacher challenged the congregation to "examine themselves" before partaking of the ordinance. He then directed the crowd's attention to the promises of God recorded only a few chapters later: "Then I will sprinkle clean water on you, and you shall be clean; I will cleanse you from all your filthiness and from all your idols. I will give you a new heart and put a new spirit within you; I will take the heart of stone out of your flesh and give you a heart of flesh" (Ezek. 36:25-26).

As Livingstone continued preaching, it began to rain lightly. When the first few drops of rain fell, people began to move away and take cover where they could find it. Even as they began moving, the preacher cried out, "If a few drops of rain so easily upset you, then what will you do in the Day of Judgment when God rains down fire and brimstone upon the Christ rejectors?" He urged people to "flee to Christ, the City of Refuge."

The sermon he'd been so reluctant to preach would never be finished. Suddenly, "the power of God came down upon the multitude." One report describes people falling under that power as though they'd been "slain as in the field of battle." Hundreds of people began crying out to God in deep agony of their souls. By the end of the day, 500 people had been converted to Christ.

Little else is remembered of the ministry of John Livingstone of the Kirk of Shotts. Little else needs to be known. The impact on the community was profound that day, but the impact on the nation would be greater in the generations to come. Throughout history, revivals have been widely reported throughout Scotland, but no revival story has been more often repeated in the Land of Heather than the story of Livingstone of Shotts and the divine visitation experienced by the Kirk of Shotts on June 21, 1630.

A Summary of the Protestant Reformation

In one sense the Protestant Reformation was not primarily a revival as judged by the technical definition used in this volume. It was primarily a protest to the Catholic Church that had implications in political, social, and economic areas, with the redrawing of geographical boundary lines. As such, the Protestant Reformation—like a revival—influenced almost every area of life it touched.

Yet there is also a sense in which the Protestant Reformation *was* a revival or an awakening. When the people were given access to the Word of God through preaching and teaching, they became a "revived" people in their walk with God. While the spiritual aspects of the Protestant Reformation were not the dominant thrust, these factors cannot be dismissed. Because of this tension between spiritual renewal and doctrinal protest, the authors ranked this era lower in revival influence than other awakenings.

The Protestant Reformation produced historical greats, but we should keep in mind their limitations. Martin Luther, for example, raged about the terrible tyranny of Rome, but if the Catholic Church had really been as powerful as he insisted it was, the Protestant Reformation could never have happened. John Calvin was an academic genius who wanted Geneva to be the "heavenly city" on earth that Rome never was, and the influence of his "reformed theology" has been lasting. Yet, in his passion for individual conscience to interpret Scripture, he was as tyrannical over private lives as Rome had ever been. He had the religious dissenter Michael Servetus arrested, tortured, and burned at the stake for following his religious convictions. Zwingli also led toward religious freedom, but he, too, with the cooperation of the Council of Zurich, executed one of the Anabaptist leaders by drowning. These reformers—not revivalists—were usually associated with the state's program of reformation, which at times clouded the purity of any revival movement that flowed in their wake.

Still, despite all they failed to do in revival, and all they did in compromise, the greatness of these leaders shines like a burning star in the blackest night. If they had not reformed, we would not live as we do today in our Protestant churches.

CHAPTER TEN

Pentecost: The Beginning of Revival, A.D. 30

Revival cannot be organized, but we can set our sails to catch the wind from heaven when God chooses to blow upon His people once again.

G. Campbell Morgan

E vangelist Charles Finney once described revival as "the people of God renewing their obedience to God." Because God's people tend to wander from him, revival may be as old as humanity itself. Using Finney's definition, we can say that accounts of revival are recorded throughout the pages of the Old Testament.

The wandering of God's people was often followed by a return to him. The story of Jacob and his sons' return to Bethel may have been Israel's first revival (see Gen. 35:1-15). Generations later there came a renewing of the nation when Moses brought the people to Mount Sinai (see Exod. 32–33). Joshua also saw Israel revived at Shechem (see Josh. 24), as did Gideon in his day (see Judg. 6–9). Samuel gathered the people to Mizpah in repentance (see 1 Sam. 7), and Elijah called Israel back to God at Mount Carmel (see 1 Kings 18).

Yet revival in the Old Testament was not limited to Israel. In what some have called "the greatest revival in history," Jonah became the unwilling prophet who brought revival to Nineveh, where an entire evil pagan city turned to God (see Jon. 3).

Other revivals were associated more with kings than prophets. Judah experienced revival during the reigns of righteous kings who initiated reform, rulers such as Asa (see 2 Chron. 15), Hezekiah (see 2 Kings 18:4-7; 2 Chron.

29–32), and Josiah (see 2 Kings 22:1–23:25; 2 Chron. 34:1–35:19).

Even after the Babylonian captivity, God raised up prophets to call the nation back to himself. A remnant experienced a revival under the preaching of Haggai and Zechariah, which energized them to begin work on a new temple (see Ezra 5–6). A later revival under the teaching priest Ezra finally broke the bondage of idolatry in Israel (see Neh. 8–9). Jewish tradition holds that during this final Old Testament revival, the Old Testament canon was established.

A New Kind of Revival

The last of the prophets calling Israel back to God was John the Baptist. His plain preaching called people to repent of sin and "prepare the way of the Lord" (Matt. 3:3). Vast crowds came out to hear John preach and to embrace his message as he travelled up and down the Jordan River.

In calling Israel back to God, the prophet Joel had made an unusual statement: "And it shall come to pass afterward that I will pour out My Spirit on all flesh" (Joel 2:28). In an age when the ministry of the Holy Spirit was limited to only a few especially chosen by God, the day of which Joel spoke must have seemed like a dream world. After all, the prophet was describing an outpouring of the Holy Spirit on people regardless of their sex, age, and socioeconomic status.

Nevertheless, this declaration was in fact the promise of God. But the promise would not be fulfilled for eight centuries. It described a new kind of revival.

The Day of Pentecost
The church itself was born in the midst of that new kind of revival among 120 followers of Christ: "When the Day of Pentecost had fully come, they were all with one accord in one place. And suddenly there came a sound from heaven, as of a rushing mighty wind, and it filled the whole house where they were sitting" (Acts 2:1-2). By the end of the day, "about three thousand souls were added" to the emerging church (v. 41).

Peter himself identified the events of that day as a prototypical fulfillment of Joel's prophecy (see Acts 2:16-21). What happened on Pentecost became the model of a new kind of revival in our present age. According to the late British pastor Martin Lloyd-Jones, "It is a truism to say that every revival of religion that the Church has ever known has been, in a sense, a kind of repetition of what has happened on the day of Pentecost."

United in Prayer

The biblical account of the Pentecost outpouring begins ten days before Pentecost with 120 men and women united in prayer: "These all continued with one accord in prayer and supplication" (Acts 1:14). One can only wonder at the self-evaluation that must have gone on during those ten days. On at least one occasion, time was taken to set in order things perceived to be out of order (see Acts 1:15-26).

It was during a prayer meeting that the church first experienced an outpouring of the Holy Spirit. History records the stories of a chain of revivals growing out of Christians united together in prayer.

Endued with power from on high, the apostle Peter and the rest preached the Scriptures. Many spoke in unlearned languages, a work of God that enabled the Pentecostal evangelists to cross linguistic barriers to preach to strangers in Jerusalem for the feast. As they preached, the Holy Spirit did his work of bringing intense conviction to those who heard. In deep anguish of soul they cried out, "Men and brethren, what shall we do?" (Acts 2:37).

When called upon to repent, 3,000 did so. Their conversions were marked by stability in the days following as "they continued steadfastly in the apostles' doctrine and fellowship, in the breaking of bread, and in prayers" (Acts 2:42). What began on Pentecost continued, "and the Lord added to the church daily those who were being saved" (Acts 2:47). In spite of hostile persecution, the church at Jerusalem was established and continued to grow.

Beyond Jerusalem

The outpouring of the Holy Spirit wasn't limited to Jerusalem. In fact, the history of the early church has been called "The Acts of the Holy Spirit" because of its continuous record of outpourings.

Philip saw a repetition of many aspects of the Pentecost outpouring when he preached the gospel in Samaria (see Acts 8:5-25). Peter acknowledged similarities between Pentecost and the phenomena accompanying the introduction of the gospel to Gentiles in Cornelius' home (see Acts 10:1–11:18). There appears to have been another outpouring in Antioch that established the prototype of missionary churches in this age (see Acts 11:19-30; 12:24–13:3).

The converted rabbi Saul of Tarsus experienced outpourings of the Holy Spirit during his first (see Acts 13:4–14:28) and second (see Acts 16:6–18:11) missionary journeys as Paul the apostle. He described aspects of revivals experienced in Thessalonica (see 1 Thess. 1:5) and Corinth in his various epistles.

Revival in Ephesus

One of the most significant revivals recorded in Paul's ministry occurred during his extended stay in Ephesus (see Acts 19:1–20:1, 17-38). The Ephesian Revival spread beyond the city limits, so that "all who dwelt in Asia heard the word of the Lord Jesus, both Jews and Greeks" (Acts 19:10). At its peak, conversions to the Christian faith so impacted the economy of the city that the idol makers themselves rioted, fearing the loss of their trade (see Acts 19:21-41).

The revivals that energized the early church tended to fade in the complacency of the established church. Even in Ephesus, Christians began wandering from their first love (see Rev. 2:4). By the end of the first century, the churches brought into being during the Ephesian Revival were rebuked by the Lord himself and called upon to repent (see Rev. 2–3).

Pentecost (A.D. 30)

Pentecost was the greatest revival known to humankind and the greatest demonstration of God's power to transform lives and influence society. Pentecost is the foundation of Christianity, separating the new, life-changing movement from its Jewish roots. Pentecost was so extraordinary that the event will never be repeated, yet the experiences of Pentecost are a challenge to any dying church that God can revive his people with his power—no matter the difficulties, no matter the circumstances.

Several demonstrations of power that were manifested on Pentecost don't appear to be normative in Christian experience. Most believers don't expect them in everyday Christian living, and most believers haven't experienced them. For example, on that day there suddenly came a tremendous sound from heaven, and a rushing wind filled the entire house where the 120 were praying (see Acts 2:2).

Did they hear a gigantic sound blasted from a heavenly stereo, and was it an actual hurricane-type gale? Whatever the miracle, we should keep in mind that in the New Testament, wind stands for the Holy Spirit, and it filled the whole house. The important fact was not the wind but the powerful presence of the Holy Spirit that everyone felt.

Next, fired licked through the air like a tongue—a split tongue—fire to burn, judge, and consume (see v. 3). Again, we shouldn't get caught up in focusing on the crackling fire in the air. It was the Holy Spirit burning away the old failures of the apostles and, from then on, forming them into bold witnesses of the message of the gospel.

Actual fire fell upon them, coming down in two (or split) flames. The fire symbolized that their speech or words would burn like fire, to judge the world for its sins and iniquity. The flames were doubled, indicating that God's gift of the Holy Spirit was double the power of anything previously experienced.

Suddenly, everyone began to speak in foreign languages not their own (see v. 4). God gave them a new ability to witness the message of Jesus Christ. Miraculously, they had the vocabulary, dialect, sentence structure, and word choice necessary to speak languages they hadn't previously known. God gave them this gift so that each listener could hear and understand the message of Jesus Christ in his or her own tongue.

During Christ's earthly ministry, multitudes heard him, and many were healed. When he died, however, many turned away from him, refusing to take up their cross in the face of scathing criticism or to follow Jesus to Calvary. After Calvary, the greatest recorded number of believers that gathered was "five hundred brethren" (1 Cor. 15:6).

In the Upper Room, approximately 120 were tarrying, praying and waiting on God for the coming of the Holy Spirit. Jesus had promised them, "But you shall receive power when the Holy Spirit has come upon you; and you shall be witnesses to Me in Jerusalem, and in all Judea and Samaria, and to the end of the earth" (Acts 1:8). They prayed for ten days that the Holy Spirit might come.

Ten days is a long time to "pray without ceasing" (1 Thess. 5:17), yet, in God's timing, they had to pray that long for him to work all things together for good (see Rom. 8:28). The Lord waited to answer their prayer until the day of Pentecost, because then they would have the greatest potential to spread their message to the known world: At least a million Jews would be present in Jerusalem for the Feast of Pentecost. Also, the "first fruits" from their farms were celebrated at this feast, and God wanted to give the "first-fruits of the Spirit" (Rom. 8:23) on that day.

There were many other reasons why the church had to wait for Pentecost. Jesus had said that the Holy Spirit would not be poured out on them in his lifetime on earth, "because Jesus was not yet glorified" (John 7:39). And why was the Holy Spirit withheld until Pentecost? Because through Christ's death, burial, and resurrection, heaven was transformed: "When [Jesus] ascended on high, [he] led captivity captive ... [and gave gifts unto] men" (Ps. 68:18; Eph. 4:8).

Jesus was the first resurrected person to enter heaven. Before this time, righteous souls who died went to "Abraham's bosom," which was also called Paradise (see Luke 16:22; 23:43). When Jesus entered triumphantly into heaven, he ushered all the saved Old Testament saints with him.

Also remember that Jesus told his disciples it was necessary for him to go away, because if he didn't leave them, the Comforter wouldn't come (see John 16:7). After Jesus entered heaven, the stage was set for the Helper to come to the disciples.

As Jesus had been with them in ministry, the Holy Spirit would do much more for them. Jesus promised, the Holy Spirit "dwells with you and will be in you" (John 14:17). When Pentecost came, the way was prepared for the Holy Spirit to indwell every believer. The only question is, *does the believer want the Holy Spirit indwelling?*

After Jesus died, the disciples knew only what Jesus had taught them. Even though Jesus was the Teacher—arguably the best Teacher of all times—still they had lingering blindness, ignorance, and doubt. Jesus had told them, "I still have many things to say to you, but you cannot hear them now. However, when He, the Spirit of truth, has come, He will guide you into all truth; for He will not speak on His own authority, but whatever He hears He will speak; and He will tell you things to come" (John 16:12-13).

So the disciples spent ten agonizing days in prayer for the Holy Spirit. For if they hadn't acted in faith that Jesus' promise would be fulfilled, there would have been no Pentecost. If they hadn't believed Jesus' words that they would "receive power" (Acts 1:8), they might have stumbled out into ministry against heathen darkness, only to fail. For ten days they prayed without getting their answer. But fifty days after the passion of Calvary (see Acts 1:3), the Holy Spirit at last came in power.

God's greatest demonstration of revival happened on a Jewish feast day because God's plan was "for the Jew first, and also for the Greek" (Rom. 1:16). The greatest revival manifested from heaven happened in a Jewish city, at a Jewish celebration, to Jewish believers. But it introduced something entirely new—the church—and the beginning of "the times of the Gentiles" (Luke 21:24). The outpouring of the Holy Spirit came on the Jewish Pentecost, empowering Jewish witnesses, resulting in 3,000 Jewish converts.

As we've noted, on Pentecost, there were miraculous signs, a powerful wind, tongues of fire, believers speaking in other languages. Instantly, the believers experienced what Jesus had promised: "Most assuredly, I say to you, he who believes in Me, the works that I do he will do also; and greater works than these he will do, because I go to My Father" (John 14:12). Instantly, they received more power than they'd received in three years of following Christ. Instantly, the Holy Spirit gave them authority to attack the dark, evil kingdom.

Previously the disciple of denial, Peter now received what Jesus had promised: "power from on high" (Luke 24:49). Peter was transformed from an evasive coward into a powerful preacher. When the crowd accused the disciples of being drunk, bold Peter stood up to say, "These disciples are not drunken, as you suppose, seeing that it is only nine o'clock in the morning" (Acts 2:15, author's translation). He boldly proclaimed, "Whoever calls on the name of the Lord shall be saved" (Acts 2:21).

But his boldness wasn't finished with the proclamation of the gospel. Peter declared, "Men of Israel, hear these words: Jesus of Nazareth, a Man attested by God to you by miracles, wonders, and signs which God did through Him in your midst, as you yourselves also know—Him, being delivered by the determined counsel and foreknowledge of God, you have taken by lawless hands, have crucified, and put to death; whom God raised up" (Acts 2:22-24). When the crowd cried out in response, "What shall we do?" Peter had only one command: "Repent, and let every one of you be baptized in the name of Jesus Christ" (Acts 2:38).

The hostile crowd mocking the disciples didn't believe that Jesus Christ was the Son of God, so courageous Peter commanded them to be converted and "be baptized in the name of Jesus Christ," which required an admission on their part that they were wrong about the deity of Christ. In baptism, they fully confessed him as their Savior and their Lord.

The Holy Spirit worked mightily in this revival meeting, because "they were all filled with the Holy Spirit" (Acts 2:4). It was only natural that the Spirit used these men, because "no one can say that Jesus is Lord except by the Holy Spirit" (1 Cor. 12:3).

The Spirit began instantly his work of drawing unsaved people to Jesus Christ. The greatest fruit of the first revival meeting was the conversion of 3,000 people: "Then those who gladly received his word were baptized; and that day about three thousand souls were added to them" (Acts 2:41). The revival continued as the new believers were "praising God and having favor with all the people. And the Lord added to the church daily those who were being saved" (Acts 2:47).

Reviving the Ephesian Church (A.D. 58)

Paul's ministry at the school of Tyrannus in Ephesus continued daily for two years, "so that all who dwelt in Asia heard the word of the Lord Jesus, both Jews and Greeks" (Acts 19:10). This approach to ministry marked a departure from previous methodology used by Paul and may be viewed as a new evangelistic strategy to bring revival. According to an early Syrian text of this passage, Paul taught the Scriptures daily from 11:00 A.M. through 4:00 P.M.

The content of Paul's teaching during these sessions was apparently communicated to others in Ephesus and other cities by those who heard him. Some believe these were the classes to which Paul referred when he later urged Timothy to train faithful men (see 2 Tim. 2:2). Using this method,

Paul trained those who in turn went to other cities and established churches in smaller towns and cities that the apostle might otherwise not have visited.

Paul's ministry during this period included not only a strong emphasis on teaching but also a number of unusual miracles (see Acts 19:11). There were occasions when people were healed and demons cast out simply because they came into contact with a piece of cloth that Paul had used. So spectacular were these and other miracles that soon those outside the Christian community attempted to duplicate them.

Many Jews recognized the reality of demon possession but relied upon the Jewish rite of exorcism to cast unclean spirits out of a possessed person. When a group of itinerant Jewish exorcists came to Ephesus, a situation arose that gave great spiritual impetus to the church. Seven sons of a Jewish chief priest named Sceva attempted to practice their rite of exorcism with near-disastrous results (see Acts 19:13-16).

When they addressed the demon "by the Jesus whom Paul preaches" (v. 13), the demon responded, "Jesus I know, and Paul I know; but who are you?" (v. 15). The demon-possessed man then turned on the seven exorcists and overpowered them. The men fled from the house naked and wounded, probably grateful that they were still alive.

Naturally, reports of this event spread through the city of Ephesus quickly. The people were overcome with fear, "and the name of the Lord Jesus was magnified" (Acts 19:17). This event shocked many believers into a renewed understanding of the reality of the spirit world and its influence in the occult religions of the day.

Many confessed their own involvement in these practices, and as an act of repentance, they brought the books they had used in these practices "and burned them in the sight of all" (Acts 19:19). The total value of the books destroyed at that time was estimated at 50,000 pieces of silver—with each silver piece probably worth a common day's wage. This response among believers resulted in continued spiritual and numerical growth in the church: "So the word of the Lord grew mightily and prevailed" (Acts 19:20).

Paul intended to remain in Ephesus until Pentecost (see 1 Cor. 16:8), but a situation arose that may have cut his stay short. The evangelistic efforts of the church were so successful that the silver industry in the city, which earned much of its profits through making silver shrines used in worshiping Diana, was beginning to suffer a financial setback. It didn't take them long to recognize a relationship between their drop in sales and Paul's evangelistic zeal.

At a meeting of the silversmith guild, one craftsman, named Demetrius, noted: "This Paul has persuaded and turned away many people, saying that they are not gods which are made with hands. So not only is this trade of ours in danger of falling into disrepute, but also the temple of the great goddess Diana may be despised and her magnificence destroyed, whom all Asia and the world worship'" (Acts 19:26-27).

The worship of Diana was the chief religious cult of the city of Ephesus. According to their myths, Diana was "born" in the woods near Ephesus at the site of her temple when her image fell down from the heavens. She was usually portrayed as a multibreasted goddess. Her temple in Ephesus was not considered her home, but rather the chief shrine where she could and should be worshiped. The silver shrines made by Demetrius and his colleagues were probably crude copies of the temple, which were normally purchased by pilgrims at the temple and carried home as worship aids in the cult.

Those engaged in the silver trade making these shrines were an integral part of the temple economy. Paul's success in the evangelization of Asia Minor meant that they were losing pilgrims to the temple, with the result that sales were diminishing. The burning of occult books probably shocked Demetrius and the others into recognizing that the decline in their trade was more than a passing phase.

If these Christians continued to be successful in their evangelistic efforts, it might well be that the magnificent temple in their city would become obsolete and even destroyed. Incensed at the prospect, the silversmiths began chanting loudly, "Great is Diana of the Ephesians!" (Acts 19:28). In the confusion that followed, most of the city filled the public theater, but they were for the most part confused as to why the meeting had been called.

Somewhere in the rush, two of Paul's companions from Macedonia, Gaius and Aristarchus, were seized by the mob and taken into the theater. Paul wanted to join his friends, but his disciples and a number of public officials sympathetic to Paul convinced him to remain outside.

In the midst of the confusion, the Jews appointed Alexander as their spokesman to address the crowd, but when he began to address them, they once again broke out in the chant, "Great is Diana of the Ephesians!" (Acts

19:34). The chanting continued in the theater for about two hours. Only then was the city clerk able to gain control of the meeting and address the crowd.

The official argued that no one was disputing the greatness of the beloved goddess, and warned them that such uprisings could result in the unwanted involvement of Rome in their civic affairs. He noted that if Demetrius and the other silversmiths had a legitimate concern, the issue could be addressed by open courts and officials. Then he managed to dismiss the assembly quietly.

After the riot ended in Ephesus, Paul realized that he'd once again become the center of a controversy that threatened to hinder the continued ministry of the church. He therefore called the Christians together and revealed his plans to leave. After he embraced those with whom he'd spent so much time, he began his journey to and through Macedonia. Later, in Jerusalem, when Paul delivered the money he'd raised for the Christians there, he was arrested and ultimately sent to Rome, where he died for his Lord.

A Summary of the Pentecost Revival

The greatest revival that ever happened took place on Pentecost when the Holy Spirit came on the 120 believers praying in the Upper Room. Because of his indwelling, they established the church, evangelized the Mediterranean world, and became the channels through whom Christianity was delivered to the world. Why was this the greatest revival? Because without it, none of the other revivals would have occurred.

Yet, even though the revival at Pentecost was great, it didn't begin with a dead church or a sinning church, as did the other nine revivals we've examined. Instead, Pentecost set the standard for Christianity, and when the church grew cold or sinned, then a revival (of the type defined in this book) was necessary to bring God's people back to their previous spiritual commitments. Thus the other revivals were divine interventions in which God had to revive a dead church—which is in some ways an even greater task than the one faced on the day the church was born.

In any case, the revival at Pentecost is listed last in this book because the authors wanted to recognize its foundational nature. It began with the church praying, and if we expect revival in our own day, we, too, must pray. The church moves from "faith to faith" because God gives us "grace for grace" (see John 1:16). Our prayer is that we will go from "revival to revival"—and experience the greatest revival ever.

Some Lessons Learned

Will you not revive us again, that Your people may rejoice in You?
PSALM 85:6

What lessons can we learn from the ten greatest revivals? Of the many we could note, perhaps these are the most important:

1. *Revival can come at any time, at any place, to any people.* God pours himself out on people for his glory whenever he pleases and wherever he pleases.
2. *Revival comes when God's people meet the conditions of 2 Chronicles 7:14:* "If My people, who are called by My name, will humble themselves, and pray and seek My face, and turn from their wicked ways ..." The greatest example of this principle is the way in which the prayers of God's people in the Laymen's Prayer Revival of 1859 led to awakening.
3. *Revival expresses itself with "several faces" as God's people demonstrate his presence in different ways in different lives.* Under Billy Graham, revival was experienced by great evangelism; under Martin Luther, revival was a return to biblical doctrine. The Canadian Prairie Revival brought great confession of sin, and the Welsh Revival led a society to clean itself up in repentance. In still other revivals, people spoke in tongues, had the "jerks," and were "slain in the Spirit."
4. *Revival begins with both the unsaved who repent* (as in the Jesus People Revival) *and the godly who spend extended times in prayer, searching for God's power* (as with Livingstone, Roberts, and Savonarola).
5. *Revival can be released when one person encounters God in a deep experi-*

213

ence (as with Billy Graham at Forest Home) *or when many people constantly live for God and seek his face* (as in the Moravian Revival).

6. *Revival is not limited by the doctrinal position of leaders.* It came to the Calvinistic Jonathan Edwards and the Arminian Charles Finney.

7. *Revival is not limited by denominational allegiance.* It came through the Methodist circuit riders of the Cane Ridge Revival, the Congregationalist pastors of New England, the Moravians of Germany, the Anglican Wesley brothers, and the founder of the Lutherans.

8. *Revival can be instigated by a crisis* (as when the banks collapsed before the Laymen's Prayer Revival) *or it can come in peaceful times* (as with the 1904 Revival and the General Awakening.)

9. *While one method may give impetus to a particular revival, all methods are not found in every revival, and revivals can exist without them.* There's a difference between the *principles* and the *methods* expressed in revival.

A *principle* is an eternal rule that governs the conditions God will bless and the ways he'll respond in all revivals, such as prayer, repentance, seeking God, and being filled with the Holy Spirit. A *method,* on the other hand, is much more narrow, being limited by time and culture. A method is the application of an eternal rule to a certain situation. It might be the school buses used in the Independent Baptist Revival or the Christian commune houses used in the Jesus People Revival.

We must remember the oft-quoted adage: *Methods are many; principles are few. Methods may change, but principles never do.*

10. *Some methods are "anointed" by God for use at particular times in a revival.* For example, Charles Finney wrote the book *Lectures on Revival,* which described the methods he used effectively in the 1800s. Some of these methods have been fruitful in later revivals, while others have not. Just as people can lose the "touch of God," so some revival methods come to a place where they are no longer useful. In the Second Great Awakening, the camp meeting was effective, but it doesn't have the same import today. Billy Graham used media and organizational techniques that weren't available to previous generations.

11. *People express their emotions and fervency in different ways in different revivals.* In the Cane Ridge Revival, emotional frenzies were common:

the jerks, running the aisle, roaring like a lion, barking like a dog, dropping "dead-like" to the floor. But in the Protestant Reformation, there seem to have been no frenzied outward displays of emotions, nor did they occur in Geneva's Second Reformation, the Korean Revival, or the Laymen's Prayer Revival.

12. *Revivals aren't always limited to an established church or a local church.* Some aspects of the Jesus People Revival seemed to be a transdenominational movement apart from the established church, even though Chuck Smith involved his followers in the Calvary Chapel movement.

13. *Some revivals seem to flow through extraordinary leaders* (such as Martin Luther, John Hus, or Savonarola), *while others are simply poured out on average believers* (as in the Laymen's Prayer Revival).

14. *Some revivals are not attached to evangelism* (such as the Thomas Road Baptist Church Revival).

15. *Some revivals seem to be geographically localized* (such as the Asbury College Revival and Thomas Road Baptist Church Revival), *while others are poured out over a large geographical area* (such as the Welsh Revival).

16. *Some revivals are poured out only on the denominational churches of an area* (such as the Independent Baptist Revival and the Wesleyan Methodist Revival of Hamilton), *while other revivals jump denominational boundaries* (such as the Cane Ridge Revival).

In short, we should put few limits on how God chooses to send revival. History demonstrates clearly that he acts sovereignly in a variety of circumstances.

Will There Be Another Worldwide Revival?

On several occasions since the close of the Baby Boomer Revival in 1975, God has poured himself out on his people. Any time God does a work, his people should celebrate the awakening and reviving of the church. Will there be another revival as great as past revivals? Is there anything happening today that could be a candidate as the eleventh greatest revival in history?

First, we'd suggest there are some evidences of revival in the ongoing work of God in South Korea, as illustrated by the emergence of the largest congregation in the history of the church: the Full Gospel Church of Seoul, South Korea, under the leadership of David Yonggi Cho. That church, and the current nationwide Korean prayer movement, reflect evidences of revival.

Second, we'd draw attention to the praise music revival that began in the 1980s. It's centered in The Church on the Way, in Van Nuys, California, and has spread throughout churches worldwide—both charismatic and non-charismatic—under the influence of that congregation's senior pastor, Jack Hayford. The use of praise worship music seems still to bring revival to churches that use it properly.

Third, we'd note the 1980s revivals in Argentina that have continued since the War of the Malvinas (Falkland) Islands in 1982. The various leaders of those revivals are listed in the book by C. Peter Wagner, *The Rising Revival* (Renew Books, 1998).

Fourth, we observe some evidences of revival in two churches in the 1990s, along with the awakening associated with each. First is the Toronto Airport Christian Fellowship and the work of the Holy Spirit called "The Toronto Blessing." Second is the "Pensacola Revival" at the Brownsville Assembly of God in Pensacola, Florida.

Any of the above awakenings might well be added in the future to the list of the greatest revivals ever. However, since the extent of God's work is measured in depth and time, we don't yet have enough perspective to determine whether these are indeed the great revivals of our day.

We aren't of the opinion that the earth can't have another revival because the evil days characterizing the end of time are upon us. As a matter of fact, we believe the opposite: The greatest revival since Pentecost can still sweep the earth before Jesus comes.

God can still do anything.

There is no sin so great that God's presence can't revive his church.

God's promises are still applicable: "If My people who are called by My name will humble themselves, and pray and seek My face, and turn from their wicked ways, then I will hear from heaven, and will forgive their sin and heal their land" (2 Chron. 7:14).

For all these reasons, revival is still up to us. Are we willing to pay the price? We can have the greatest revival in the history of Christianity if we will only seek it.

Church History Surveys

Cairns, Earle E. *Christianity through the Centuries.* Grand Rapids, Mich.: Zondervan, 1979.

Latourette, Kenneth S. *A History of Christianity.* New York: Harper & Brothers, 1953.

Porter, Douglas. *An Analysis of the Relationship between Revival and Evangelism* (D.Min. Thesis). Lynchburg, Va.: Liberty Baptist Theological Seminary, 1991.

Schaff, Philip. *History of the Christian Church.* New York: Charles Scribner's Sons, 1910.

Waugh, Geoff. *Fire Fell: Revival Visitations.* Brisbane, Australia: Renewal, n.d.

The Day of Pentecost (A.D. 30)/The Ephesian Revival (A.D. 60)

Towns, Elmer. *What the New Testament Is All About: A Study of the History Makers of the New Testament.* Lynchburg, Va.: Sunday School Heritage 1995.

England's Lollard Revival (1382)

Peters, Edward. *Heresy and Authority in Medieval Europe.* Philadelphia: University of Pennsylvania Press, 1980.

The Burning of John Hus (1415)

Hutton, J.E. *A History of the Moravian Church.* London: Moravian Publication Office, 1909.

Revival in Florence (1481-98)

Lawson, J. Gilchrist. *Deeper Experiences of Famous Christians.* Anderson, Ind.: Warner, 1978.

The Protestant Reformation (1517)

Bainton, Roland H. *The Reformation of the Sixteenth Century.* Boston: Beacon, 1952.

The Communion Revival at Shotts (1630)

Stewart, James Alexander. *William Chalmers Burns: A Man With a Passion for Souls.* Alexandria, La.: Lamplighter, n.d.

The Great Awakening (1727)

Wood, A. Skevington. *The Inextinguishable Blaze: Spiritual Renewal and Advance in the 18th Century.* Grand Rapids, Mich.: Eerdmans, 1960.

The Moravian Revival (1727)

Greenfield, John. *Power from on High.* Edinburgh: Marshall, Morgan and Scott, 1927.

Hutton, J.E. *A History of the Moravian Church.* London: Moravian Publication Office, 1909.

Weinlick, John R. *Count Zinzendorf: The Story of His Life and Leadership in the Renewed Moravian Church.* N.P.: Moravian Church in America, 1989.

The Surprising Work of God in Northhampton (1734)

Winslow, Ola Elisabeth, ed. *Jonathan Edwards: Basic Writings.* New York: New American Library, 1966.

The Fetter Lane Watch Night Revival (1739)

Hutton, J.E. *A History of the Moravian Church.* London: Moravian Publication Office, 1909.

Lelievre, Matthew. *John Wesley: His Life and His Work.* A.J. French, trans. London: Charles H. Kelly, n.d.

Telford, John. *The Life of John Wesley.* New York: Eaton & Mains, n.d.

Wesley, John. *Journals.* Nashville: Abingdon, 1993.

The Crossweeksung Indian Revival (1745)

Edwards, Jonathan. *Memoirs of the Rev. David Brainerd.* New Haven, Conn.: S. Converse, 1822.

Cornwall's Christmas Revival (1781)

Wood, A. Skevington. *The Inextinguishable Blaze: Spiritual Renewal and Advance in the 18th Century.* Grand Rapids, Mich.: Eerdmans, 1960.

The Second Great Awakening (1792)/
The Third General Awakening (1830)

Orr, J. Edwin. *The Eager Feet: Evangelical Awakenings, 1970-1830.* Chicago: Moody, 1974.

The Cane Ridge Revival (1801)

Cleveland, Catharine C. *The Great Revival in the West 1797-1805.* Gloucester, Mass.: Peter Smith, 1959.

Lawson, J. Gilchrist. *Deeper Experiences of Famous Christians.* Anderson, Ind.: Warner, 1978.

The Yale College Revival (1802)

Orr, J. Edwin. *Campus Aflame: A History of Evangelical Awakenings in Collegiate Communities.* Wheaton, Ill.: International Awakening Press, 1994.

The Bridgewater Revival (1816)

Porter, E. *Letters on the Religious Revivals which Prevailed About the Beginning of the Present Century.* Brooklyn, N.Y.: Linde, 1992.

Thornbury, J.F. *God Sent Revival: The Story of Asahel Nettleton and the Second Great Awakening.* Grand Rapids, Mich.: Evangelical Press, 1977.

Geneva's Second Reformation (1816)

Haldane, Alexander. *The Lives of Robert Haldane of Airthrey, and His Brother, James Alexander Haldane.* Edinburgh: Andrew Elliot, 1855.

Finney's Rochester, New York, Revival (1830)

Finney, Charles G. *Memoirs of Charles G. Finney.* New York: Fleming H. Revell, 1876.

The Hawaiian Revival (1836)

Coan, Titus. *Life in Hawaii: An Autobiographic Sketch of Mission Life and Labors (1835-1881)*. New York: Anson D.F. Randolph & Company, 1882.

The Kilsyth Anniversary Revival (1839)

Stewart, James Alexander. *William Chalmers Burns: A Man with a Passion for Souls*. Alexandria, La.: Lamplighter, n.d.

The Laymen's Prayer Revival (1857)

Orr, J. Edwin. *The Fervent Prayer: The Worldwide Impact of the Great Awakening of 1858*. Chicago: Moody, 1974.

Hamilton's Wesleyan Methodist Revival (1857)

Palmer, Phoebe. *The Promise of the Father*. Boston: Henry V. Degen, n.d.
Wheatley, R. *The Life and Letters of Mrs. Phoebe Palmer*. New York: n.p., 1876.

The Jamaican Revival (1860)

Orr, J. Edwin. *Evangelical Awakenings in Latin America*. Minneapolis, Minn.: Bethany, 1975.

Moody's British Campaign (1873)

Chapman, J. Wilbur. *The Life and Work of Dwight L. Moody*. New Haven, Conn.: Butler & Alger, 1900.
Moody, W.R. *The Life of Dwight L. Moody*. Murfreesboro, Tenn.: Sword of the Lord, 1980.

The 1904 Revival (1904)

Orr, J. Edwin. *The Flaming Tongue: The Impact of 20th Century Revivals*. Chicago: Moody, 1973.

The Welsh Revival (1904)

Evans, Eifion. *Revival Comes to Wales*. Fort Washington, Pa.: Christian Literature Crusade, 1979.

Matthews, David. *I Saw the Welsh Revival.* Chicago: Moody, n.d.

Asuza Street (1906)

Cox, Harvey. *Fire from Heaven: The Rise of Pentecostal Spirituality and the Reshaping of Religion in the Twenty-First Century.* New York: Addison-Wesley, 1995.

Kulbeck, Gloria Grace. *What God Hath Wrought: A History of the Pentecostal Assemblies of Canada.* Toronto: Pentecostal Assemblies of Canada, 1958.

Miller, Thomas William. *Canadian Pentecostals: A History of the Pentecostal Assemblies of Canada.* Mississauga: Full Gospel Publishing House, 1994.

The Mizo Outpouring (1906)

Orr, J. Edwin. *Evangelical Awakenings in Southern Asia.* Minneapolis, Minn.: Bethany, 1975.

The Korean Pentecost (1907)

Goforth, Jonathan. *When the Spirit's Fire Swept Korea.* N.P.: Bethel, 1984.

The Manchurian Revival (1915)

Goforth, Jonathan. *By My Spirit.* London: Harper & Brothers, n.d.

Goforth, Rosalind. *Goforth of China.* Chicago: Moody, n.d.

Goforth, Rosalind. *How I Know God Answers Prayer: The Personal Testimony of One Lifetime.* Lincoln, Neb.: Back to the Bible, n.d.

The World War II Revival (1935)

Anderson, Neil, and Elmer L. Towns. *Rivers of Revival.* Ventura, Calif.: Regal, 1997.

Orr, J. Edwin, et. al. *Revival in Our Time: The Story of the Billy Graham Evangelistic Campaigns.* Wheaton, Ill.: Van Kampen, 1950.

The Ngaruawahia Easter Revival (1936)

Orr, J. Edwin. *All Your Need: 10,000 Miles of Miracle through Australia and New Zealand.* London: Marshall, Morgan & Scott, Ltd., 1936.

Billy Graham's Los Angeles Crusade (1949)

Graham, Billy. *Just As I Am*. New York: Harper & Row, 1998.

Pollock, John. *To All the Nations: The Billy Graham Story*. New York: Harper & Row, 1985.

The Lewis Awakening (1949)

Campbell, Duncan. *God's Answer: Revival Sermons*. Edinburgh: The Faith Mission Publishing Department, 1960.

Campbell, Duncan. *God's Standard: Challenging Sermons*. Edinburgh: Faith Mission Publishing Department, 1964.

Peckham, Colin N. *Heritage of Revival*. Edinburgh: The Faith Mission Publishing Department, 1986.

Woolsey, Andrew A. *Channel of Revival: A Biography of Duncan Campbell*. Edinburgh: Faith Mission Publishing Department, 1982.

The Baby Boom Revival (1965)

Anderson, Neil, and Elmer L. Towns. *Rivers of Revival*. Ventura, Calif.: Regal, 1997.

The East Timor, Indonesian Revival (1965)

Orr, J. Edwin. *Evangelical Awakenings in Southern Asia*. Minneapolis, Minn.: Bethany, 1975.

Peters, George W. *Indonesia Revival: Focus on Timor*. Grand Rapids, Mich.: Zondervan, 1975.

The Jesus Revolution (1966)

Graham, Billy. *The Jesus Generation*. Grand Rapids, Mich.: Zondervan, 1971.

The Independent Baptist Revival (1969)

Hindson, Edward E. *Glory in the Church: The Coming Revival*. New York: Thomas Nelson, 1975.

Towns, Elmer. *Ten Largest Sunday Schools*. Grand Rapids, Mich.: Baker, 1969.

The Asbury College Revival (1970)

Coleman, Robert E. *One Divine Moment.* Old Tappan, N.J.: Fleming H. Revell, 1970.

Orr, J. Edwin. *Campus Aflame: A History of Evangelical Awakenings in Collegiate Communities.* Wheaton, Ill.: International Awakening Press, 1994.

The Saskatoon Revival (1971)

Blackaby, Henry T., and Claude V. King. *Experiencing God: Knowing and Doing the Will of God.* Nashville, Tenn.: The Sunday School Board of the Southern Baptist Convention, 1990.

Lutzer, Erwin W. *Flames of Freedom.* Regina, Saskatchewan: Canadian Revival Fellowship, 1992.

The Ten Greatest Revivals Ever

Which of the Ten Greatest Revivals most
influenced your ministry and why?

Bill Bright
Campus Crusade for Christ, Orlando, Florida
All of the revivals have influenced my life. I would consider the most important ones to be Pentecost, the Protestant Reformation, and the Second Great Awakening.

Gerald Brooks
Grace Outreach Center, Plano, Texas
It was the Jesus Movement that reached me. This revival was characterized by a move of God that went beyond the existing paradigms of the established church. It brought the gospel to unusual places and unconventional people. Though unwelcome in traditional churches, these young people whom God had touched were warmly embraced by Chuck Smith and the other leaders of the Jesus movement. Thank God for revival!

David Yonggi Cho
The Full Gospel Church, Seoul, Korea
To me, the three most important revivals are the 1857 Laymen's Prayer Revival, the 1904 Revival, and the 1965-70 Baby Boomer Revival. The 1904 Revival swept the whole of Korea and established Korea as a Christian country in the Far East.

Robert Coleman
Billy Graham Center Institute of Evangelism, Wheaton, Illinois
It was during the post World War II period in 1950 that I first experienced revival. I was a student at Asbury Seminary when a spontaneous revival came to the college, and I was one who knelt at the altar to receive a deeper experience with the Holy Spirit, which heightened my understanding of the supernatural workings of God. Since that time I have witnessed a number of powerful movements of the Spirit in various parts of the world, all of which have contributed to a yearning in my soul for a mighty world revival and the fulfillment of the Great Commission.

James O. Davis
National Evangelism Director, Assemblies of God, Springfield, Missouri
I believe the most important revival took place on the Day of Pentecost. Indeed this Pentecostal revival has radically impacted my ministry because it fostered the foundation necessary to birth, build, and broaden a "Holy Spirit outpouring" in our world today. On the Day of Pentecost, the roles and goals of revival were actualized through evangelizing the sinner, equipping the saint, and exalting the Savior. Pentecost moved the early church from sitting to standing and

from weakness to witness. We are still experiencing the influence and impact of this mountain-moving, devil-defying, life-changing revival.

Lewis Drummond
Beeson Divinity School, Birmingham, Alabama
The most influential revival in my experience was the World War II Revival, 1935-50. It was not because of its profundity compared to other great awakenings, but rather because it was in that context that I began my ministry and became aware of what revival truly is. The revivalist who most influenced my early ministry is Charles G. Finney. I do not see either as the most significant in the entire history of the church, but they personally impacted me most profoundly.

Dale Galloway
Asbury Theological Seminary, Wilmore, Kentucky
Without a doubt the greatest influence on my life was Billy Graham and the crusade he did in Columbus, Ohio, in the early 1960s. I had been brought up on camp meetings and had experienced revivals because of my Nazarene background, but the crusade was one of the foundational events of my life. There I saw for the first time Dr. Graham effectively reaching people of all ages, races, and backgrounds.

Eddie Gibbs
Fuller Theological Seminary, Pasadena, California
Each of these ten revivals was significant in its own way. In terms of the worldwide advance of the gospel, I believe that the 1904 revival has made the greatest impact, with

Pentecostalism becoming the third great force in Christendom. I believe that the second most influential revival would be the Laymen's Prayer Revival because of its urban impact and lay initiative.

Jack Hayford
The Church on the Way, Van Nuys, California
The revivalists that have most influenced my ministry are John Wesley (because of his passion and intellect, joined with crystal clear clarity in focus), Aimee Semple McPherson (because of the mighty miracles, the multitudes that she evangelized, and the global evangelistic movement that was born), and Billy Graham (because of his steadfastness in Bible-centered preaching, his constancy in integrity, and his creativity in reaching the masses as well as shaping leaders).

Charles Kelly
New Orleans Baptist Theological Seminary, New Orleans, Louisiana
The revival that most influenced my ministry was the Baby Boomer Revival. I saw and was a part of a dramatic movement of God on my college campus. It taught me forever that God can do profound, amazing things and that there is no environment the power of God cannot change. George Whitefield is the revivalist who most influenced me. God used his hard work, deep praying, and forceful, eloquent preaching to stir two nations in a mighty way.

D. James Kennedy
Coral Ridge Presbyterian Church, Fort Lauderdale, Florida
We have gone from approximately 20,000 converts per day worldwide in 1980 to approximately 200,000 per day by the end of this year. This has been the largest ingathering in the history of the church and the only one that I have had the opportunity of being personally involved with.

Ron Phillips
Pastor, Central Baptist Church, Hixson, Tennessee
Having been a student of the Cane Ridge Revival and its impact, especially on Baptists in Tennessee and Kentucky, I found myself transported by the description of those camp meetings in chapter three. Having been in a revival atmosphere for nearly six years, our church has experienced many of the manifestations so described.

Alvin Reid
Southeastern Baptist Theological Seminary, Wake Forest, North Carolina
The Jesus Movement in the 1970s made a radical impact on my life. I came to Christ during that period. I have never gotten over what God did in those days, transforming hippie freaks into Jesus freaks! Much of my ministry is devoted to spiritual awakenings. No doubt my hunger for a mighty outpouring of God's Spirit began in those days.

Chuck Smith
Calvary Chapel of Costa Mesa, Santa Ana, California

The revivalist who most influenced my ministry is Billy Graham. He sets a great example of integrity and humility and fiscal responsibility. His message is clear and straightforward: All men have sinned and God has provided only one remedy, the shed blood of his Son, Jesus Christ. Through his Schools on Evangelism, he has sought to pass on the torch to thousands of others.

Tommy Tenney
Evangelist, Pineville, Louisiana

The revival that most influenced my life would be the 1904 Azusa Street Revival. My family's denominational background descends directly from Azusa. On the other hand, the revival that most influenced my ministry was the World War II Hebrides Revival. Reading the accounts and even listening to rare tapes of Duncan Campbell have had incredible impact upon me. Duncan Campbell said that 75 percent of the conversions in the Hebrides Revival happened outside a church setting. If we are to reach this "unchurched" generation, that's the kind of revival I want to see in my day—a revival that isn't confined within the walls of a church but that flows into the bars, shopping malls, and streets of our cities.

C. Peter Wagner
World Prayer Center, Colorado Springs, Colorado

The pentecostal revival at the beginning of the twentieth century has influenced my ministry more than any of the others on the list. When I first went to Bolivia as a missionary, I was anti-pentecostal. But over the years, because of the vitality of the pentecostal churches in Latin America, I began to experience a paradigm shift in my ministry so that the Third Person of the Trinity became a reality rather than just a shadow cast by the Second Person of the Trinity. Now I see fruit in my ministry that would have been inaccessible to me had not those early pioneers paid the price and allowed the revival fire to burn.

Steve Wingfield
Evangelist, Harrisonburg, Virginia
My life and ministry have been impacted by a number of these revivals. For instance, where would we be without the Protestant Reformation? I was reared in the home of an old-time Methodist minister, so I thank God for the First Great Awakening and the birth of Methodism. Men such as Jonathan Edwards, Peter Cartwright, Charles Finney, Dwight Moody, and Billy Graham, who were raised up as spiritual leaders in different revivals, have greatly influenced my life and ministry. I gave my life to Christ in the midst of the Baby Boomer Revival in 1970. Words cannot describe what God did in my life during those days.

INDEX OF NAMES

233

269.2409
T747

10043